To Declan + Maureen,
Happy Mardi Gras!
Hal

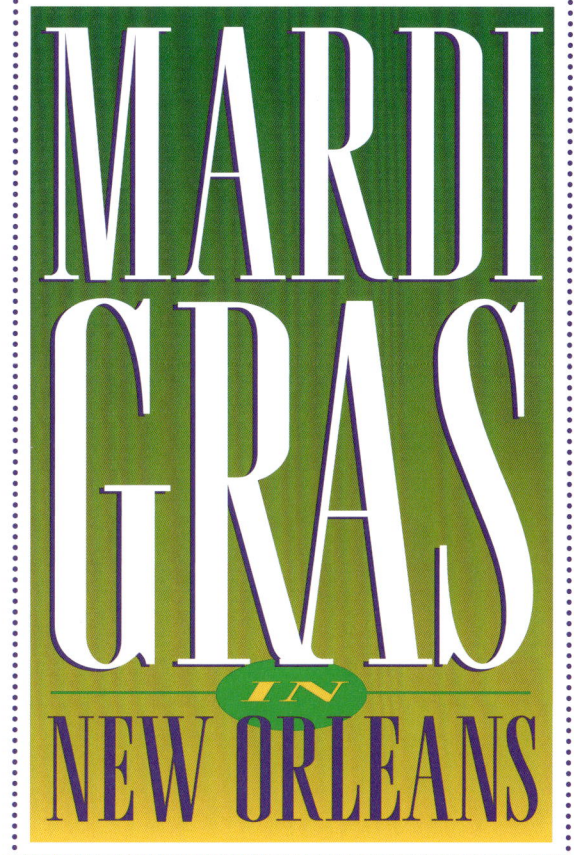

An Illustrated History

by Arthur Hardy

Second Edition

Dedication—

To the memory of Don Lee Keith 1940-2003

Art Director: David Johnson
Editor: Don Lee Keith
Typography: Barbara O'Neal Aitken

Acknowledgments

I gratefully acknowledge the help of the following people in the compilation of this volume: David Johnson, Don Lee Keith, Barbara O'Neal Aitken, Lorraine Buchta, Marvel LeBreton, Iggy Christiana, Herbie LeBlanc, Sidney Hebert, Henri Schindler, Judy Fischer, Jimmy Clark, Collin Hamer Jr., Wayne Phillips, Pat Reicke, James Sefcik, John Magill, Dr. Wilbur Meneray, Jamie Montgomery, Neal Foy and Jan Freeman.

Arthur Hardy, New Orleans, September 2003

Library of Congress Control Number: 2001118886

ISBN 0-930892-62-3

Copyright © 2003 by Arthur Hardy Enterprises, Inc.
All rights reserved

Printed in Canada

Arthur Hardy Enterprises, Inc.
602 Metairie Road
Metairie, LA 70005

Memorabilia from the Arthur Hardy Collection unless otherwise noted:

Photo/art credits:
p. 5 map, Sidney Hebert; p. 11 Comus illustration, Henri Schindler; p. 63 Louis Armstrong by car, Celeste Broadway; Time cover, © AOL-Time Warner; p. 66 "Rex Rules," Ray Cresson; p. 67 Pete Fountain, Pete Fountain; p. 69 Danny Kaye, Z. J. Montz; p. 70 Zeus photo, Phil Lundgren; Endymion, Bob Stempel; p. 71 newspaper, The Times-Picayune Publishing Corporation. All rights reserved; p. 72 National Guard, Keith Thienemann; p. 73 1978 Mardi Gras poster by Charest & Brousseau © 1978 ProCreations Publishing Company; On Strike, © Christopher R. Harris, All rights reserved; Children, George Long; p. 74 Lundi Gras, John Drury; Police, Bevil Knapp; King Kong, Syndey Byrd; p. 75 Caesar, Syndey Byrd; p. 76 Boston Club, Syndey Byrd; Mardi Gras World, Blaine Kern Artists; p. 77; Harry Connick Jr, Krewe of Orpheus; Leviathan, Sidney Hebert; p. 78 Barkus, Syndey Byrd; p. 80 Flambeaux, Mardi Gras Indian, Christopher Veo; Krewe de Vieux, Syndey Byrd; p. 82 Chaos, Muses, Petronius Ball, Syndey Byrd; p. 83 Meeting of the Courts, Bourbon Street, Hermes, Syndey Byrd; Proteus, Sidney Hebert; back endsheet, Syndey Byrd.

Herbie LeBlanc:
p. 15 TNR program; p. 16 Rex 1874 invitation; p. 22 Momus 1902 pin; p. 24 parade, p. 44 Rex medal; p. 46 Canal St.; p. 51 Consus pin; p. 67 Rex 1960 doubloon art; p. 65 Rex float; p. 67 Mardi Gras pennant

Historic New Orleans Collection:
p. 14 Mother Goose TNR parade THNOC 1975.114.4
p. 26 Audubon TNR tableau THNOC 1975.117.10

Confederate Memorial Hall:
p. 12 Confederate flag; p. 27 Winnie Davis portrait

Special Collections, Tulane University:
p. 11 Comus 1857 invitation; p. 26 Momus 1877 floats; p. 39 Teunisson 1896 photo; p. 43 Rex 1887 parade; p. 63 Louis Armstrong on float

Louisiana State Museum:
p. 5 Iberville portrait; p. 21 Downman photograph; p. 24 Charles Darwin; p. 33 Comus 1874 Carnival Bulletin; p. 39 flambeau; p. 41 Richardson portrait; p. 43 French Opera House photo; p. 45 Wild West ad; World's Fair broadside; p. 49 Well Known invitation; p. 52 1909 scepter; p. 57 1925 crown. p. 77 1881 crown

New Orleans Public Library:
p. 22 Momus card, invitation; p. 23 Momus dance card; p. 35 TNR 1875 invitation; p. 36 Proteus 1891 dance card; p. 57 Mystic invitation; p. 66 Sepia Mardi Gras; p. 70 French Quarter scene

Contents

- 4 In the Beginning
- 6 New Orleans Adopts Mardi Gras
- 10 The Birth of Comus
- 14 Twelfth Night Revelers
- 16 Rex Rules the Day
- 18 A Love Affair That Wasn't
- 20 The Monday King
- 22 The Knights of Momus
- 24 Satire on Parade
- 28 The Carnival Ball
- 32 The 1870s: History on Parade
- 36 The Krewe of Proteus
- 40 The 1880s: Golden Invitations
- 44 Rex at the World's Fair
- 46 The 1890s: Presenting the Tableau
- 52 Carnival Turns the Century
- 56 Roaring with the Twenties
- 58 1930-1949: Every Man a King
- 62 A Media Event
- 64 Mid-Century Merriment
- 66 Something Old, Something New
- 68 The Super Krewes Arrive
- 70 A Time of Change
- 76 A New Landscape
- 115 Index

Mardi Gras Reference Guide

- 84 Mardi Gras Dictionary
  Mardi Gras Q & A
- 86 Current Parade Themes, Royalty
- 100 Defunct Parade Themes, Royalty
- 105 Oldest Ball Krewe Queens
- 108 African American Balls
  Mardi Gras Indians
- 109 Kiddie Krewes
  Krewe Name Derivation
  Krewes with Most Parades
  Little Rascals Themes, Royalty
  Oldest Active Parades
  Parade Theme Categories
  Truck Parades
  Walking Clubs
- 110 Ball Krewes
  Gay Carnival Clubs
  Mardi Gras Archives
  Mardi Gras Collectibles
  Memorabilia on Display
  Oldest Ball Krewes
- 111 Carnival Celebrity Guests
- 112 Doubloon Kings
  Economic Impact
  Float Builders/Designers
  Foreign Language Mottoes
  Parade Components
  Royal Oddities
  Same Name, Different Krewes
  Sponsoring Organizations
  St. Tammany Parades
- 113 Mardi Gras Cancelations
  Mardi Gras Dates by Day
  Mardi Gras Dates by Year
  Parade Growth
- 114 Fat Tuesday Weather
  Mardi Gras Reading List

In the Beginning

The true genesis of Mardi Gras has been debated by historians for centuries, though few would deny the fact that man's need for celebration and repentance is universal and timeless. Some theorists find its roots in tribal fertility rites that welcomed the arrival of spring. Certainly, for primitive man mere survival through the winter was cause enough for celebration. The Roman poet Ovid reported that 5,000 years ago Greek shepherds in Arcadia held a spring festival on March 15. Later in France, the Druids sacrificed young bulls in their *Fete du Soleil* as an offering to the gods who might bless them with more fertile women and more productive livestock. Some sources claim that farmers threw flour upon the fields in a symbolic gesture for a more fruitful harvest. Other scholars insist there is no direct linkage between these celebrations and Mardi Gras. A closer connection can be documented with the Saturnalia and Bacchanalia rituals. The conquering Romans transformed an ancient Greek celebration into the Lupercalia. This event, which featured the sacrifice of an ox, was held annually on February 15 until the end of the 5th Century A.D.

Masquerades and street festivals were held in France during the reign of Louis XIV (1643-1715), and under Louis XV (1723-1774), masked balls reached their zenith. In 1789 the French Revolution put a temporary prohibition on masking and revelry. In 1805 Napoleon brought back Carnival by an official decree, but by the 1870s the celebration began to die out in France, while it continued in many other European countries.

Carnival spread throughout Catholic countries, and in the Middle Ages it flourished in France and Italy. As early as 1512 an important element of the French celebration was the boeuf gras *(fatted bull), symbolic of the last meat eaten before the fasting of Lent.*

The anonymity offered by the mask eventually caused the Roman festival to degenerate into a circus-like orgy replete with pain and pleasure. Often the distinction between classes was completely suspended, causing further debauchery.

Enter the Catholic Church

Church leaders tried desperately to rid converts of their heathen ways. When the priests' best efforts met with resistance, they decided to direct those pagan rituals into Christian channels. One new celebration would be sanctioned, with the condition that it be followed by a time of abstinence and penance. This 40-day period of fasting would be called Lent and it would begin on Ash Wednesday, the day when subjects were admonished by Mother Church, "Remember, man, that thou art dust and unto dust thou shalt return." The time of feasting that preceded the Lenten fast would come to be known as "Carnival," from the Latin *carnelevamen,* which loosely translates as "farewell to flesh." The climactic day of the pre-Lenten Carnival celebration would gain acclaim under its French name, *Mardi Gras* — Fat Tuesday.

The Carnival "season" would later have an official opening date, January 6 (Twelfth Night), and it too would have a Christian connection, since this is the liturgical Feast of the Epiphany when Christ was visited by the Magi.

The Carnival celebration is followed by a period of penance.

Mardi Gras in North America

Pierre leMoyne, Sieur d'Iberville

In 1682, Rene Robert Cavelier, Sieur de la Salle, claimed a vast portion of North America for France and named it Louisiana, after Louis XIV, the "Sun King." During the final year of the 17th Century, Mardi Gras, in name and in spirit, was introduced to the continent. Thirty-eight-year-old French Canadian Pierre leMoyne, Sieur d'Iberville, was commissioned to explore the Mississippi River. According to his journal, on March 3, 1699, he and his men camped for the night at the river's first large bend. "I came to sleep on a turn that the river makes on the west, 2 leagues from the mouth on a point to the right of the river." In tribute to the festive holiday being celebrated that day in France, Iberville named the spot *Pointe du Mardi Gras* and the adjoining channel *Bayoue du Mardi Gras.*

Bayoue du Mardi Gras appears on many early maps of Louisiana, including this one from 1764.

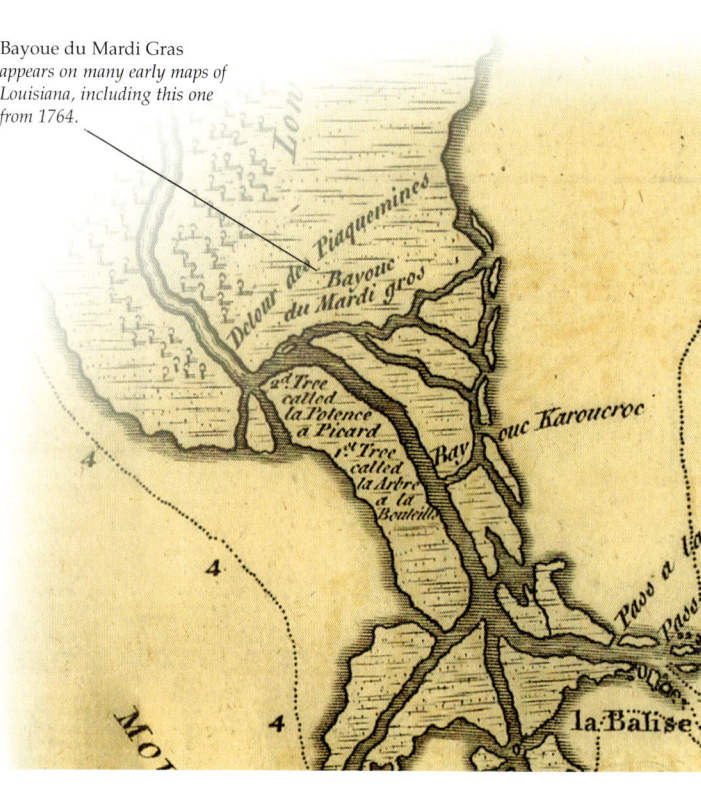

New Orleans Adopts Mardi Gras

Several themes that defined the European Carnival found parallels in New Orleans. Mardi Gras was celebrated privately and publicly by people of varied social ranks, and excesses occurred on both sides of the cultural divide. Governments tried to suppress, or at least control, the festivities. And they failed, because the need to dance, to sing, and to celebrate was so deeply entrenched in the collective memory of the populace that it could not be contained. But Mardi Gras did not march smoothly through the centuries. Because of violence, the press periodically called for an end to the celebration.

Persons of mixed races were common in New Orleans. "Quadroon" women — females who were one-quarter black — were known for their exquisite beauty. In 1805, a series of Quadroon balls began. These affairs attracted men of society who would use the secrecy of the mask to attend these forbidden soirees.

THE DATE OF MARDI GRAS

The Catholic Church established the moveable dates for Mardi Gras when it developed the formula for the date of Easter, which may occur as early as March 22 or as late as April 25. Mardi Gras is then scheduled 47 days before Easter. (Forty days of Lent plus six Sundays, which are not considered part of the penitential season). Mardi Gras can be as early as February 3 or as late as March 9.

THE DATE OF CARNIVAL

The Carnival season always starts on January 6, Twelfth Night, the Feast of the Epiphany, and ends on Mardi Gras. Depending on the date of Fat Tuesday, the Carnival season can vary in length from 28 to 63 days.

Little Cause for Celebration

When New Orleans was founded in 1718 by Iberville's brother, Bienville, the city was nothing more than a colonial outpost. With its hot climate and hostile environment, there was little reason for jubilation. Yet only 25 years later, Mardi Gras was first celebrated in Louisiana.

- *1743* Governor Marquis de Vaudreuil presented an elegant Carnival ball.
- *1762* Governor Don Antonio Ulloa issued a law to suppress public masking.
- *1781* New ordinance prevented "colored" people from masking.
- *1790* Twelfth Night parties held on Louisiana plantations.
- *1792* The first public ball room, La Salle Conde, opened in French Quarter.

While public masking was prohibited for most of the years 1806-1827, The Gazette, a New Orleans paper, reported in 1824 "magnificent society balls" at the Salle d'Orleans, while other masked balls took place at the Theatre St. Phillipe. It is likely that the first maskers to appear on the street were on their way to such *bals masques*.

In 1804 when a dispute erupted between Creoles and Americans over the type of music to be played at a Carnival ball, Governor William Claiborne was called in to restore order. This incident was a manifestation of the bad feelings shared by the two groups that would last for decades. Canal Street provided a boundary between the territory of the feuding neighbors, and the median in the center is still referred to by locals as the "neutral ground."

During the 1830s street festivities on Fat Tuesday became more common.

In 1837 and again in 1838, the newspapers printed documentation of parades of maskers on foot. The French custom of tossing sugar-coated peanuts to the crowds became popular, but pranksters sometimes ruined the day by throwing bags of flour and soiling the clothing of bystanders.

The first mention of a float-like vehicle appeared in 1839. *The Daily Picayune* described it as "a giant fighting cock, six feet tall, drawn in a carriage by two horses."

A highlight of Creole Carnival occurred in 1840. Auber's opera *Le Bal Masque* featured a grand march of maskers. The audience, also in costume, joined the performers on stage for the finale on Mardi Gras night. The union of cast and audience was repeated in several subsequent years.

With the exception of a spectacular 1852 parade of a thousand men masked as Bedouin Arabs on foot, on horseback, and in wagons, Mardi Gras in New Orleans was in a general decline from 1845 to 1855. Dismal weather in consecutive years, coupled with growing violence, appeared to sound the death knell for Carnival.

The balcony of the Theatre d'Orleans collapsed during a Mardi Gras ball in 1854, killing several attendees.

CARRIAGE FOR HIRE

A half-century before the first official float parade was held in New Orleans, citizens enjoyed Mardi Gras in a variety of ways.

It was common for a reveler to rent a carriage and driver for the festivities, as indicated in this classified ad from the January 5, 1808, *Louisiana Gazette*:

> A neat coach with a pair of good horses and a careful driver…may be had by application to the subscriber, every evening during Carnival — it is suggested that four families might find their interest in taking it together, it will then be sacred to them for the time they engage it.

— John Dawson No. 34 St. Louis Street

The Picayune observed in 1837, "... sugar plums, kisses and oranges were lavishly bestowed by these good natured jokers. However, an unpopular prank among early revelers was the throwing of flour onto unsuspecting bystanders." This sort of mischief spoiled the day for its unlucky victims and supported the belief of many that Mardi Gras was out of control.

A FORCE TO BE RECKONED WITH

The chaotic and often violent nature of the festivity in the early 19th Century caused the local government and the press to campaign hard against it.

In 1850, the Creole newspaper *The Bee* editorialized: "We are not sorry to see that this miserable annual exhibit is rapidly becoming extinct. It originated in a barbarous age and is worthy of only such."

However, the celebrations continued undeterred, surviving even the yellow fever epidemic of 1832-33, which claimed 10,000 lives.

The earliest photograph of a Mardi Gras celebration was almost taken in 1840. The Daily Picayune reported, "We had our Daguerreotype reflectors ready to take a proof of the procession as it passed our office, but our devil ran away to look at the show..."

One-eyed Michael Kraft, founder of the Cowbellian deRakin Society in Mobile, Alabama. His group's spontaneous street celebration in 1830 is the earliest known Mardi Gras parade in North America.

The Mobile Connection

Although their parades on Fat Tuesday did not begin until 1866, the claim that the city of Mobile makes as the motherland of Mardi Gras parades in the United State is a viable one. Some Alabama historians view the annual *Masque de la Mobile* feasts as Carnival celebrations. These events were presented annually on August 25 by the Societe de la Saint Louis (1704-1842). A stronger case can be made for two other groups: the Boeuf Gras Society (1711-1861), which gathered on Fat Tuesday, and the Spanish Mystic Society, which appeared on Twelfth Night (1793-1833). But Mobile's most significant contribution to Mardi Gras dates from New Year's Eve 1830. Pennsylvania-born Michael Kraft and a group called the Cowbellian deRakin Society — named after the cowbells and rakes used as noisemakers — walked the streets in a spontaneous celebration. The Mobile party grew in size and fame each year to the point that in describing a local foot parade of boisterous masqueraders in New Orleans in 1837, *The Picayune* called them "Cowbellians." In 1840 the Mobile Cowbellians added floats and paraded with the theme *Heathen Gods & Goddesses*. Two other "mystic societies" were founded in Alabama before New Orleans joined the parading fraternity: the Strikers (1842) and the Tea Drinkers (1846). In 1852, members of the Cowbellians marched in New Orleans, and the next year the men participated in a local *bal masque*.

New Orleans' first Mardi Gras organization, the Mistick Krewe of Comus, was founded by former "Cows" Thad Smith and Joseph Ellison. Along with co-founder Charles Churchill, they received considerable help from the Cowbellians and the Strikers. The theme of Mobile's New Year's Eve 1856 Cowbellian's parade was *Pandemonium Unveiled*. Fifty-five days later, with borrowed floats and costumes, Comus' first parade and ball were entitled *Demon Actors from John Milton's Paradise Lost*. Cowbellians attended both events as guests of the Mistick Krewe.

The Cowbellian deRakin Society was named for the cowbells and rakes members used as noisemakers.

The Birth of Comus

On January 10, 1857, a group of 19 men met in a room above the Gem, an establishment on Royal Street in New Orleans. The result of that gathering was the birth of the Mistick Krewe of Comus, which not only saved Carnival from the near-fatal abuses of the 1850s, but also became the model for the future celebration of Mardi Gras in New Orleans.

The group coined the word "krewe" and was the first to form a secret Carnival society and to choose a mythological namesake. The Comus procession on Tuesday, February 24, 1857, was the first themed parade with floats and costumed maskers. The torch-lit street procession was followed by a masked ball during which four tableaux (theatrical scenes) were presented.

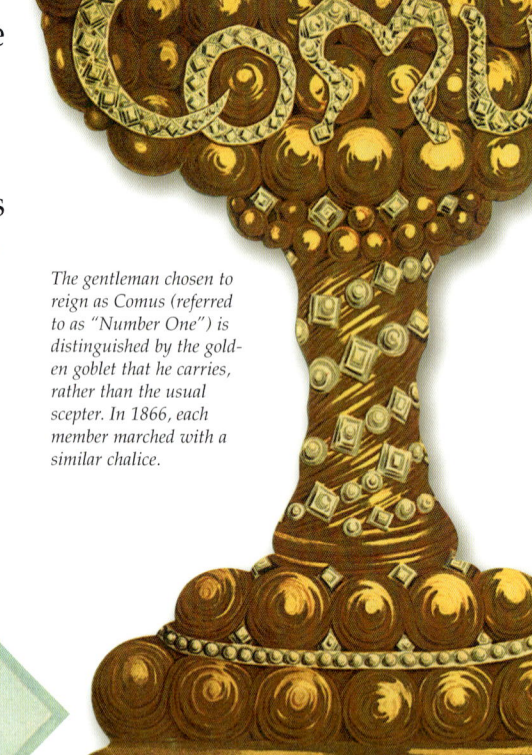

The gentleman chosen to reign as Comus (referred to as "Number One") is distinguished by the golden goblet that he carries, rather than the usual scepter. In 1866, each member marched with a similar chalice.

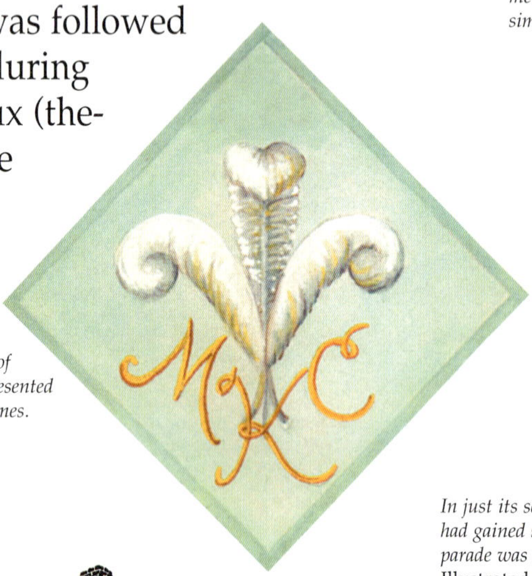

The Mistick Krewe of Comus is often represented by three ostrich plumes.

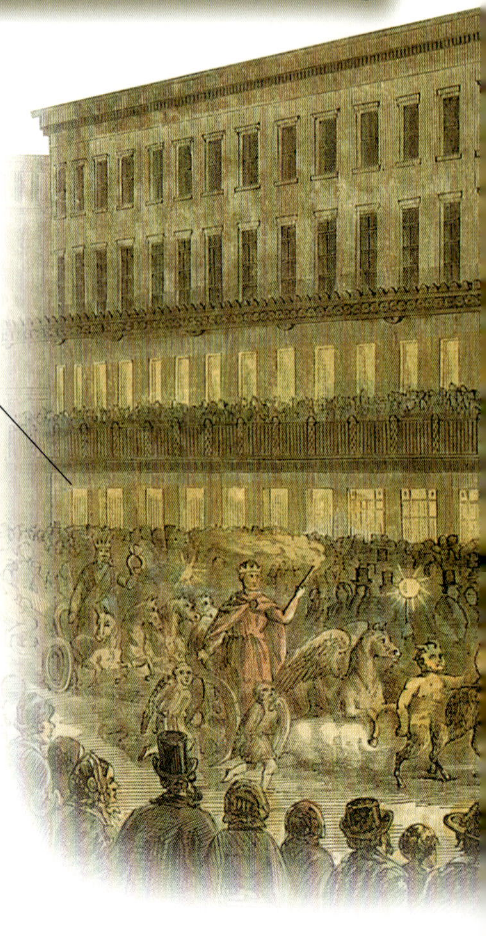

In just its second year, Comus had gained such fame that its parade was depicted in the Illustrated London News. *The theme of the 30-float procession was* Mythology.

N. O., Jan. 4, 1857.

You are requested to meet a few of your friends at the "Club Room" over the Gem, Royal street, on Saturday evening, the 10 inst., at 7 o'clock.

S. M. TODD.
L. D. ADDISON.
J. H. POPE.

F. SHAW, JR.
JOS. ELLISON.
WM. P. ELLISON.

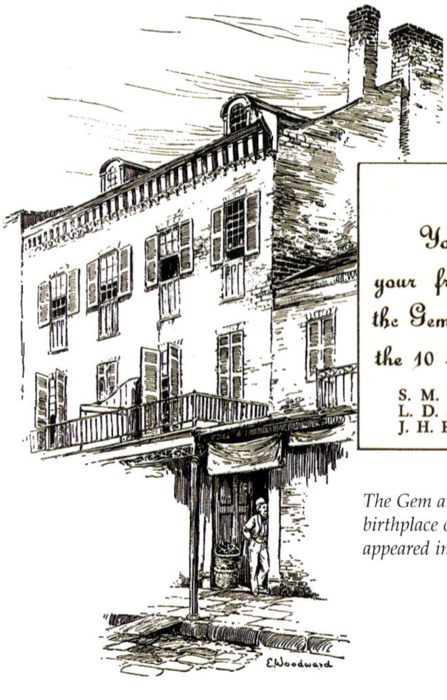

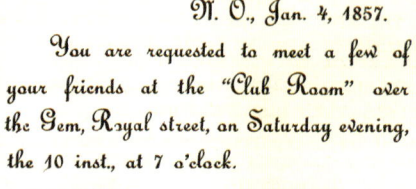

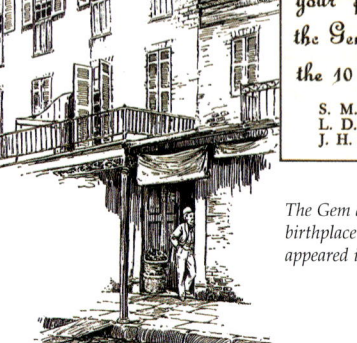

The Gem at 127 Royal Street, birthplace of Comus, as it appeared in 1857.

The first Comus parade received a glowing review from *The Daily Crescent*:

Led by the festive Comus high on his royal set, and Satan high on a hill, far-blazing a mound with a pyramid and towers from diamond quarries hewn, and rocks of gold, the palace of great Lucifer was followed by devils large and devils small, devils with horns and devils with tails, and devils without either.

After the parade, the men retired to Crisp's Variety Theater, where exquisite tableaux were staged under a gaslight banner that proclaimed *Vive La Dance*. New Orleans Mayor Charles Waterman led off the first quadrille.

Invitation to the first Comus ball.

Who was Comus?

The Greek *komus* means to revel, or a company of revelers. Komus was the god of festive mirth; he sprang from the union of Bacchus and Circe.

Comus co-founder, pharmacist Dr. John H. Pope, is credited with naming the new group. He was a classical scholar and an admirer of the poet John Milton, who wrote *The Masque of Comus*, and the classic *Paradise Lost* — the theme of the first Comus parade and ball. Comus is also mentioned in several other 17th Century works, including Thomas Gray's *Elegy in a Country Church Yard*, in which the line "Comus and his midnight crew" appears.

Mobile's Carnival groups were called "mystic societies." The men who formed Comus wanted to add a similar sense of secrecy to their club, so the spelling was changed to "Mistick." To give the group a pseudo Old English flavor, "crew" became "krewe." Although not every organization would use it, "krewe" would eventually serve as the generic term for all Carnival organizations.

11

Civil War Cancels Comus

The first of several Carnival cancelations during wartime came in 1862, when the country was engulfed in the Civil War. Comus issued this proclamation calling for a hiatus from the festivities:

···

GREETINGS !

WHEREAS, War has cast its gloom over our happy homes and care usurped the place where joy is wont to hold its sway. Now, therefore, do I, deeply sympathizing with the general anxiety, deem it proper to withhold our Annual Festival in this goodly Crescent City and by this proclamation do command no assemblage of the

-MISTICK KREWE-

Given under my hand this, the 1st day of March, A. D. 1862.

COMUS.

···

On March 6, 1862, Comus donated $100 to feed the destitute families of Confederate veterans.

In 1866, the krewe returned with a single float bearing Comus, followed by maskers on foot. The theme — *The Past, The Present and The Future* — reflected on the just-ended War Between the States. The Past was represented by war; The Present, by industry, commerce, science, history and art; The Future, by expressions of peace and hope.

Invitation to the 1861 Mistick Krewe of Comus Festival, The Four Ages of Life.

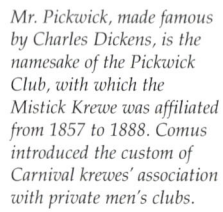

Mr. Pickwick, made famous by Charles Dickens, is the namesake of the Pickwick Club, with which the Mistick Krewe was affiliated from 1857 to 1888. Comus introduced the custom of Carnival krewes' association with private men's clubs.

The Varieties Theatre was home to many early Comus balls.
In 1860, P. G. T. Beauregard, a future Confederate General, restored order at the ball after a gate crasher yelled "fire" in the hope of gaining admission.

CARNIVAL TRADITION

PARADES AND FLOATS

Parades are typically held in conjunction with holidays and seasonal celebrations such as Christmas, New Year's Day, Thanksgiving and Independence Day. The tradition of parading can be traced to the days of the Roman Empire when tremendous military and coronation processions were held. The Egyptians and Chinese also staged parades. Religious pilgrimages sometimes took on the trappings of parades, with sacred statues being promenaded on decorated carts or wagons.

Floats are an essential ingredient in a parade. Some etymologists claim that the word "carnival" is itself derived from *carrus navavlis* — literally, "ships on wheels." The Phoenicians put wheels on their small ships and pulled them through the streets in victory parades. In Spain, the same custom prevailed, and these small ships were called *flotas*, thus the Spanish flotilla. The fact that boats on wheels were used in Carnival celebrations is documented by action taken in 1595 by the Council of Ulm. The Catholic Church was so troubled by the scandalous behavior of the populace during one such festival that it prohibited the use of boats on wheels during a local German Carnival parade.

The 1867 Comus parade, Triumphs of Epicure, *featured maskers on foot in an array of costumes representing food and beverages.*

Twelfth Night Revelers

Thirteen years after the Mistick Krewe of Comus premiered, a second Carnival association debuted in New Orleans. Twelfth Night Revelers, so named because their pageants took place twelve days after Christmas (on the Feast of the Epiphany), presented their first parade on January 6, 1870. The nine-float procession was followed by a ball at the French Opera House.

TNR is credited with the introduction of the first queen of a Mardi Gras krewe and with a unique selection procedure for its royalty. Borrowing from a centuries-old European custom, the men roll out a giant cake and distribute slices to young ladies at the ball. The lucky young woman who receives the golden bean hidden inside the cake is declared queen; the remaining women receive silver beans and serve as maids in her majesty's court.

During the 19th Century, Twelfth Night Revelers presented six parades and 19 balls. In time their January 6 presentations were considered the official opening event of the annual Carnival season.

A GOODLY HUMOR, IS IT NOT, MY LORDS?

- First Carnival queen, Emma Butler (1871).
- First to feature grand march as an element of the tableau ball (1870).
- First to present a parade that featured political satire (1873).
- First to permit newspaper accounts naming ladies in attendance at balls (1872).
- First to be cited in the press as tossing trinkets from a float when a TNR member masked as Santa Claus dispensed gifts (1871).
- First krewe to abandon parading and focus solely on presenting balls (1876).

The king of Twelfth Night Revelers is known as the Lord of Misrule and he is usually accompanied by a group of cooks. Carnival's second organization was initially associated with the Chalmette Club. TNR disbanded and regrouped twice in the 19th Century.

The modern day TNR cakes are made of wood and are used as ceremonial props. In the 19th Century, edible versions of the cake were featured at the ball.

King Cake in History

In ancient times, tribes that survived the harshness of winter celebrated by baking a crown-shaped cake, using the preceding year's wheat. Within the cake was placed a seed, bean or nut. Later, the Romans chose a king for their festivals by drawing lots. The Catholic Church linked these ancient customs to the Feast of the Epiphany in the 4th Century.

During the 17th and 18th Centuries, the *Roi de la Fève* (King of the Bean) was celebrated in both art and literature in Europe. "Twelfth Cakes" were annually featured in England.

Twelfth Night rituals took place in Creole homes in New Orleans when its French settlers brought the *gateau des rois* (king cake) custom with them. In 1870 the Twelfth Night Revelers formalized the Mardi Gras connection with its first parade and ball.

CARNIVAL TRADITION

KING CAKE IN MODERN TIMES

With a plastic baby doll tucked inside, the oval-shaped cinnamon dough brioche is covered in granulated sugar in the Mardi Gras colors of purple, gold and green. Custom dictates that whoever receives the tiny favor buys the next cake or gives the next party.

By the late 20th Century, more than 500,000 king cakes were consumed locally each year, with another 75,000 shipped out of state via overnight couriers.

The "Frozen Charlotte" was the first doll to be inserted in the king cake. Legend has it that the tiny China doll was inspired by a pious little girl who froze to death seeking the Christ child.

Rex Rules the Day

Mardi Gras served as a brief escape from the grief that permeated the post-Civil War South during Reconstruction. For several years maskers had gathered along the principal streets of New Orleans on Fat Tuesday. An attempt in 1871 to collect these groups into an orderly parade failed, but businessmen continued to recognize the need to present such an organized procession. The next year, an impromptu visit to New Orleans by Russian Grand Duke Alexis Romanoff provided the justification to try once again.

The leader of that event on February 13, 1872, when the King of Carnival first reigned, was called Rex (Latin for king), and the influence of the organization that crowned him would shape the direction of Carnival in New Orleans in ways unimagined. Rex would introduce the colors of the celebration, as well as its flag and its anthem. And he would transform Mardi Gras into an official Crescent City holiday. The edicts and proclamations he issued, as well as those sent forth from his royal household — Bathurst (Lord High Chamberlain) and Warwick (Earl Marshal of the Empire) — called for the closing not only of schools, the post office, the Custom House, and of all businesses normally open on Fat Tuesdays, but also for the shutting down of operations of the Louisiana Lottery.

In time Rex would help turn Mardi Gras into a tourist attraction, with hundreds of thousands traveling annually to the city by train and steamboat — and eventually, by automobile and airplane — to witness his grand procession.

The king appeared on horseback from 1872 to 1874. The costume for the first Rex, Lewis Salomon, was borrowed from Shakespearean actor Lawrence Barrett, who was appearing in Richard III *at the Varieties Theater.*

Rex ball invitations were very plain and were typeset in French the first two years.

CARNIVAL TRADITION

PURPLE, GOLD AND GREEN

The colors of Carnival were likely chosen in 1872 with no particular meaning in mind, other than the need to follow the general rules of heraldry. The Rex organization later declared that purple, gold and green signified justice, power and faith, respectively. The inspiration for this interpretation was the 1892 Rex parade, *Symbolism of Colors*, in which each float's color was assigned a specific meaning.

Revelers without a cause: The first Rex parade in 1872 would offer an outlet for maskers who annually gathered on Canal Street in search of a celebration.

The boeuf gras, the ancient symbol of Fat Tuesday, appeared in every Rex parade from 1872 to 1909.

The sponsoring organization of the Rex parade and ball is called the School of Design. The club's coat of arms was introduced on the invitation to the Rex ball of 1875.

17

A Love Affair That Wasn't

In 1872, Lydia was a 36-year-old English show girl; Alexis, 14 years her junior, was a royal visitor on a cross-country tour of the United States. Legend has it that the Russian Grand Duke was so smitten by her that he rearranged his schedule to follow her to New Orleans. While the addition of the city to his itinerary was a last-minute decision, there is no evidence that Lydia and Alexis paired up in New Orleans. His attention was diverted instead to another actress, Lotta Crabtree, Lydia's main competition, who was also performing in the Queen City of the South.

Alexis, fourth son of Tzar Alexander II, visited some 32 cities. At every stop he was treated with pomp and ceremony. He hunted buffalo in Nebraska with George Custer, Buffalo Bill Cody and General Philip Sheridan. After his American trip, he became nothing more than a footnote to Russian history, while in New Orleans he has been incorrectly credited as being the sole inspiration for the Rex parade.

Lydia Thompson (1836-1908) performed in New Orleans on a regular basis, starting in 1869. She was so popular that a local baseball team was named after her.

The London-born Lydia performed in venues that included Moscow, Berlin, St. Petersburg, and Paris before embarking on her first American tour in 1868.

Bon vivant Grand Duke Alexis Alexandrovitch Romanoff (1850-1908) distinguished himself more as a ladies' man than as a military officer in his native Russia.

The Royal Anthem

The whimsical tune chosen by Rex as his anthem was written by George Leybourne and published in London in 1871. British star Lydia Thompson adopted it for her burlesque show *Bluebeard*, which she brought to America. The song was a hit in New Orleans months before the arrival of the Grand Duke, who also was fond of it, having heard Miss Thompson sing *If Ever I Cease to Love* at the Olympic Theater in St. Louis in January, 1872. Playful New Orleanians added the line, "May the Grand Duke Alexis ride a buffalo in Texas, if ever I cease to love."

IF EVER I CEASE TO LOVE

In a house, in a square, in a quadrant
In a street, in a lane, in a road
Turn to the left on the right hand
You see there my true love's abode
I go there a courting
And cooing my love like a dove
And swearing on my bended knee
If Ever I Cease to Love

If Ever I Cease to Love
If Ever I Cease to Love
May sheepheads grow on apple trees
If Ever I Cease to Love

May fish get legs and cows lay eggs
If Ever I Cease to Love

May dogs wag their tails in front
If Ever I Cease to Love

May we all turn into cats and dogs
If Ever I Cease to Love

Grand Duke Alexis Romanoff reviewed the Rex and Comus parades from a special stand erected at City Hall on St. Charles Avenue. The royal Russian declined to occupy the throne that had been prepared for him, preferring instead to sit next to Governor Henry Clay Warmoth.

The Monday King

For most of the years from 1874 to 1917, Rex made a grand entrance into New Orleans aboard a ship on the Monday before Fat Tuesday. The Mississippi River steamboat *Robert E. Lee* served as his personal carrier for several years. Often the "Monday King" was a stand-in for the man who would reign as Rex the next day. This king would assume the role of a historical character, such as Louis XIV, Charles II or Charlemagne.

Rex, 1907, on his way to City Hall in the royal carriage the day before Mardi Gras.

A 1915 publication reported:

Thousands lined the levees to watch Rex make his journey to the city by way of the river on his "Royal Yacht"... accompanied by tugs and merchant steamers. The arrival of the gaily decorated flotilla, amid the booming of cannon and the loud sounds of music...should not be missed. On his landing, Rex and his retinue, in brilliant military and civic procession, escorted by a crack military organization, proceed to City Hall, where he receives the keys to the city.

Robert H. Downman, Rex 1907, and his delegates disembark his steamship.

New Orleans artist John Pemberton depicted Rex arriving at Gallier Hall on Monday, February 11, 1907. For more than 135 years, the historic St. Charles Avenue building would serve as the official reviewing stand for most New Orleans Mardi Gras parades.

Sketch for "First Day King" costume, designed exclusively for Rex's Monday arrival.

Rex's royal yacht, bearing full Mardi Gras regalia.

The Knights of Momus

Patterned after Comus and Twelfth Night Revelers, but with a younger membership, the Knights of Momus debuted on New Year's Eve of 1872. As crowds gathered on Royal Street, Momus appeared on horseback, preceded by maskers on foot and followed by four floats that depicted Sir Walter Scott's *Talisman*. Momus' second parade was also staged on New Year's Eve. After a two-year hiatus, in 1876 the men moved their pageant to the Thursday before Fat Tuesday where, with two exceptions, it remained for 115 years. Momus paraded only 11 times during the 19th Century, but the club made international news with its 1877 parade, *Hades, a Dream of Momus*, which ridiculed President Grant's administration.

Invitation and admit card to the first Momus ball held at the French Opera House, where the Knights would stage 38 such events from 1872 until 1917.

Beautifully crafted dance cards were commonly provided for the ladies at the ball. Often more elaborate than the invitations themselves, they were intended to be tucked into scrapbooks as mementos of the occasion.

Who Was Momus?

Momus, the Greek god of laughter, mockery and ridicule, was the sireless son of Night. His job was to needle the other Olympian deities. In 1870 a Carnival group called the Knights of Momus had staged their first parade and ball in Galveston, Texas. Since this group shared the same motto as its New Orleans cousin — *Dum Vivimus, Vivamus* (While we live, Let us live) — it is assumed that there is some connection between the two groups, although no documentation exists.

In 1884 Momus appeared as the son of Night enthroned on an imaginary moon in a parade and ball entitled The Passions.

The theme of the second Momus ball and parade was The Coming Races. *That same year the Carnival group became associated with the Louisiana Club.*

In 1878 the invitation to the Knights of Momus' fifth annual ball, The Realm of Fantasy, *was lithographed in Paris.*

Satire on Parade

The War Between the States canceled four Mardi Gras celebrations, but the Reconstruction Era that followed had a longer effect on Carnival. The people of New Orleans resented the political and social order imposed on them by the forces that had triumphed over the Confederacy. The local and national Republican administrations provided thematic material for hard-hitting, satirical parades presented by TNR, Comus, and Momus. Conditions in New Orleans were so explosive that in 1875, those three, along with Rex, canceled their balls and parades.

In the 1880s and 1890s, the daughters of Confederate President Jefferson Davis and Confederate Generals Robert E. Lee, Stonewall Jackson, and D. H. Hill were honored at tableau balls presented by Comus and Momus.

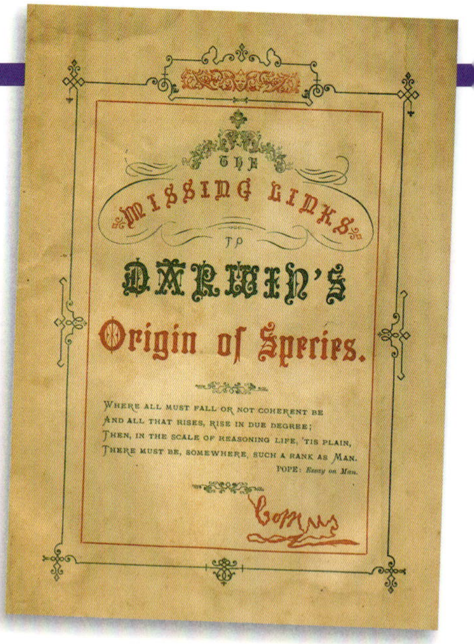

Charles Darwin was not very impressed with the Comus parade that carried his name. Shortly after the parade, he wrote to the Mistick Krewe:

Dear sir:
As I suppose that Comus and the newspapers were sent in good faith, I thank you for your kindness and for your letter. The abusive article in the newspaper amused me more than Comus: I can't tell from the wonderful mistakes in the article whether the writer is witty, ignorant, or blunders for the sake of fun.

Yours faithfully,
Ch. Darwin.

The 1873 Comus procession, which received full-page treatment in the Canadian Illustrated News, *was the first parade constructed completely in New Orleans. In previous years, all props came from France. Swedish lithographer Charles Briton designed this parade and the 1877 Momus parade, which also spoofed Reconstruction figures.*

A hyena carrying a large spoon bore the face of Union General Benjamin "Spoons" Butler, so named because of his alleged theft of silverware from New Orleans homes.

The Missing Links to Darwin's Origin of the Species

The Comus ball and parade of 1873, *The Missing Links to Darwin's Origin of the Species*, was a satire on Carpetbag rule and Darwinian theory. While many people enjoyed the humor, the parade was met by an angry mob on Canal Street. Fearing violence, the Mistick Krewe altered its parade route by avoiding the French Quarter and instead, marched directly to the Varieties Theater for its *bal masque*.

Among the many caricatures featured in the 1873 Comus procession was one of Ulysses S. Grant. The 18th president was portrayed as a tobacco grub because of his fondness for cigars.

As indicated on this invitation, Rex canceled his ball and parade in 1875, as did Comus, Momus and Twelfth Night Revelers. Post-Civil War conditions in New Orleans were so volatile that these organizations refused to take part in a festival of merry-making.

The 1873 Twelfth Night Revelers parade and ball, The World of Audubon, *were, for the most part, subtle parodies on local politicians. However, two floats — "The Political Barnyard Meeting" and "The Crows in the Council" — were direct in their mocking of the Louisiana State Legislature.*

Hades, a Dream of Momus

Carnival historians consider the Knights' 1877 parade, *Hades, a Dream of Momus*, the most sensational ever presented. Garbed in the guise of demons from mythology and the Bible, Momus maskers portrayed prominent national and local officials. President Ulysses Grant, who was depicted as Beelzebub, and his administration were taunted and ridiculed by the procession. The ensuing controversy reverberated all the way to Washington, D.C. and prompted the Louisiana Governor, Democrat Francis T. Nicholls, to apologize to the new Republican administration for the parade, claiming (falsely) that the procession was "universally condemned and regretted by the whole community." The parade was delayed because the floats were too wide to pass through the doorway of the den where they had been constructed.

The final two floats in the legendary 1877 Momus parade lampooned the Carpetbag Government and indivual legislators.

26

Daughters of the Confederacy

Comus had reigned without a queen since his first appearance in 1857. In 1884 at a tableau ball held at the French Opera House, the organization honored Mildred Lee and Mary Lee, daughters of General Robert E. Lee; Varina Davis, daughter of President Jefferson Davis; Nannie Hill, daughter of General D. H. Hill; and Julia Jackson, daughter of General Thomas "Stonewall" Jackson. Though not officially designated as such at the time, the "Daughters of the Confederacy" are considered to have been Comus' first court and Mildred Lee, the krewe's first queen.

Varina "Winnie" Davis, daughter of Confederate President Jefferson Davis, reigned as queen of the Knights of Momus in 1883 and was queen of the Mistick Krewe of Comus in 1892. When Mildred Lee, daughter of Robert E. Lee, reigned as queen of Comus in 1884, Winnie Davis served as a maid in her court.

Costumed in Japanese dresses to reflect the theme, Nippon, the Land of the Rising Sun, *the 1892 Comus court included (from left, standing) maids Nettie Miller, Josephine Maginnis; (seated) Emma Sinnott, Queen Winnie Davis.*

The Carnival Ball

The celebration of Carnival in New Orleans is made up of two equally important components. There is a public face and a private face.

Souvenir pins emblazoned with the krewe's name or initials were often presented to ladies at Carnival balls.

To the general populace, Mardi Gras consists of masking and street parades, to which of course no admission is charged. But there is yet another side of the festivity, and admission to that element is not for sale. It is the social world of the Mardi Gras ball. A hundred years before Carnival parades officially began rolling in the Crescent City, the city saw its first Carnival ball. The love of the dance was the primary attraction that *bals masques* provided in those early days. In the year 1850, more than 200 such events were presented, and they were not limited to the Carnival season. And in the century and a half that was to follow, ten times as many balls would be staged as parades would roll.

Invitation and envelope to the Rex ball, 1892. The twelve leaves folded out in the form of an artichoke.

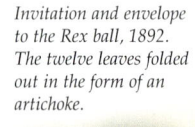

Costume De Rigueur

Unlike a masked ball, a Carnival ball requires full formal wear for all who attend. Admission is by non-transferable invitation issued in the name of each guest. These invitations and other ephemera generated by balls — admit cards, dance cards, krewe favors, and pins — are highly prized by collectors.

In 1899, The Ladies Home Journal *used these photographs to illustrate a story on Creole women of the Crescent City.*

Krewe favors, such as this 1899 Rex hand mirror, were often distributed as gifts at the balls.

High Society

The Carnival connection to the debutante scene in New Orleans is a long-standing one. Queens and maids of the older societies are almost always debutantes, while kings are prominent members of the club. In most of these organizations, with the notable exception of Rex, the king's identity is never revealed.

Elaborate staging and scenery enhanced the entertainment at the early balls. The 1880 tableau of Comus featured the Aztec people and their conquest by Cortez.

The Tableau Ball

The tableau ball introduced an element of theater to the festivities and ushered in the use of a ball theme, normally based on mythology or history, that is acted out by krewe members who appear in costumes and masks. And Carnival added still another feature to the ball, that of mock royalty, with kings, queens, royal courts and regal ceremony.

"Triumph of Bacchus," a tableau scene from the 1873 ball of Comus, Scenes from the Metamorphosis of Ovid.

1878 masquerade ball at the St. Charles Hotel.

The Ball Houses of New Orleans

New Orleans boasted many grand theaters in the 19th Century and most were well suited as venues for the *bals masques*, which were held year-round.

Exposition Hall, so named because it housed the Grand Industrial Exposition in 1872, was the home of every Rex ball from 1873 through 1906. Rex called it his Imperial Palace. The three-story building, which was bought by the Washington Artillery in 1880, was located on St. Charles Avenue between Girod and Julia Streets.

The Odd Fellows Hall, built at Camp and Lafayette Streets in 1852, was the ball site for several prominent Carnival organizations, including the Phunny Phorty Phellows, Two Well Known Gentlemen, the Carnival German and the Young Men's Society.

The Academy of Music and the St. Charles Theatre were popular sites for many *bals masques*.

The Athenaeum, located on St. Charles Avenue at Calliope Street, was the scene of hundreds of balls from 1896 until 1937. Rex presented his annual receptions here for 27 years. The krewes of Olympians, Athenians, Mystery, Osiris, Mystic, Harlequins, and Prophets of Persia presented their first balls here. Twelfth Night Revelers, Momus, Proteus, Atlanteans, Oberon, Nereus, and Mithras also used the Athenaeum.

For more than 60 years, the French Opera House, on Bourbon Street, corner Toulouse, was at the very center of cultural and Carnival life in New Orleans. It was designed by noted architect James Gallier in 1859.

The 1870s: History on Parade

Despite the political turmoil that canceled Carnival in 1875, and the yellow fever epidemic limiting the celebration in 1879, Mardi Gras grew rapidly in grandeur and in popularity during the 1870s. The Mistick Krewe of Comus was joined by Twelfth Night Revelers, Rex and Momus; collectively they presented 28 parades during the decade. While some processions lampooned political figures, most centered on historical events. Visitors flocked to New Orleans to see these moving spectacles.

Admit cards to the first eight Comus balls directed guests to the Varieties Theater.

In the early days of Comus, ball invitations occasionally memorialized themes of the current and past parades. In 1871, four black stars represented the Civil War years, which had darkened the Carnival celebration in New Orleans.

The King and Queen of Carnival receive their royal guests at the 1873 Rex ball, held at the Carnival Palace.

A scene from the 1874 Twelfth Night Revelers' ball, Dolliana and Her Kingdom, held at the French Opera House.

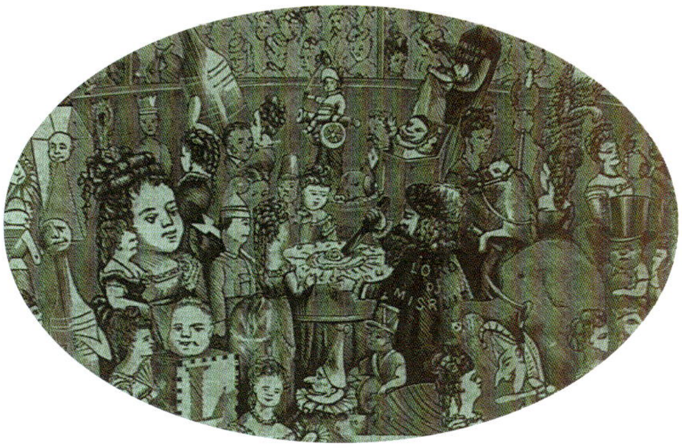

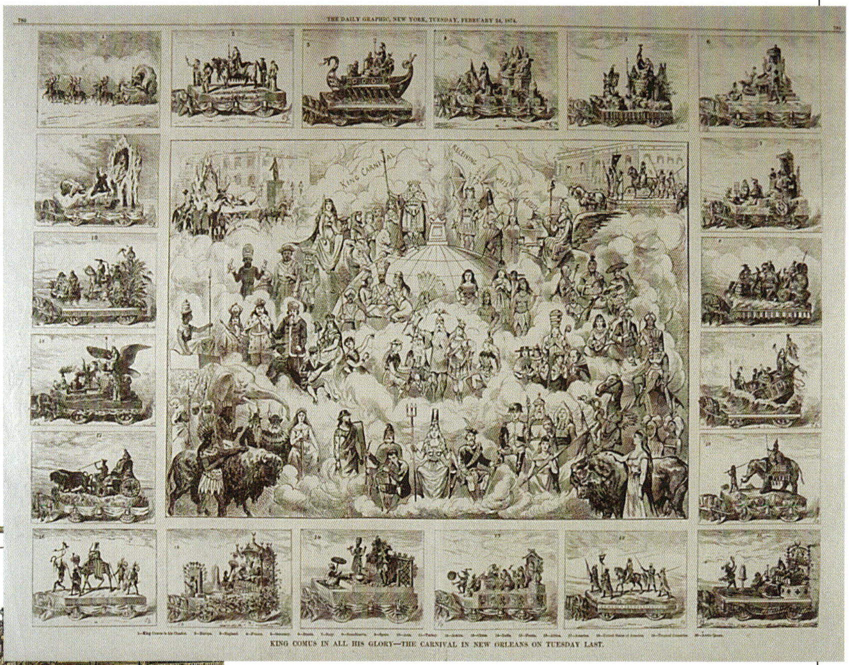

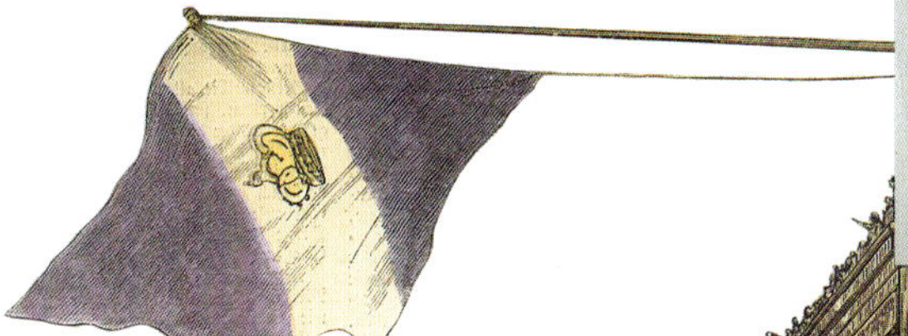

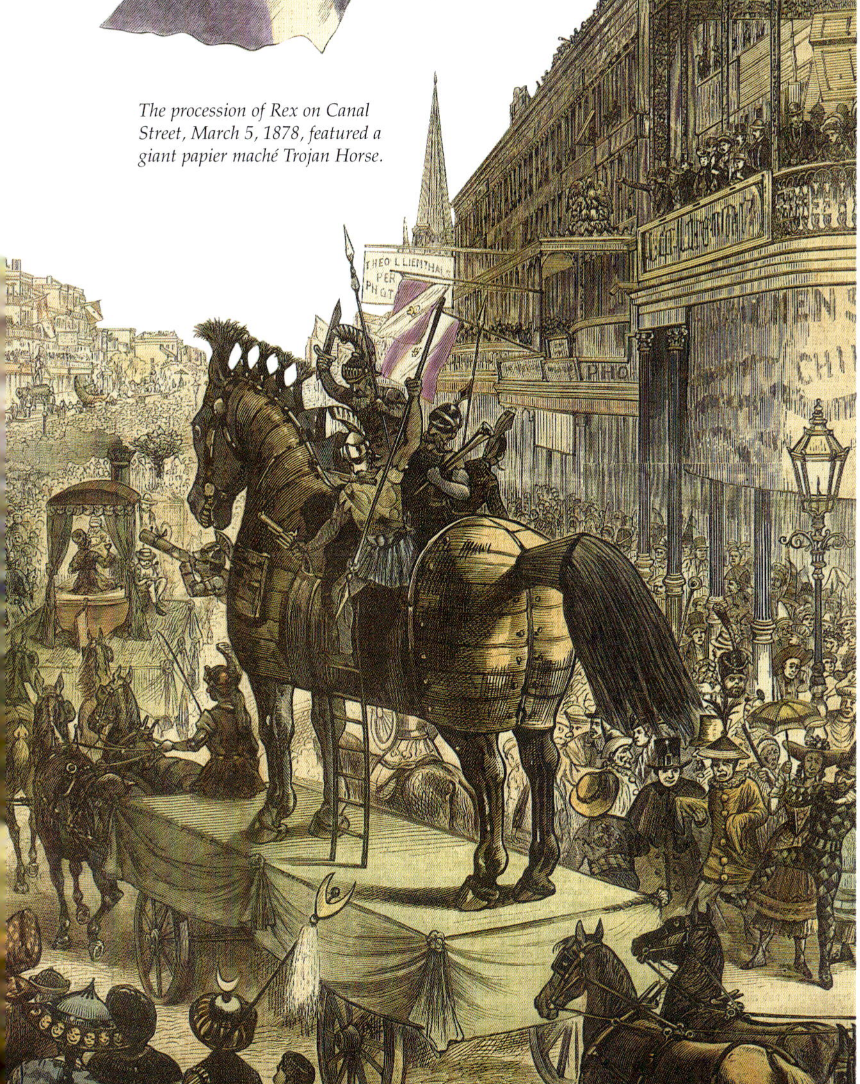

The procession of Rex on Canal Street, March 5, 1878, featured a giant papier maché Trojan Horse.

Parading Past History

In 1874, the first in a continuing series of parade papers was produced. These fold-out "Carnival Bulletins," originally printed in black and white, then in full-color, illustrated all of the floats in each parade. The last set of these chromolithographs was produced in 1941.

HAND BOOK

—OF—

THE CARNIVAL

CONTAINING

MARDI-GRAS

ITS ANCIENT AND MODERN OBSERVANCE;

History of the Mystick Krewe of Comus,

The Twelfth Night Revelers,

& Knights of Momus,

WITH ANNALS OF THE REIGN OF HIS MAJESTY,

The King of the Carnival

IN NEW ORLEANS.

Entered according to Act of Congress in the year 1873, in the Office of the Librarian of Congress at Washington.

NEW ORLEANS:

John W. Madden, Printer and Stationer, 73 Camp street.

1873.

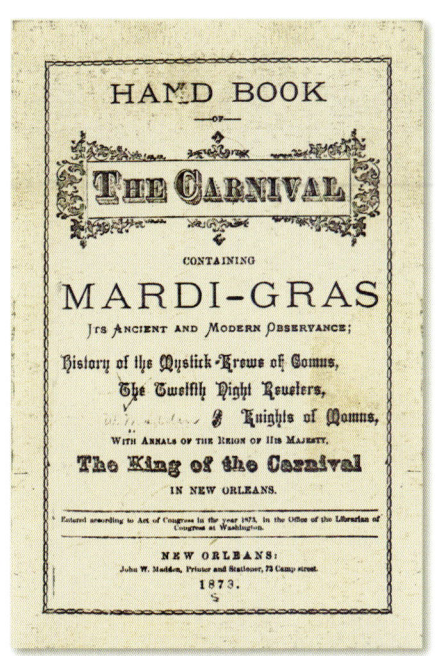

The first history of Mardi Gras, a 144-page volume, was published in New Orleans by John Madden in 1873. That same year, in an attempt to attract passengers to the Crescent City, the Western & Atlantic Railroad in Atlanta issued a condensed version of this book.

The foldout invitation to the 1879 Rex ball illustrated important historical events.

Adam and Eve and Noah's Ark were depicted as Rex presented a comical look at The History of the World *with his seventh parade in 1879.*

Costumes and papier maché props for the 1878 Comus parade, Scenes from the Metamorphosis of Ovid, *were made in Paris and assembled in New Orleans.*

Two invitations like this one were the subject of an announcement in an 1877 edition of The Daily Picayune. *The reward went unclaimed and the invitations unused.*

REWARD — $2000 ! !
Whereas, two invitations to my festival, each numbered 22, have been stolen by some disloyal subject, now, therefore, be it known, that a reward of $1,000 each will be paid by the keeper of my privy purse for the return of the same to the custodian of our royal archives.
  This done in the twentieth year of our reign, anno domini, 1877.
    — COMUS

In 1878, Frank Leslie's Illustrated Weekly, *published in New York, devoted three full pages to its coverage of the Rex parade in New Orleans. In* The Gods Modernized, *the King of Carnival spoofed Olympic deities and local institutions.*

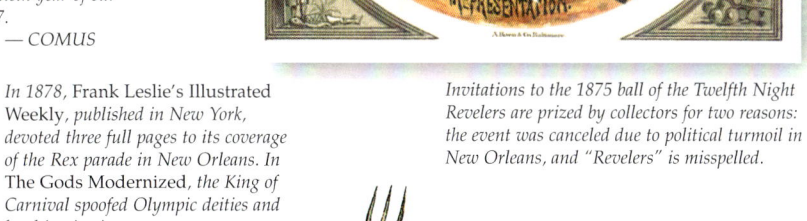

Invitations to the 1875 ball of the Twelfth Night Revelers are prized by collectors for two reasons: the event was canceled due to political turmoil in New Orleans, and "Revelers" is misspelled.

35

The Krewe of Proteus

Because of long waiting lists for membership in the Mistick Krewe of Comus and the Knights of Momus, a group of young men, mostly from the New Orleans Cotton Exchange, created their own organization, the Krewe of Proteus. In Greek mythology, Proteus was the son of Poseidon, and the shepherd of his seals. Proteus possessed the gift of prophecy and the ability to change shape at will.

In 1882, the new Carnival club made its debut with a 17-float procession entitled *Ancient Egyptian Theology*. Just months after the first parade, Proteus was chartered under the name, the Crescent Club.

1896 Proteus queen, Miss Vira Boardman.

Invitation to the first Proteus ball in 1882.

1891 Proteus dance card.

- First to have a queen at its initial ball (1882).
- First to parade for 36 consecutive years (1882-1917).
- First to introduce the call-out section of reserved seats (1893).
- First to be snowed out (1899). First to be rained out (1927).
- First krewe with a Creole captain and a sizeable Creole membership.
- First parading krewe to use the Municipal Auditorium for its ball (1930).
- First krewe with a female designer, Carlotta Bonnecaze (1884).
- Only krewe to stage balls at French Opera House for 36 consecutive years.

Title float and king's float from Proteus' 1882 inaugural parade, **Ancient Egyptian Theology.**

Proteus introduced a new feature to the tableau ball in 1893. The krewe announced in the newspapers' society sections, "In order to (accommodate) the ladies who have been specially invited to take part in the maskers' dances…. Proteus will set apart for them the parquette seats…." This area of reserved seating came to be known as the "call-out" section.

The 1892 Proteus invitation is an outstanding example of the lavishly illustrated and die-cut ball invitations of the period.

When Comus withdrew from the parade scene in 1885, the Krewe of Proteus moved its parade from Monday to Mardi Gras night. Five years later Comus returned to reclaim his position on Fat Tuesday evening. Both parades planned to traverse Canal Street. However, because several Comus floats had broken down, the Mistick Krewe had not cleared Canal and Bourbon Streets when Proteus was set to turn into the French Quarter on its way to the Opera House. It appeared that Proteus would cut through the middle of the Comus parade. A heated exchange took place between the captains of both clubs before Proteus yielded to its older cousin.

Where's My Costume?

In 1883 costumes for the Proteus ball and parade, along with those for Rex and Momus, were late in arriving from Europe when foul weather kept the ship *Dryburg Abbey* at sea. Momus borrowed costumes from Comus, which was not parading that year, while Rex and Proteus scurried around town to round up appropriate outfits. Proteus officials admitted that their costumes were "shabby and did little to represent their French theme." The next year, all costumes were produced locally.

Proteus' second parade in 1883 celebrated the History of France.

CARNIVAL TRADITION

THE FLAMBEAUX

Gas-fueled torches, or flambeaux, had been used to illuminate night parades starting with the first Comus parade in 1857. Hundreds of them once provided the only source of lighting for the Comus, Momus, and Proteus processions.

In 1880, British journalist George Augustus Sala visited New Orleans and reported, "The Americans have vastly improved on these primitive (European) flambeaux. Their so-called torches are carried on tall poles…fed by petroleum…the illuminating power of which is increased by immense reflectors…"

Less than 50 original units survive. Their use in a half-dozen 21st Century parades is strictly ornamental. In modern times, appreciative parade viewers often toss coins at the feet of the flambeau carriers, who dance along the parade route while twirling the lighted torches.

A traditional gas-fueled flambeau. Competition is fierce among the African-American men who vie for the right to carry the lighted torches.

19th Century flambeau illustration from the March 8, 1884, Harper's Weekly.

The scene from Proteus' 1898 parade, A Trip to Wonderland *— the earliest known nighttime photo of a Mardi Gras parade — was captured by New Orleans photographer, J. N. Teunisson.*

In this oil painting by noted New Orleans artist John Pemberton, flambeau carriers prepare to take up their positions alongside the floats in the Proteus parade of 1907.

39

The 1880s: Golden Invitations

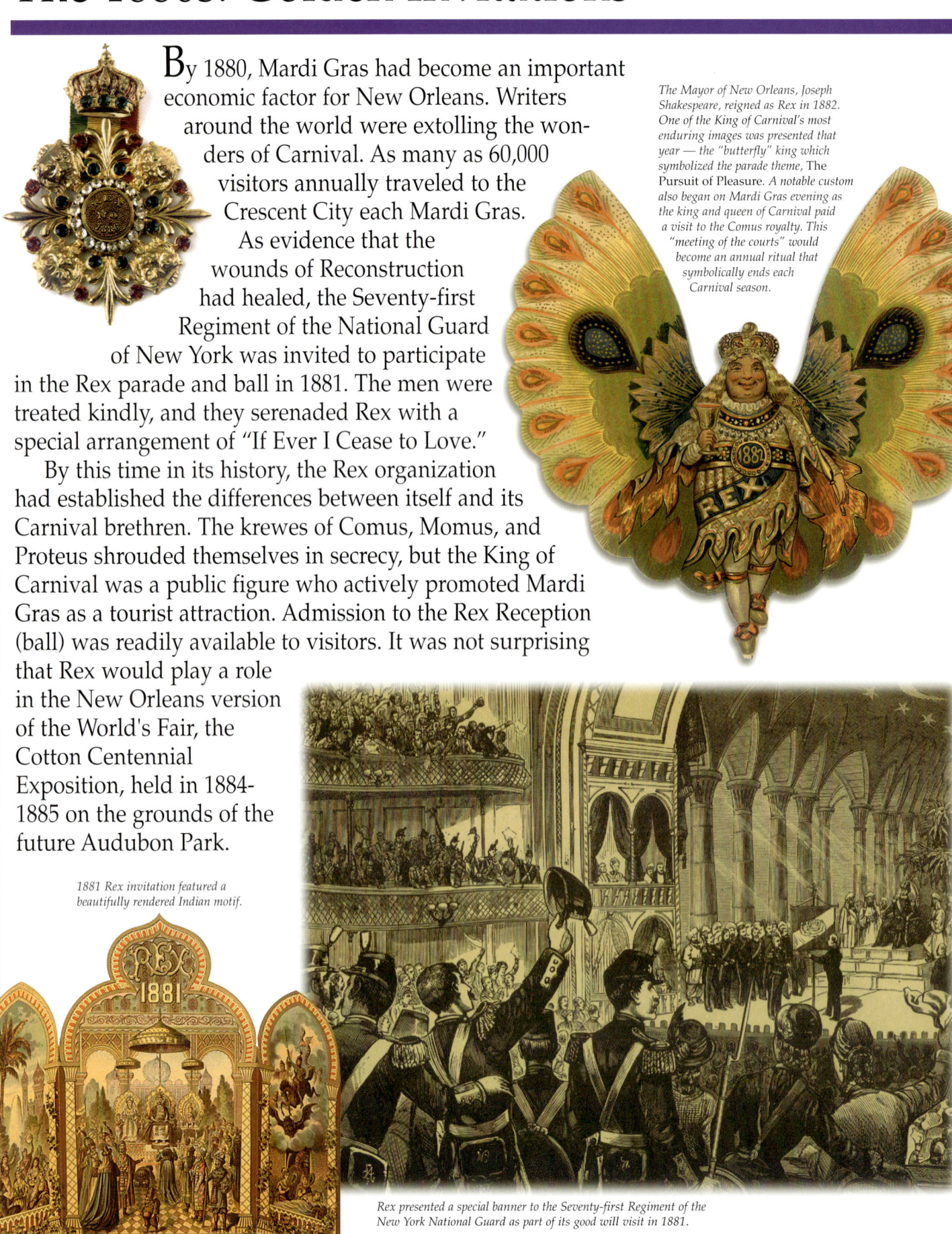

By 1880, Mardi Gras had become an important economic factor for New Orleans. Writers around the world were extolling the wonders of Carnival. As many as 60,000 visitors annually traveled to the Crescent City each Mardi Gras. As evidence that the wounds of Reconstruction had healed, the Seventy-first Regiment of the National Guard of New York was invited to participate in the Rex parade and ball in 1881. The men were treated kindly, and they serenaded Rex with a special arrangement of "If Ever I Cease to Love."

By this time in its history, the Rex organization had established the differences between itself and its Carnival brethren. The krewes of Comus, Momus, and Proteus shrouded themselves in secrecy, but the King of Carnival was a public figure who actively promoted Mardi Gras as a tourist attraction. Admission to the Rex Reception (ball) was readily available to visitors. It was not surprising that Rex would play a role in the New Orleans version of the World's Fair, the Cotton Centennial Exposition, held in 1884-1885 on the grounds of the future Audubon Park.

The Mayor of New Orleans, Joseph Shakespeare, reigned as Rex in 1882. One of the King of Carnival's most enduring images was presented that year — the "butterfly" king which symbolized the parade theme, The Pursuit of Pleasure. *A notable custom also began on Mardi Gras evening as the king and queen of Carnival paid a visit to the Comus royalty. This "meeting of the courts" would become an annual ritual that symbolically ends each Carnival season.*

1881 Rex invitation featured a beautifully rendered Indian motif.

Rex presented a special banner to the Seventy-first Regiment of the New York National Guard as part of its good will visit in 1881.

James H. Maury, Rex 1885, greets spectators on Canal Street on Fat Tuesday. The parade theme was Tales of Ivanhoe.

The first "one-hit-wonder" in Carnival circles was the Mistick Merry Bellions, which paraded only once, in 1884. The group satirized popular culture.

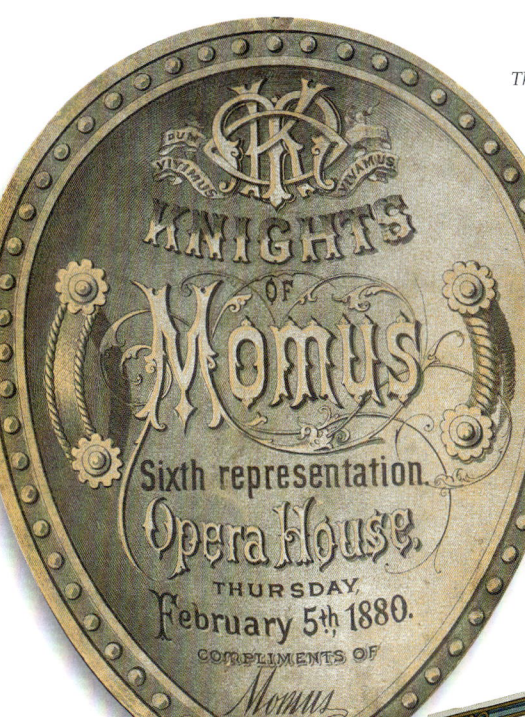

The 1880 Momus parade was heavily criticized in the press. With the theme, A Dream of Fair Women, *the men appeared in feminine costumes and masks, much to the displeasure of the crowds.*

Many of the debutantes who reigned as Carnival royalty would later travel to Paris to sit for a portrait in their royal gowns. Noticeably absent here are the royal jewels, which could only be worn during her reign as queen.

Portrait of Miss Susie Richardson, Queen of Carnival 1883.

Starting in 1878, a group of fun-loving gentlemen decided to spoof the volunteer groups that annually assembled in New Orleans every March 4 for a mammoth firemen's parade. Masking as the "Rex Volunteer Fire Company #40," they followed the King of Carnival's procession with a satirical collection of floats and maskers. The king of these Phunny Phorty Phellows was known as "The Boss," and he rode at the head of the parade.

41

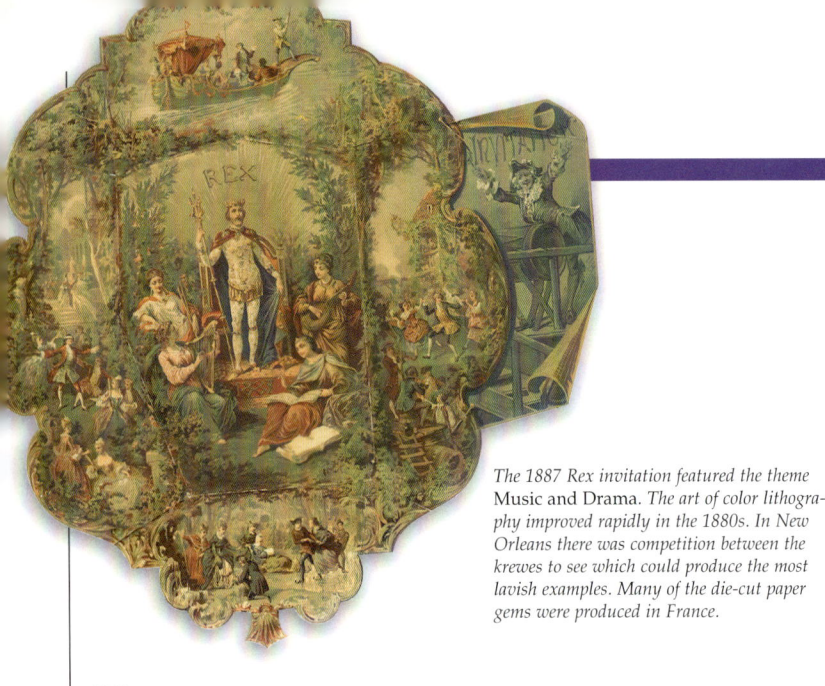

The 1887 Rex invitation featured the theme Music and Drama. *The art of color lithography improved rapidly in the 1880s. In New Orleans there was competition between the krewes to see which could produce the most lavish examples. Many of the die-cut paper gems were produced in France.*

The success of Carnival in New Orleans did not go unnoticed by some other cities that also tried to capitalize on Mardi Gras as a tourist attraction. In the late 1870s, Natchez, Vicksburg, and Memphis scheduled large celebrations on Fat Tuesday. The Rex organization lent its help to a pair of other Carnival groups — the Orioles in Baltimore in 1881 and the Order of Cincinnatus in Cincinnati the next year.

Not all Mardi Gras organizations flourished within this period, however. Because of financial difficulties, Comus and Momus managed a total of only 11 parades during the 1880s, and Twelfth Night Revelers ceased operations. The decade ended with a less than spectacular Knights of Electra parade, a disappointing attempt by the Edison Company to present an electric light procession.

Artisans at the French Opera House, circa 1880, constructing props for an upcoming Mardi Gras ball.

Sponsored by the Edison Company, the Knights of Electra announced a procession of 308 characters, all connected by concealed wires. Eight horses were to pull the dynamo and steam engine that powered the incandescent globes. The twice-postponed 1889 parade finally rolled on Ash Wednesday and did not live up to its pre-parade publicity.

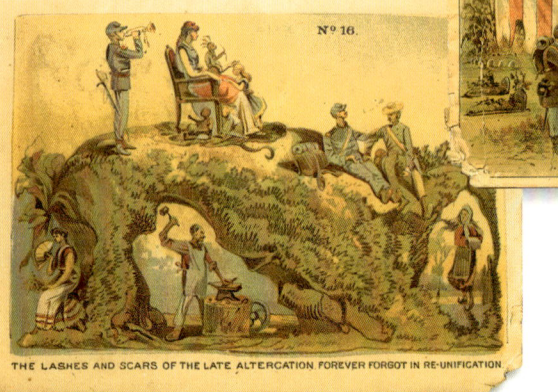

The Independent Order of the Moon, founded in 1883 and patterned after the Phunny Phorty Phellows, presented a 16-float parade in 1887 entitled This Yankee Nation, *a poetic salute to life in the United States. Float No. 16 represented "The Lashes and Scars of the Late Altercation Forever Forgot in Re-unification."*

42

The King of Carnival saluted blossoms and blooms from the garden of the Roman goddess Flora with his 1888 parade, The Realm of Flowers.

Art and geometry combine to make this 1882 Momus invitation a standout. When folded, the star becomes an octagon.

The scene from the Rex parade of 1887 on St. Charles Avenue is the earliest known photograph of a day parade.

43

Rex at the World's Fair

Exactly two months after the official opening of the New Orleans World's Industrial and Cotton Centennial Exposition, the King of Carnival brought Mardi Gras to the Fair. On Monday, February 16, 1885, Rex arrived by Illinois Central Railways; then, dressed as France's Charles VII, he rode a white stallion at the head of a military pageant that paraded from City Hall to the foot of Canal Street. There the regal entourage boarded the steamer *Edward Richardson* and led an 18-vessel naval parade up the Mississippi River as thousands of citizens cheered from the levees.

The first Rex medallion was struck in Philadelphia for the World's Industrial and Cotton Centennial Exposition in 1884-1885.

From the February 17, 1885, *Daily States*:

RECEPTION OF REX AT THE EXPOSITION

   The scene at the great Exposition yesterday was one which will pass into the annals of history written upon one separate page in the brightest colors memory can picture. Such an occasion never was before presented, and probably never will be again. The Exposition in its magnitude and beauty was of itself a sufficient attraction for the throng … but the sight of the reception of Rex, held in the spacious Music Hall, must have been one of unequaled beauty….
Who can describe that throng, or estimate the number? For hours before, every available seat, perch, position or standing place anywhere near the immense Music Hall had been held by the lucky first-comers. By bodily force an opening was made in the packed vestibule, the troops formed a line, and Rex and the dukes of his realm, in their gay regalia, proudly advanced to their throne room, concealed by a drawn curtain…The royal party in a few minutes were seated, the curtain was drawn aside, and a shout went up from the multitude as the scene of royal grandeur burst upon their enraptured gaze.

1885 Rex invitation.

The 1885 Rex parade depicted the Tales of Ivanhoe, *but the King of Carnival also paid tribute to the World's Fair.*

Later that day Rex and his subjects were entertained at the Music Hall on the Exposition grounds by a band led by a young conductor named John Philip Sousa. Rex's Fat Tuesday procession depicted the *Adventures of Ivanhoe*, but the World's Fair did not go unacknowledged as mounted maskers carried the flags of all participating nations. The King of Carnival appeared as the "Ruler of Industry" and was surrounded by female figures representing Agriculture, Mining, Navigation, and Trade. The second float honored Louisiana, the host state of the Exposition. While about half of the exhibitions remained open on Mardi Gras, newspaper reports likened the grounds to a ghost town. Rex had out-drawn the World's Fair!

The main building of the World's Fair of 1884-85 covered 33 acres at the future site of Audubon Park.

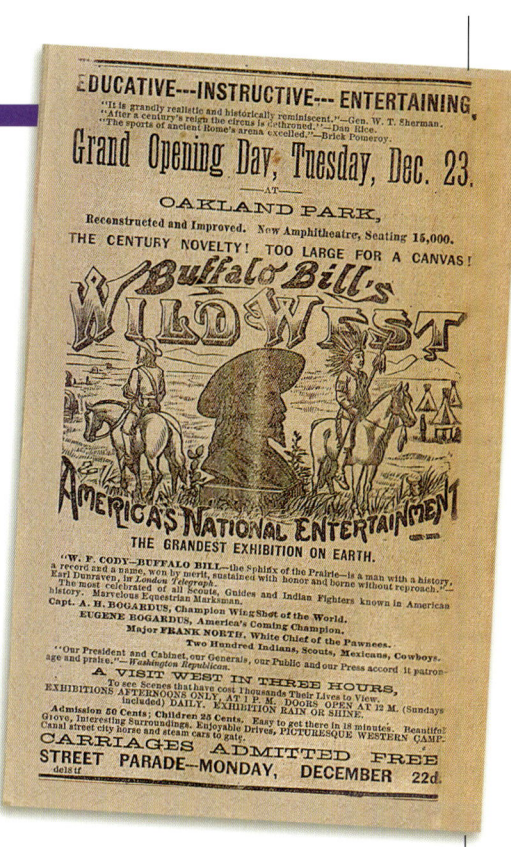

Buffalo Bill's Wild West extravaganza spent several months in New Orleans. The show's opening was advertised in the December 21, 1884 issue of the New Orleans States.

Mardi Gras Indians

The origin of African-Americans' participation in Carnival in New Orleans was unfortunately not recorded, but the rich tradition of the black Mardi Gras Indians dates from at least the mid-1880s. These small, beautifully costumed groups do not function as traditional Carnival krewes. Evidence suggests that local blacks were influenced by Plains Indians who appeared in New Orleans with Buffalo Bill's Wild West Show in 1884. The oral history of the Creole Wild West Indian tribe indicates that Becate Batiste, of African, Choctaw, and French descent, founded the group in 1885.

The 1890s: Presenting the Tableau

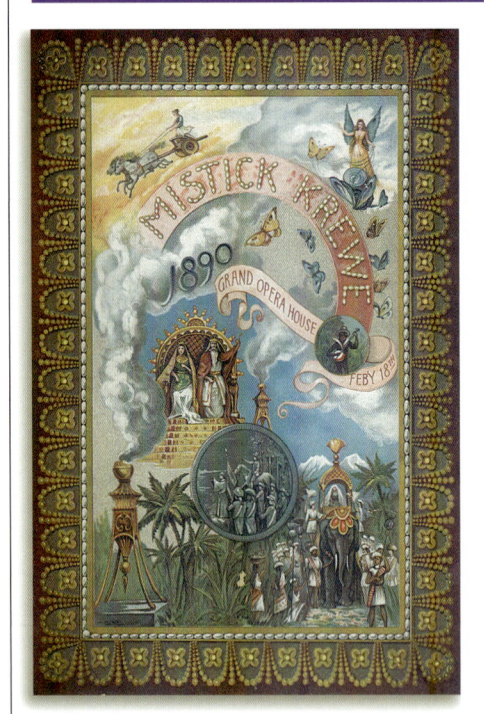

The final decade of the 19th Century was one of expansion in the number of Carnival organizations, but not in the number of parading krewes. Emphasis shifted toward clubs whose sole interest was in staging elaborate tableau balls. Four such society krewes destined to continue into the 21st Century were founded: Atlanteans (1891); Elves of Oberon (1895); Nereus (1896); and the High Priests of Mithras (1897). The Krewe of Consus (1897-1906) presented some of the most spectacular balls in history.

Also born during the period was the first krewe made up of celebrants on foot (Jefferson City Buzzards, 1890); the first Mardi Gras organization for African-Americans (Illinois Club, 1895), and the first Carnival club for women (Les Mysterieuses, 1896).

While Rex, Proteus, and Comus prospered, the Knights of Momus withdrew from the parading fraternity from 1888 until 1900. However, the men continued to produce balls, and one was perhaps their most memorable. In 1896, the stage of the French Opera House was decorated with papier maché scenes of Canal Street, complete with replicas of the Boston and Pickwick Clubs. A procession of 18 miniature floats amazed the thousands who had gathered in honor of Momus' 20th tableau ball.

After a five-year hiatus, Comus returned in 1890 with a 23-float parade entitled Palingenesis of the Mistick Krewe, *a salute to Comus processions of the past.*

Ladies in attendance at the King of Carnival's ball in 1890 received a foldout invitation that doubled as a fan.

1890 Proteus dance card measured six inches long and opened at the center.

In 1891 the Rex organization issued the largest Mardi Gras ball invitation ever produced. Measuring 20 inches x 15 inches, the colorful piece was delivered by hand by the Boylen Security Service.

Why Mardi Gras?

An 1890 publication, *The Current Magazine*, had this to say about the value of Mardi Gras: "Mardi Gras is a great educational factor, for the devices and make-up of the processions are refined and intellectual; and lookers-on are treated without fee or reward to public pageants as splendid, brilliant and beautiful as the genius and skill of man and the lavish expenditure of money can make them. Pages from mythical and modern histories are explained by gorgeously illuminated cars of wit, satire, humor, and intellectual feasts."

The Grand Opera House was the scene for the first three tableau balls presented by the new Krewe of Atlanteans, which debuted in 1891 with a lavish reenactment of The Destruction of Atlantis.

Fancy dress was the order of the day for those reviewing the Rex parade from a Canal Street balcony in 1892.

Walking Clubs

Semi-organized groups of maskers had appeared in Carnival for years, but the only group to survive more than a decade was the Jefferson City Buzzards, which incorporated in 1890. They were named for a suburban section of New Orleans known as the Faubourg Jefferson City. In place of masks, these costumed revelers appeared in blackface.

Justice, Power & Faith

One of the few official things about Mardi Gras is its colors: purple, gold and green. Rex chose them prior to his first appearance in 1872 for reasons that remain unknown. Perhaps they were selected because they were visually pleasing or were chosen to comply with the general rules of heraldry which dictate the various fields of metals and colors that comprise a tri-colored flag. In any case, in 1950, when Rex decided to assign a meaning to each, he looked back to his 1892 parade, *Symbolism of Colors*, in which each float's color carried a theme. Rex thereby decreed that purple stands for justice, gold for power, and green for faith.

1893 Proteus dance card from the ball, The Myths of Finland.

The 1898 Krewe of Nereus invitation was an elaborate creation, complete with the keys to the gates of Hell.

In Shakespeare's A Midsummer Night's Dream, *Oberon was the King of Fairyland. The Elves of Oberon presented their first ball at the Grand Opera House in 1895. The krewe was hailed as a welcome addition to the small group of tableau societies.*

Original Illinois Club

In 1895, former Chicago resident Wiley Knight formed Knight's School of Dancing in New Orleans and then organized the Illinois Club for the purpose of staging formal balls for African-Americans. Annual highlights of the Illinois ball are the introduction of debutantes and a father-daughter minuet-style dance called the "Chicago Glide."

Considered by the press as "lascivious" at the time, the balls of the Two Well Known Gentlemen were populated by prostitutes who gathered annually at the Odd Fellows Hall for these popular Carnival events.

Leap year brought with it a giant jump for women in New Orleans in 1896 with the founding of the first female Carnival organization, Les Mysterieuses.

Miss Emily Poitevent, Queen of Comus, 1895.

Miss L.W. Fairchild, Queen of Carnival, 1895.

Frank T. Howard, Rex 1895.

A Royal Wedding

Rex saluted *Chronicles of Fairyland — Fantastic Tales for Young and Old* in his 1895 pageant. Rex that year, Frank T. Howard, would be the only King of Carnival to eventually marry his queen. Her name was Lydia Fairchild.

Created by noted Carnival designer Bror Andrews Wikstrom, the Heavenly Bodies *1896 parade and ball occasioned a fold-out invitation that featured a celestial backdrop through which Rex charged forth.*

After an absence of eleven years, the Phunny Phorty Phellows made a triumphant return in 1896 with a parade and ball entitled Phads and Phancies.

More than a dozen Mardi Gras-inspired songs were published prior to 1900, including George Rosey's King Carnival March *in 1898. The sheet music for this cakewalk was printed in New York and distributed throughout the United States and Europe.*

This invitation is to one of the six balls presented by the Harmony Club, a Carnival organization that lasted only those half-dozen years. Its luxurious stone and marble clubhouse on St. Charles Avenue survived well into the 20th Century.

The High Priests of Mithras, a club named after a Persian mythological figure, debuted in 1897 with a ball at the French Opera House. The next year, a fire would disrupt their evening presentation at the French Quarter landmark.

The undersea world was the domain of the Krewe of Nereus, which debuted in 1896. In his second presentation, Nereus depicted Coral Groves and Grottoes. The ball featured a 100-foot long sea monster that belched fire.

This 1899 Comus dance card was the final Carnival memento of the 19th Century.

The Krewe of Consus presented its first ball in 1897. The club lasted only ten years, but Consus reigned supreme as the presenter of the most extraordinary balls of the period.

Mardi Gras 1899 saw New Orleans covered in snow. Temperatures dipped to an all-time low of 6.8 degrees the Sunday before Fat Tuesday. Legend has it that Rex paraded with a frozen mustache. Proteus postponed its parade until the Friday after Ash Wednesday.

51

Carnival Turns the Century

The period from 1900 to 1929 witnessed many changes in Carnival. Mardi Gras survived World War I (despite being canceled in 1918 and 1919), Prohibition and the closing of the beloved French Opera House, home of Carnival balls for more than a half-century. Mardi Gras' most famous African-American organization, the Krewe of Zulu, was founded in 1909. Rex abandoned his Monday river arrivals, the distribution of favors and die-cut ball invitations, and he removed from Mardi Gras its oldest tradition — the live boeuf gras in its parade — because it was "not in harmony with the beautiful displays which are produced in this era."

The Krewe of Nereus attempted a Carnival first during the first year of the new century — an entire parade mounted on streetcars.

Many short-lived tableau societies sprang up in the first third of the 20th Century, including Amphictyons, Apollonians, Argonauts, Artemesians, Empyreans, Titanians, Falstaffians, Indra, Mittens, and the Mystic Maids. Among the more popular were the Asian-inspired Krewe of Nippon, and Yami, a female group, whose krewe utilized a Hindu motif.

Famous visitors

Chinese ambassador Ting Fang Wu received a warm welcome to the Crescent City in 1900 and attended the Proteus ball at the French Opera House. In 1903, Alice Roosevelt, daughter of President Teddy Roosevelt, attended the Atlanteans ball. In 1920, General John J. Pershing, Commander of the American troops in Europe in WWI, was a guest of the city. Rex named the distinguished officer, the Duke of Victory. Six years later, President-Elect Taft enjoyed Mardi Gras. In 1928 *The Times-Picayune* stated, "New York Mayor Jimmy Walker quickly found out that the main purpose of Mardi Gras is to have a good time and no subject of Rex spent a more riotous day than the New York Mayor."

William Howard Taft

For the only time in history, the Rex organization published a special booklet in 1900 that included illustrations of each of its 19 floats.

Scepter carried by the Queen of Carnival 1909, Miss Edith Libby.

52

Birth of Zulu

As early as 1901, a group called The Tramps marched on Fat Tuesday. They were one of many "benevolent aid societies" that functioned as insurance providers and burial societies in the black community. The inspiration for the name Zulu came about in 1909 when a group of these African-American laborers went to the Pythian Temple Theater to see a musical comedy entitled "The Smart Set." The production included a skit about a Zulu tribe called "There Never Was A King Like Me." William Story, the first Zulu king (1909), in a parody of Rex, wore a lard can as his crown and ruled with a banana stalk in place of a scepter. Floats mounted on wagons and decorated with palmetto leaves and moss were added to Zulu's walking parades in 1915. The next year the men officially incorporated as the Zulu Social Aid and Pleasure Club.

King Zulu 1927, Arnold L. Moss.

A crowd of black maskers gathers on South Claiborne Avenue on Fat Tuesday, 1915.

Rex was not the only royalty to arrive by water. King Zulu and his entourage traveled by tug boat on the New Basin Canal.

ZULU FIRSTS
- First Mardi Gras parade by African-Americans.
- First krewe to feature a signature throw, the Zulu coconut.
- First krewe to feature a celebrity monarch, Louis Armstrong.
- First krewe to integrate.

Zulu members (left to right) John L. Metoyer Jr., James Russell, Leopold LeBlanc, Ovide Steward and John Kelly.

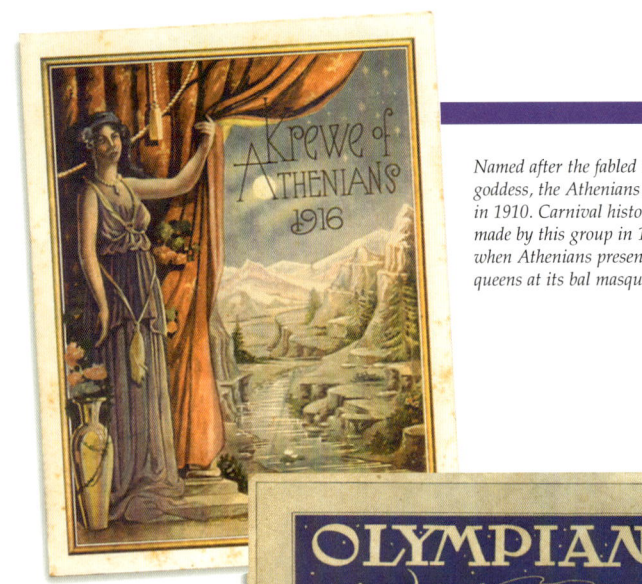

Named after the fabled Greek goddess, the Athenians started in 1910. Carnival history was made by this group in 1933 when Athenians presented 10 queens at its bal masque.

What started in 1899 as the "Youth Literary Society" developed in 1903 into the Krewe of Olympians. This collection of Creole gentlemen disbanded in 1918 but reorganized in 1934.

The sidewalk-to-sidewalk throngs that appeared on Canal Street in the Teens would turn into sparse and unenthusiastic crowds when Prohibition removed one of the season's more pleasurable elements. By the mid-1920s, however, the spirit of Mardi Gras had returned. Fat Tuesday again saw a mixture of well dressed citizens and an odd collection of maskers all lined up to see the Rex parade.

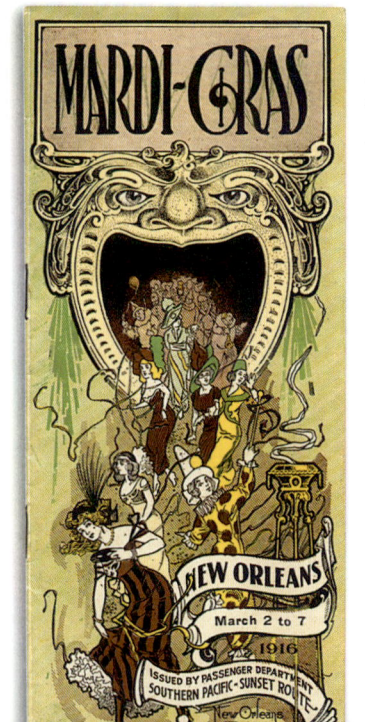

Elaborately illustrated travel brochures, like this 1916 Southern Pacific pamphlet, were produced annually by the railroads to entice visitors to the city.

All social classes join in the fun of masking for Carnival. For one day of the year, a pauper can become a prince and a debutante can become a clown.

A sea of derbies and bonnets on Canal Street (circa 1910) reveals that Mardi Gras was not then the casual affair it would become.

Carnival Balls' Home Burns

On the morning of December 4, 1919, the city lost is cultural crown jewel when the 60-year old French Opera House burned to the ground. Popular New Orleans author Lyle Saxon wrote in *The Times-Picayune*:

"Gone, all gone....The opera house has gone in a blaze of horror and glory. There is a pall over the city; eyes are filled with tears and hearts are heavy....The heart of the old French Quarter has stopped beating."

Roaring with the Twenties

The Fraternal Order of the Druids mounted eight parades in the 1920s and became a highlight of Fat Tuesday. Major ball organizations founded included Harlequins, Mystic Club, Prophets of Persia, Apollo and Les Marionettes. Two clubs that would eventually stage parades were also started, the Krewe of Iris and the Seventh District Carnival and Pleasure Club. A faction of the Illinois Club broke off and formed the Young Men Illinois Club in 1926. That same year the Children's Carnival Club was founded as the first Mardi Gras ball organization for youngsters.

CARNIVAL TRADITION

THROW ME SOMETHING, MISTER!

In 1921, the Rex organization added an element that changed the face of Mardi Gras when it began the custom of throwing strands of beads to the crowds. Individual float riders had occasionally tossed favors in previous parades, but Rex formalized the practice with all members participating.

For many years, elementary school teacher and Newcomb College graduate Louis Andrews Fisher designed the parades of Rex and Momus.

First aerial shot of Mardi Gras in 1929.

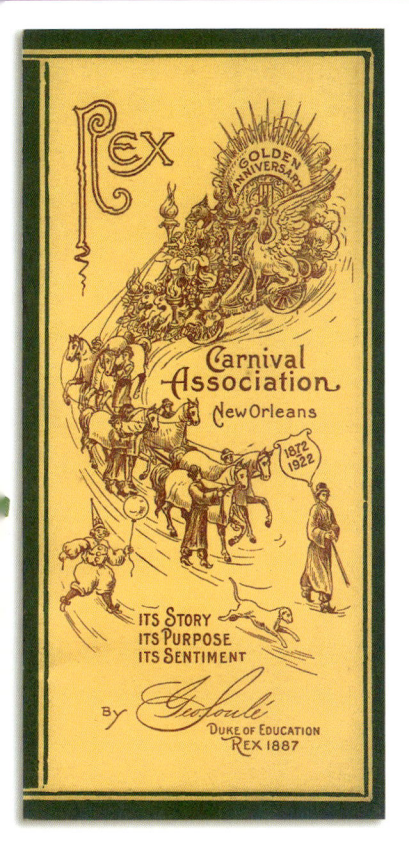

Col. George Soulé, Rex 1887 and founder of Soulé College.

Crown worn by the King of Carnival, Leonidas M. Pool, in 1925.

For the Public Good

As part of its 50th anniversary in 1922, the Rex organization issued a brochure penned by the "Duke of Education," George Soulé, who reigned as Rex in 1887. The former king explained that the purpose of Rex was to operate *Pro Bono Publico*, for the public good.

"The magnificent pageants presented by the Rex Association are of great social and civic value, for they bring together in joyous mood the people of the North, the South, the East, and the West, and by this interstate social intercourse, political animosities are subdued, personal prejudices are dethroned, and lasting friendships are formed."

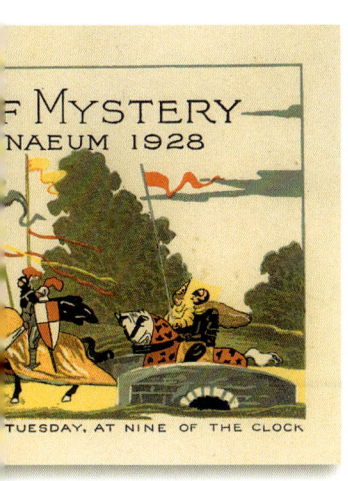

In 1912 a small group of young men started the Krewe of Mystery, an organization that presented spectacular masquerade balls each year on the Wednesday preceding Fat Tuesday.

In an effort to attract visitors to the Crescent City, the Rex organization produced broadside proclamations which were posted in train depots across the country.

The Mystic Club would be the last of the elite society balls to be founded. From its first presentation in 1929, the group gained a reputation for staging well-orchestrated balls, usually based on historical themes. Mystic is unique in that its queen is always married.

1930-1949: Every Man a King

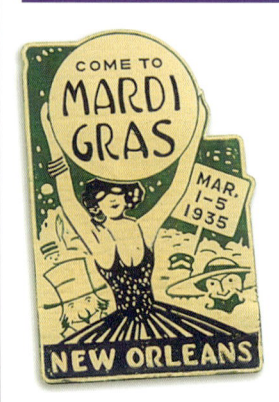

The period 1930-1949, which encompassed the Great Depression and the Second World War, was one of profound change for Carnival in New Orleans. Highlights included the 1930 opening of the Municipal Auditorium — the new home of virtually every Carnival ball — and the appearance of Louis Armstrong as king of the 1949 Zulu parade.

More than three dozen ball krewes debuted. Twelve major new parading clubs were also founded, including the first for children, the first for women, and the first to feature truck floats. These new organizations, some of which limited their activities to neighborhood parades, opened up Mardi Gras to participation by the middle class.

Extended media coverage was marked by the first nationwide radio broadcast of a Mardi Gras parade in 1930 and the first telecast in 1949. The most important Mardi Gras history ever published, *The Mistick Krewe*, was released in 1931.

In 1947, a young artist named Blaine Kern constructed his first parade. He would become the most prominent float builder of the 20th Century.

Local coverage of the 1930 Proteus parade by NBC affiliate WSMB radio was aired throughout the country, making it the first national broadcast of a Mardi Gras parade.

The first opportunity for children to participate in a Mardi Gras parade was offered by the Krewe of NOR (New Orleans Romance), which paraded from 1934 to 1949. Made up entirely of grammar school age kids, the processions featured as many as 100 miniature floats constructed by students from the city's public and parochial schools. Each year King and Queen NOR were chosen by lot.

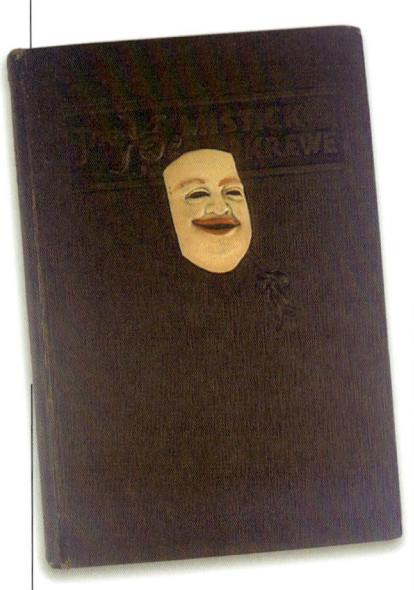

In 1931, Perry Young produced the most comprehensive history of Mardi Gras ever published, The Mistick Krewe. *The 270-page volume remains the definitive source of all Mardi Gras research.*

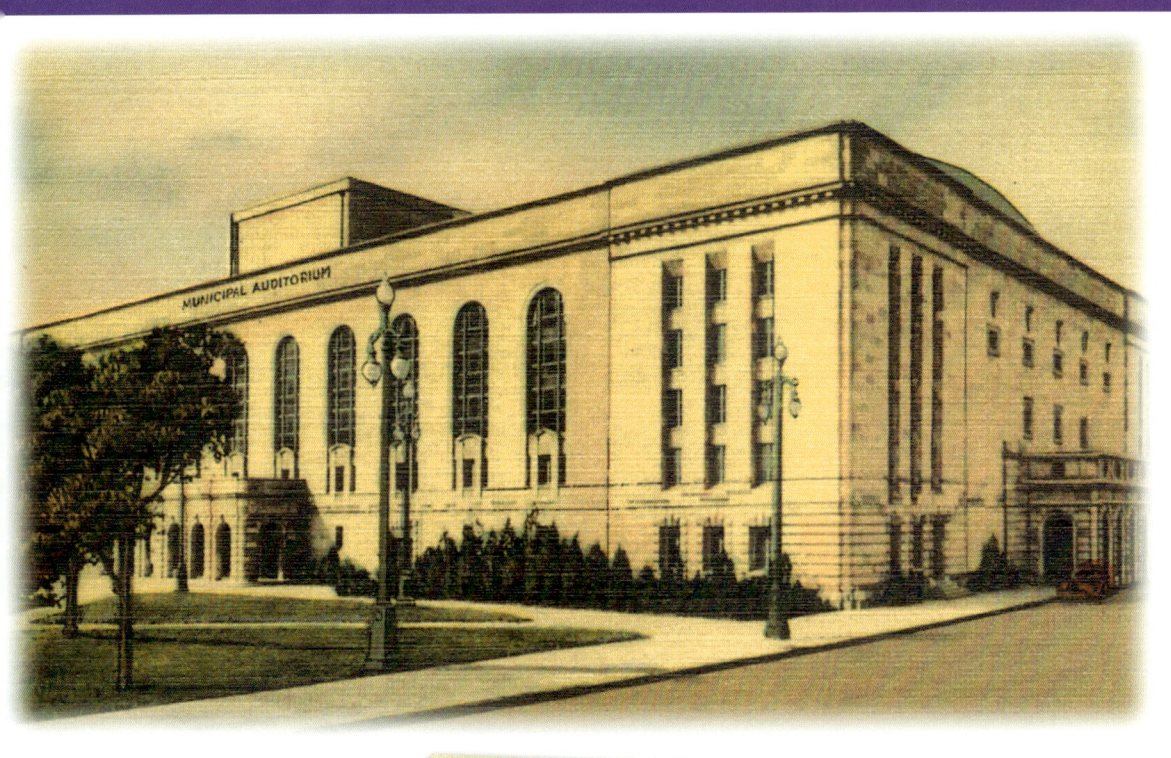

The Elves of Oberon enjoyed the distinction of presenting the first Carnival ball at the Municipal Auditorium, which opened in 1930. The 10,000-seat facility, located on the edge of the French Quarter, would serve as the primary home for most Carnival balls into the 21st Century. From 1930 to 1949, the following krewes staged balls at the Auditorium: Achaens, Alhambra, Alla, Alpheus, Athenians, Atlanteans, Babylon, Bards of Bohemia, Caliphs of Cairo, Carrollton, Children's Carnival Club, Comus, Dorians, Eros, Harlequins, Hermes, Iris, Les Marionettes, Mid-City, Mithras, Momus, Moslem, Mystery, Mystic, Naiads, Nereus, Niobeans, Oberon, Olympians, Omardz, Osiris, Prometheus, Prophets of Persia, Proteus, Rex, Twelfth Night Revelers, and Venus.

The artwork for the 1931 Comus ball invitation almost seems a metaphor for the economic conditions that the city would soon experience. The stock market crash of October 29, 1929, and the Great Depression that followed, had a deep effect on Carnival. Floats, which traditionally had been completely redesigned from year to year, were suddenly reused with only minor modifications. Cutbacks in the quality and size of the processions were obvious. Momus was unable to parade from 1933 to 1936.

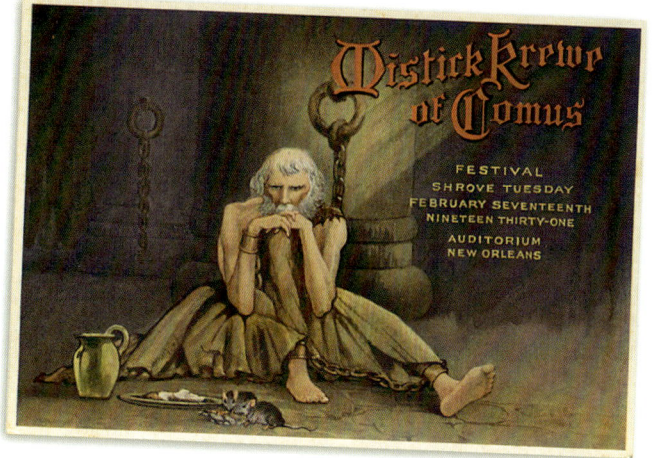

Carnival Further Diversifies

Two significant ball organizations were also founded in the 1930s. The Capetowners, an African-American group, formed in 1935 for the purpose of providing entertainment for guests and visitors. Four years later, the first krewe of Italian-Americans was organized when the Virgilians debuted with opera diva Marguerite Piazza as queen. The club quickly gained a reputation for presenting the most extravagant balls of the period, and invitations to their annual events were perhaps the most sought-after in Carnival. The Virgilians disbanded in 1964.

Other important krewes founded in the Thirties include the Bards of Bohemia, Eros, Omardz, Elenians, Moslem, Caliphs of Cairo, Noblads, Dorians, and Prometheus.

The Old Reliable Club formed the Krewe of Choctaw, which reigned on the West Bank (1939-1998).

In an attempt to spur tourism in the city, the Krewe of Hermes was formed in 1937. The club featured lighthearted themes and included more float riders than the older krewes. Rather than masked royalty, Hermes' king and dukes wore beards and make-up. The krewe is credited with the introduction of neon lighting to parades.

One of the most popular of all neighborhood parades began in 1934 with the Krewe of Mid-City. With its themes selected with children in mind, Mid-City was a hit with families.

The West Bank community of Algiers joined the parading fraternity in 1933 with the formation of the Krewe of Alla, an abbreviation for Algiers, Louisiana. In addition to its street parade, for many years Alla presented a parade of boats on the Mississippi River.

The first place winner in the "Best Truck" contest in the first Elks Orleanians parade in 1935.

Truckin'

The introduction of automobiles and trucks to American life offered a new opportunity for revelers to celebrate. Often on Fat Tuesday families and friends would don costumes and masks and ride through the city aboard open trucks. In 1933, when Rex experienced its only rain-out, rendering Fat Tuesday "paradeless," a young man named Chris Valley decided to organize these independent groups into a unified parade. The result was the formation of the Krewe of Elks Orleanians, which paraded first in 1935. In 1947, the Crescent City truck parade would begin. Both groups follow the Rex parade on Mardi Gras.

WWII Cancels Carnival

For the third time in history, war brought a halt to the celebration of Mardi Gras. From 1942 to 1945, the city turned its attention to the war overseas. Floats stayed in their dens and the ball stage at the Municipal Auditorium remained dark.

The Knights of Babylon debuted in 1940 with a 15-float parade entitled Travelogue. *The initial pageant on the Wednesday before Fat Tuesday extended the parade season to one full week.*

The first parade presented by a female club was staged by the Krewe of Venus in 1941. Despite light rain and heavy criticism by some male krewes, Venus was a huge success. Venus was the first krewe to rent floats from another Carnival club.

1941 Venus royalty: Miss Gerry Mills and Mr. Irwin J. G. Janssen.

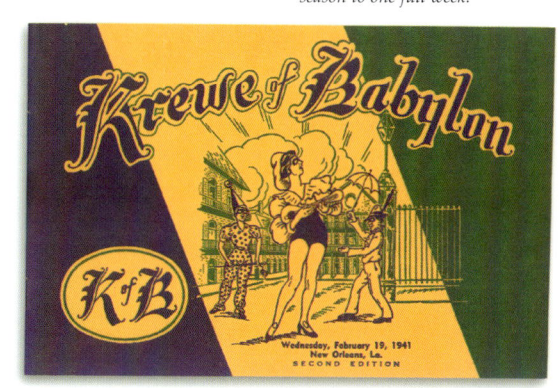

In 1947, former members of the Seventh Municipal Carnival and Pleasure Club, which had marched in its neighborhood since the 1920s, organized the Krewe of Carrollton. The third float in the 1953 Carrollton parade, entitled Songs, *saluted "God Bless America."*

A Media Event

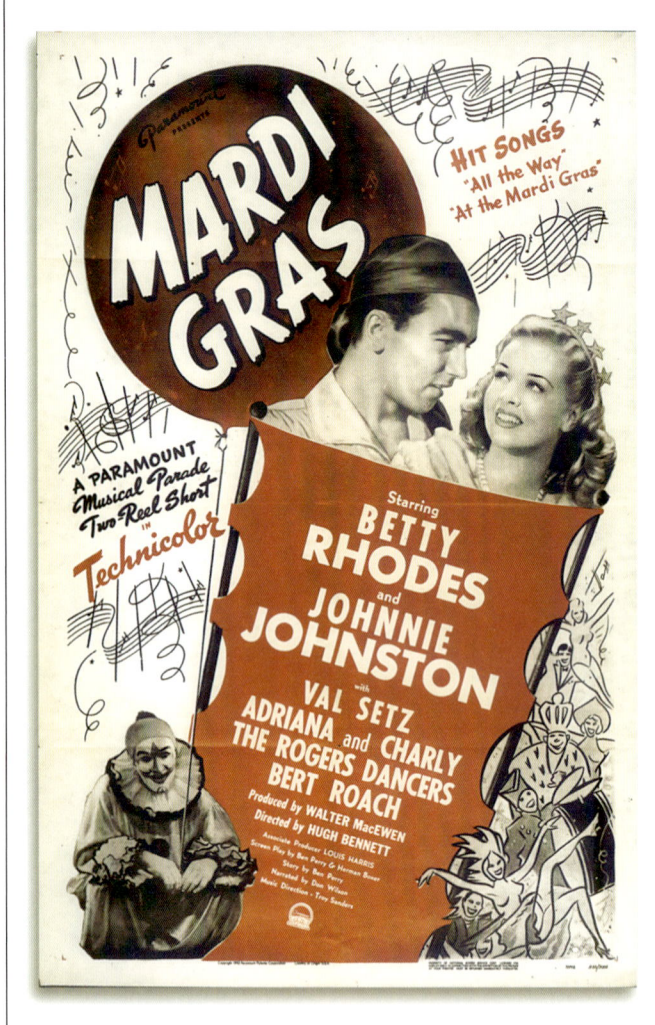

Mardi Gras is the backdrop of countless Hollywood films, but the 1948 short Mardi Gras *holds the distinction of being nominated for an Academy Award as the best short film of the year. It did not win.*

WDSU, Louisiana's first television station, broadcast its first parade and ball in 1949. For more than two decades, announcer Mel Leavitt provided coverage of night parades from the station's balcony at 520 Royal Street in the French Quarter.

In the Neighborhood

Two small neighborhood krewes started up in the late Forties and each would contribute to Carnival. The Krewe of Grela (for Gretna, LA) brought a daytime parade to the Jefferson Parish city of Gretna on the West Bank with its first procession in 1948 entitled *Floweramia*. The uptown Krewe of Thoth began with a five-float effort in 1947. The club would soon become known as the "krewe of shut-ins" because it directs its parade route to pass in front of a dozen institutions that care for persons with disabilities and illnesses.

In 1947, float builder Blaine Kern worked on his first parade for the Krewe of Alla. During the next half-century, Kern would become known as "Mr. Mardi Gras" and would supply floats for more than 60 krewes, including Rex, Zulu, Bacchus, Orpheus, and Endymion.

Louis Armstrong Reigns as Zulu

When the Zulu Social Aid & Pleasure Club selected native son Louis Armstrong to reign as king on March 1, 1949, it was more than a simple honor. Satchmo told *Time* magazine, "There's a thing I've dreamed of all my life, and damned if it don't look like it's about to come true — to be King of the Zulu's parade. After that, I'll be ready to die." His connection to the club was long standing. He had ridden in the parade three years earlier, and on a visit home in 1933, Armstrong had bought the Zulu baseball team a new set of uniforms. On the final Fat Tuesday of the decade, thousands of African-Americans and whites gathered to get a glimpse of the jazz giant. Along the route, Armstrong dismounted his float to greet his aging grandmother, Josephine. The king's golden float fell apart before the end of the parade, and souvenir hunters rendered it an unrecognizable hulk.

In conjunction with his reign as King of Zulu, Time magazine honored Satchmo by making him the first jazz musician to be featured on its cover.

A highlight of Armstrong's visit was his performance at a special evening concert. During the intermission, Louis and his queen, Bernice Oxley, were crowned as king and queen of Zulu.

Mid-Century Merriment

The decade of the Fifties began in dramatic fashion with an appearance by the Duke and Duchess of Windsor at the 1950 Rex and Comus balls. Ten months later, a fire at the Rex den destroyed floats, costumes and precious records of the School of Design, the krewe's sponsoring organization.

The Korean conflict canceled many Carnival activities in 1951. By 1952, the mules that had pulled Carnival floats for nearly a century were replaced by tractors. In 1958, the Babylon parade was postponed for a most unusual reason — snow in New Orleans. That same year Mardi Gras expanded to the Jefferson Parish suburb of Metairie with the inaugural parades of Helios and Zeus. Rex ended the decade by reintroducing, after a 50 year absence, the boeuf gras. First parades were staged by Okeanos, Iris, Poseidon, Arabi, and Freret. The krewes of Bal Masque and Ancient Scribes joined the Municipal Auditorium calendar during the decade, and four short-lived parading krewes debuted: Midas, Orion, Cronus, and Gemini.

Life magazine covered the royal couple's visit to Mardi Gras in its March 6, 1950, issue.

The Royal Treatment

When the Duke and Duchess of Windsor attended the balls of Comus and Rex in 1950, the question in the minds of those present was, Would the royal couple follow Carnival protocol and bow before the "make-believe monarchs"? As anticipation engulfed the hushed crowd, the regal pair bowed and curtsied.

The last of the mule-driven floats had been phased out by 1952.

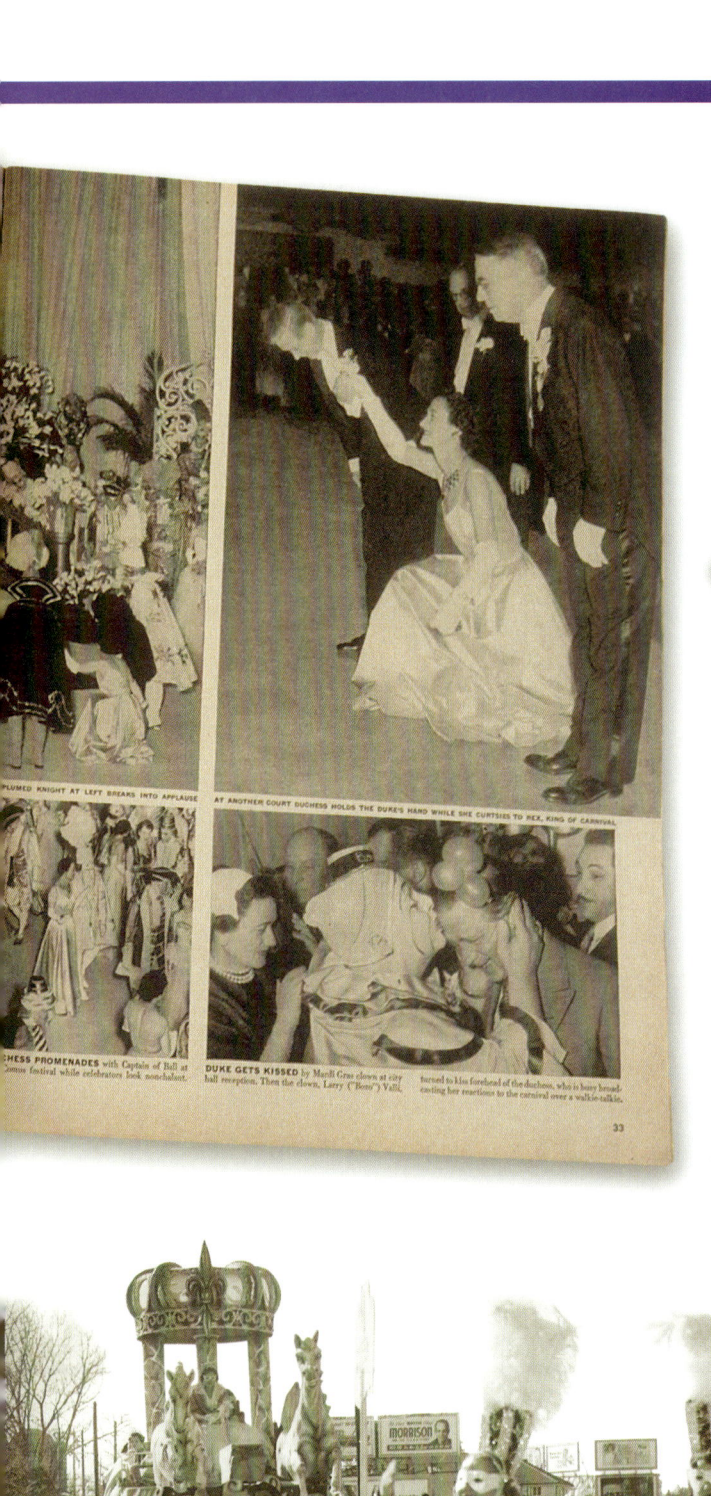

William Waller Young, Rex 1952, was presented with a special replica of the King of Carnival's float. This foot-long ceramic piece was hand painted in Japan.

In 1951, the majority of Carnival krewes in New Orleans did not parade because of the Korean conflict. In place of Rex, a 20-float parade, consisting of units from canceled parades, rolled down Canal Street on Fat Tuesday. U.S. Marine and Korean War veteran Lindsay Alexis Larson Jr. rode as King of Patria. The theme of the parade on that cold, rainy day was **The Freedoms**.

The Krewe of Helios staged Jefferson Parish's first Mardi Gras parade on Metairie Road in 1958.

Something Old, Something New

Boeuf Gras Returns

The boeuf gras, the ancient symbol of the last meat eaten before Lent, returned to the Rex parade after a half-century's absence. While a live version of the fatted bull had appeared in earlier parades, Rex presented a papier maché figure in his 1959 procession.

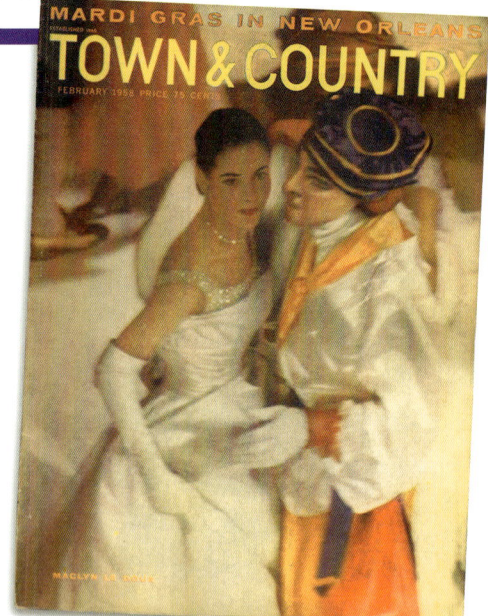

The nation was provided its first behind-the-scenes look at Carnival balls in 1958 when the prestigious Town & Country *magazine published a cover story on Mardi Gras in the Crescent City. The 22-page, heavily illustrated feature was the talk of the town for weeks.*

The first recording of the traditional anthem of Mardi Gras, "If Ever I Cease to Love," was released by Johnny Wiggs in 1954. That same year, another classic, "Mardi Gras Mambo," by the Hawkettes, also debuted.

Nat King, who reigned as King Zulu in 1955, also published the first definitive guide to African-American Carnival in the Crescent City. The publication detailed nearly 100 black Mardi Gras organizations.

In 1954, local photographer Ray Cresson snapped this picture that was judged by one local magazine as the best Mardi Gras photograph of the decade.

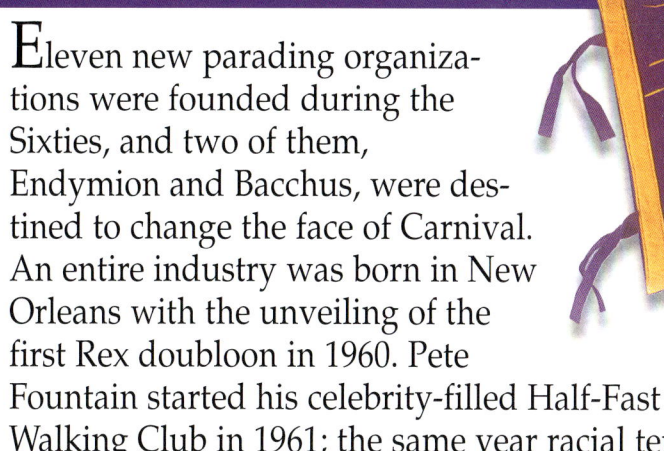

Eleven new parading organizations were founded during the Sixties, and two of them, Endymion and Bacchus, were destined to change the face of Carnival. An entire industry was born in New Orleans with the unveiling of the first Rex doubloon in 1960. Pete Fountain started his celebrity-filled Half-Fast Walking Club in 1961; the same year racial tension almost caused Zulu to disband. The next year the first official ball presented by a gay Carnival club was staged in Metairie by the Krewe of Yuga. The first parading club to include men and women was formed in 1969 by the Krewe of Amor in St. Bernard Parish. Other krewes to debut included Aphrodite, Mecca, Mokana, Sprites, Jason, Pegasus, Pandora, Tucks, Diana, Hercules, and Jupiter.

Sharpe's original sketch for the 1960 Rex doubloon was very close to the finished product.

A Sharpe Concept

In 1960 when local engraver H. Alvin Sharpe convinced the Rex organization to toss his new creation — the aluminum "doubloon" — a new era in Carnival was ushered in: that of krewe-specific throws. Previously, generic trinkets and necklaces were tossed to parade goers. By the decade's end, the doubloon would be the primary throw of all parading groups. Later, Mardi Gras krewes would produce other logo merchandise, but no item ever surpassed the appeal of the shiny metal coins.

H. Alvin Sharpe, father of the Mardi Gras doubloon.

New Orleanian Pete Fountain had participated in Mardi Gras since he marched in the Warren Easton High School Band in the mid-1940s. In 1961, he formed his own krewe, the Half-Fast Walking Club. The group annually walks on Fat Tuesday from Commander's Palace in the Garden District to the French Quarter, preceding the Rex parade through most of its route.

Glass beads imported from Czechoslovakia were a popular throw of the 1950s and 1960s.

The Super Krewes Arrive

Endymion

Endymion started out in 1967 as a meager parade that rented floats from the Krewe of Carrollton and paraded near the Fair Grounds Race Track. It would soon develop into a super parade, patterning itself after its younger cousin, Bacchus. In a few short years, Endymion would become the largest Carnival club in history.

It took less than 10 riders to fill this float from the inaugural Endymion parade.

Endymion I, Harry P. Rosenthal, poses with his royal dukes at the Jung Hotel in 1967.

Endymion calls its doubloons "tokens of youth." Babe Ruth was featured on the first token with the theme, Take Me Out to the Ball Game.

The Krewe of Mid-City unveiled its Greatest Bands in Dixie contest in 1963. Judging took place during the parade. Local businesses sponsored the competition which attracted bands from several states. The winning band — like the Abbeville High Band from South Carolina — received a huge trophy and bragging rights as the best band in the South.

68

Bacchus

The Krewe of Bacchus would be declared "the most innovative and most imitated krewe founded in the 20th Century." The 12 businessmen who founded the club in 1969 unveiled concepts that, at the time, were revolutionary. With its super-sized floats and its open admission policy for its after-parade ball, the krewe immediately grabbed the attention of the press and the people. Bacchus further defied Carnival tradition by annually presenting a Hollywood celebrity in place of a local king. Danny Kaye was the first to reign, leading a 20-float parade entitled *The Best Things in Life*. The procession ended inside the Rivergate Convention Center, another first for a Mardi Gras parade.

Danny Kaye, Bacchus I, was the first celebrity to reign as a Carnival king since Louis Armstrong in 1949.

Canal Street is ground zero for the celebration of Mardi Gras. From the mid-1940s through the late 1960s, the city annually decorated all the light standards on the famous parade route.

During the 1960s, several gay Carnival clubs presented their first balls, including Yuga, Petronius, Amon-Ra and Armeinius. In 1965 a popular gay costume contest was begun in the French Quarter. Called the Bourbon Street Awards, the annual event would attract entrants from across the country.

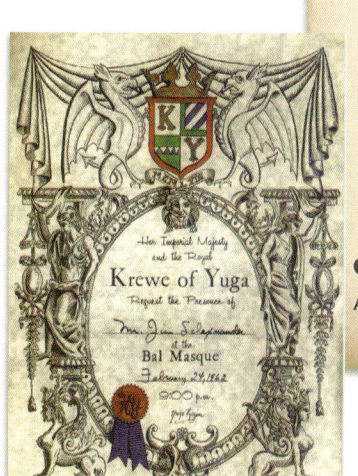

A Time of Change

During the 20-year period from 1970 to 1989, Mardi Gras in New Orleans experienced its largest expansion. The schedule that included 30 parades in 1970 grew to 58 processions by 1989. The celebration spread into New Orleans East, and more parades were added on the West Bank and in St. Bernard Parish. In 1974, for the first time ever, a Fat Tuesday parade came to Jefferson Parish.

Fueling Carnival's growth was the new availability of rental floats that started in the late 1960s, enabling upstart clubs to parade with a smaller investment. But the unparalleled growth also created widespread instability. During the period, 52 parading clubs were formed and 33 folded, most of them lasting only three years. This revolving door of Mardi Gras krewes, coupled with the general increase in the number of parades, caused the City of New Orleans to issue a moratorium on new parade permits.

As membership in Mardi Gras krewes became more accessible to the general public, the fundamental character of many balls and parades underwent a transformation. The ball calendar at the Municipal Auditorium, which had peaked at 68 balls in 1973, dwindled to 38 by 1989, with most new krewes casting aside the tableau balls in favor of less traditional forms of entertainment.

There were many empty hotel rooms in 1971 due to rumors of a violent "hippie" invasion of Mardi Gras.

Because of the growth in the size of floats, and of the crowds that gathered to see them, in 1973 Mardi Gras parades were banned in the French Quarter, ending a 117-year tradition.

Endymion morphed into a super parade in 1974, and eight years later moved its after-parade party into the Louisiana Superdome. International media and corporate America finally discovered Mardi Gras in the 1980s, turning the event into a larger tourist attraction than had been previously imagined.

March of Dimes 1976 poster child receives a special doubloon from Zeus King XIX, Philip Lundgren. In addition to their fun-filled Mardi Gras activities, many Carnival organizations are very active in charitable causes.

In 1970 the Krewe of Venus issued the first in a series of Mardi Gras collector stamps.

Krewes vied to attract guest celebrities that would, in turn, draw the public to their parades. Bob Hope reigned as Bacchus in 1974, and in 1980, a dozen parades featured guest stars. By 1989, only three krewes continued to present celebrity monarchs.

Tragedy hit Carnival in 1970 when a tornado struck the Carrollton parade, resulting in the death of a rider who was thrown to the ground. After two youngsters were crushed beneath floats in 1981, the Mayor of New Orleans formed an advisory committee that would work toward improving safety measures.

Connie Stevens, Argus Empress VI. The Krewe of Argus, which brought the first Fat Tuesday parade to Metairie in 1973, featured female guest celebrities in each of its processions from 1975 to 1984. In addition to Stevens, others to reign included Barbara Eden, Kay Starr, Phyllis Diller, Shirley Jones, Loretta Swit, Diane Ladd, Cathy Lee Crosby, Shari Lewis and Lee Meredith.

Dolly Parton was a popular attraction in Endymion's 1988 parade. Highlights of the parade and the Extravaganza were featured on Dolly's nationally televised program on ABC.

Marching bands, such as the St. Augustine Marching 100, are a favorite feature of most Mardi Gras parades. However, the addition of new parades has caused a shortage of marching bands, so many suburban clubs have turned to dance groups that are followed by sound trucks.

National Guardsmen good-naturedly kept the peace during the police strike of 1979.

As the super krewes outgrew the Municipal Auditorium and the Rivergate, they began holding their extravagant blowouts at the Louisiana Superdome. The Krewe of Bacchus first paraded in the dome in 1977.

On Strike

Perhaps the most unsettling event of the period occurred in 1979 when union members of the New Orleans Police Department went on strike just before the parade season commenced. Orleans Parish krewe officials voted not to parade and backed the city's position of not allowing Carnival to be used as a pawn in the negotiations. Thirteen parades were canceled, and a dozen others were rescheduled in the suburbs. The action deprived the city of its parades for one season, but it also created a renewed appreciation for Mardi Gras, which many had taken for granted.

The Mardi Gras Mask-a-thon began its annual family-oriented costume contest on Canal Street in 1985.

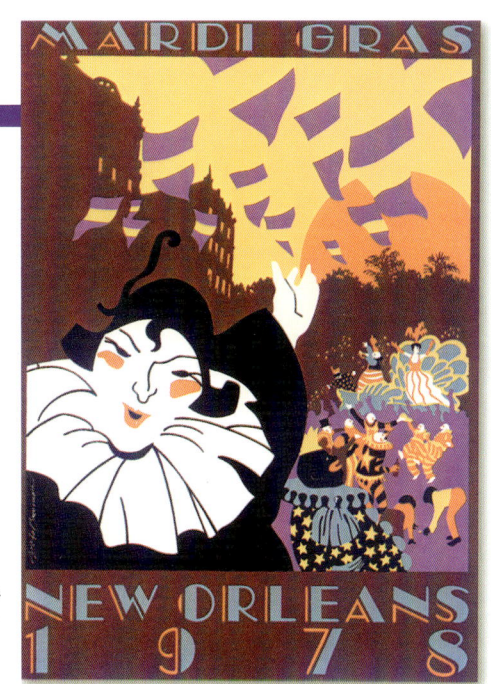

Pro-Creations' 1978 Mardi Gras poster, the first in a series of Carnival collectibles. Few Carnival visitors return home without a Mardi Gras poster or T-shirt.

Sell Me Something, Mister!

While it was still forbidden within the parades, commercialism grew on the periphery, with beer companies and radio stations leading the way in capitalizing on the celebration. Since there is no licensing body to declare any item as "official," Mardi Gras developed into an entrepreneur's paradise as the marketplace alone decided the success of a product. Dozens of companies and individuals produce posters, T-shirts, and throw items, and sell them to krewe members and to the general public. Local bakeries started exporting Mardi Gras by shipping king cakes via overnight couriers.

Among the many national corporations that capitalize on Mardi Gras in a positive way are beer companies Budweiser, Coors, and Miller; soft drink makers Coke and Pepsi; liquor manufacturers Taaka, Seagrams, Gallo, and Crown Royal; and pharmaceutical firms such as Bristol-Myers Company, which promotes its headache remedies to those who imbibe too much.

Parade ladders are standard equipment for most families with children in New Orleans. These modified creations include carpeted seats that provide ideal vantage points for parade viewing.

The strike by union members of the New Orleans Police Department did not cancel Mardi Gras, but it did keep 13 parades off the streets.

73

The King of Carnival's Lundi Gras arrival is a cooperative venture sponsored by the Rex organization, the City of New Orleans, and the Riverwalk Market Place.

Lundi Gras Returns

In 1987 a century-old custom was revived when Rex arrived on the Mississippi River on Lundi Gras, the day before Fat Tuesday.

The evening has turned into a media event and includes fireworks and a free concert. The Zulu organization also participates in Lundi Gras, starting with its Gold Nugget Festival at Woldenberg Park on Monday morning. That evening, King Zulu welcomes Rex as the countdown to Fat Tuesday begins.

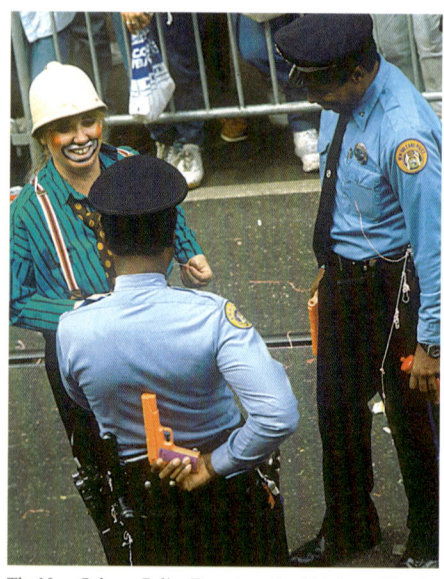

The Growth of the Gras

Sixty-seven krewes presented their first or final parades from 1970 to 1989. Among those from the 1970s that would prosper were Aquila, Argus, Atlas, Cleopatra, Gladiators, Isis, King Arthur, NOMTOC, Pontchartrain, Rhea, Shangri-La, and Thor. Long-lasting clubs to parade first in the 1980s included Aphrodite, Bards of Bohemia, Caesar, Centurions, Mercury, Napoleon, Saturn, Sparta, and Ulysses.

Rex and Bacchus were the first krewes to feature a series of "signature" floats that would be presented every year and would become synonymous with the krewes themselves. In addition to the gorilla menagerie — King Kong, Queen Kong and Baby Kong — Bacchus introduced the Baccha-Whoppa, a giant whale, and the Bacchusaurus, a friendly dinosaur.

The New Orleans Police Department, which has achieved world-wide acclaim for its expertise in crowd management, has also gained a reputation for its friendly interplay with citizens and visitors during the Carnival season.

The new Phunny Phorty Phellows include more than 40 members and not all are men. The club uses a king cake to choose its king — the "boss" — and its queen during its streetcar ride through uptown New Orleans.

The first krewe-emblemed cup was thrown by the Krewe of Mardi Gras in 1979.

Carnival Keepsakes

As the doubloon declined in popularity, competing companies developed new krewe-insignia items, including embossed cups, coasters and bikinis. Plastic beads from Hong Kong replaced the glass necklaces from Czechoslovakia that were so popular in the 1950s and 1960s.

In 1980 Solomon Signal and Angela Celeste Baranco reigned over the Original Illinois Club's ball entitled "Robins Come Back to Nest."

While members of krewe royalty customarily viewed their parade from an official reviewing stand, new clubs presented their maids and dukes within the parade aboard special mini-floats. The tuxedoes and gowns traditionally worn by the court were replaced by feathered costumes with enormous headpieces and collars. For the first time, some krewes presented both the king and queen within the parade. Captains became more public, abandoning the low-profile horses usually ridden by krewe leaders, and instead presented themselves aboard special floats.

The Jefferson City Buzzards, the area's oldest walking club, marches in front of the Zulu and Rex parades on Fat Tuesday.

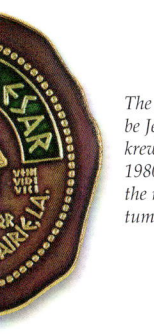

The Krewe of Caesar, destined to be Jefferson Parish's first super krewe, debuted in Metairie in 1980. Caesar presents some of the most exquisite court costumes in all of Carnival.

75

A New Landscape

Comus bid farewell to his Fat Tuesday night parade in 1991.

The final decade of the 20th Century was one of the most volatile in the history of Mardi Gras. Claiming that membership criteria of Carnival's oldest parading organizations discriminated against African-Americans, in 1991 New Orleans City Councilwoman Dorothy Mae Taylor introduced an ordinance requiring krewes that paraded on public streets to open their membership to minorities. This controversial legislation tore the community apart. While Rex invited a handful of African-Americans to join, the krewes of Comus and Momus canceled their 1992 parades in protest. Proteus joined the boycott the next year and did not return until 2000. Protracted litigation eventually confirmed the private clubs' rights to parade, but Momus and Comus stayed off the streets.

The Nineties also saw the demise of 16 clubs, including several that had existed for more than two decades: Venus, Diana, Freret, Hercules, Pandora, Amor, Nefertari, and Choctaw (which returned in 2003).

The geography of Carnival shifted during the 1990s, with Saturn, Pontchartrain, Shangri-La, and King Arthur moving their processions from neighborhoods to downtown. The popularity of downtown New Orleans as the premiere parading grounds gave birth to another phenomenon: back-to-back parades on the same route.

In 1994, when Harrah's temporary casino opened in the Municipal Auditorium, Carnival balls moved elsewhere. (Many returned in 1998 when the gambling hall closed.) The Pontchartrain Center in Kenner became the home for a half-dozen major krewes. Meanwhile, the Ernest N. Morial Convention Center started hosting the annual Zulu ball. The Bacchus and Orpheus parades now end inside the facility. Endymion attracts more than 15,000 to its after-parade party inside the Louisiana Superdome.

In the face of the anti-discrimination legislation in 1991, private men's clubs sought to distance themselves from Mardi Gras. Accordingly, the toast to the Queen of Carnival by Rex at the Boston Club — a 100-year tradition — was terminated in 1992. Since then, Rex has saluted his consort from a special reviewing stand at the Hotel Inter-Continental.

Mardi Gras World, opened by Blaine Kern in 1984, offers visitors the chance to see floats under construction.

During the mid-Nineties, Jefferson Parish experienced an upturn in the number of parades and in the size of the crowds that gathered to enjoy them. The all-male Krewe of Caesar became Metairie's first super krewe. By the decade's end, however, several clubs were experiencing financial difficulty. Jefferson Parish officials wrestled with enforcement of minimum standards since some parades had problems paying for the requisite number of bands and floats. Similar problems occurred on the West Bank in the City of Gretna.

Impressive debuts were made by the Ancient Druids (1999), the Krewe of Muses (2001), the Knights of Chaos (2001), Excalibur (2002), and Morpheus (2002). Gretna's Krewe of Poseidon folded in 2003 after 55 years.

Endymion became the first krewe to surpass the 2,000-member mark, while other clubs also experienced growth. Krewes such as Alla, Iris, Thoth, Hermes and Tucks, once small affairs, doubled in size.

Krewe of Orpheus founder Harry Connick Jr. rides at the head of his parade and entertains at the post-parade Orpheuscapade.

Birth of Orpheus

Founded in 1994 by native son Harry Connick Jr., the Krewe of Orpheus debuted in spectacular fashion. Orpheus was the first super krewe to include women. Its large number of minority and out-of-town members also made it unique. Orpheus further distinguished itself by depicting classical themes, by attracting top-flight national celebrities such as Sandra Bullock, Stevie Wonder, Whoopi Goldberg and Glenn Close, and by annually saluting local musical legends.

The fire-breathing Leviathan, one of Orpheus' signature floats, was the first to feature fibre-optic lighting.

As the first decade of the 21st Century neared the mid-point, Mardi Gras in New Orleans showed its resilience and its flexibility by adjusting to changes from within and without. The horrific events of September 11, 2001, impacted Mardi Gras by greatly reducing the number of visitors in 2002. Fifteen parades were pushed back one week to avoid a conflict with the rescheduled NFL Super Bowl in New Orleans. In a hotly negotiated settlement, Orleans Parish krewes whose parades were displaced were reimbursed $20,000 each for their losses.

The prevailing movement of the early 2000s was one of consolidation. Citing a dramatic rise in the demand for city services —police, sanitation, emergency —local governments sought ways to raise revenue and reduce costs.

In 1977, more than two dozen parade routes were used by the 52 krewes that rolled. By 2003, those routes had been standardized to the point where only five basic parade routes are utlilized. Furthermore, 37 krewes now parade as part of double- and triple-header processions. The City of Gretna compressed its parade calendar from four days to two, while Jefferson Parish removed one Saturday from its east bank parade calendar. To eliminate the possibility of further expansion in the parade schedule, Orleans and Jefferson Parishes issued moratoriums on new parade permits.

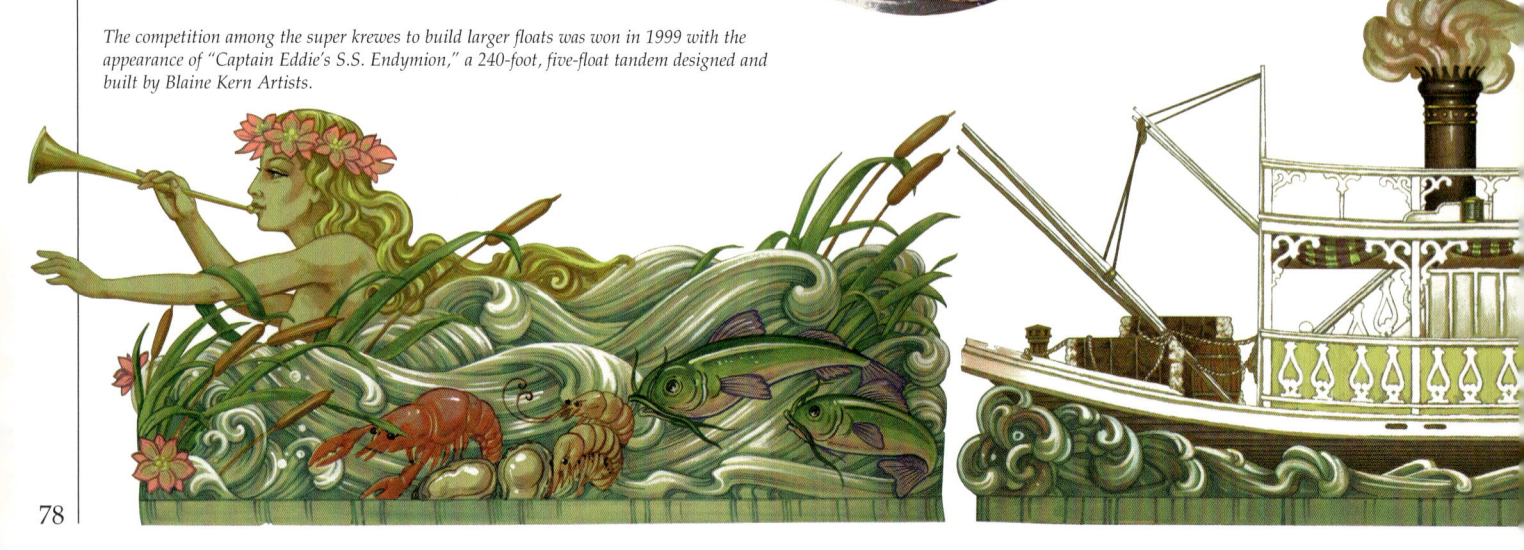

The Mystic Krewe of Barkus, a parade of canines that promenades through the French Quarter, began in 1993. With whimsical themes such as "Tailhouse Rock," "Joan of Bark," "Tailtanic," "Jurrasic Bark" and "Lifestyles of the Bitch and Famous," the annual procession features hundreds of costumed dogs of every size and breed.

The competition among the super krewes to build larger floats was won in 1999 with the appearance of "Captain Eddie's S.S. Endymion," a 240-foot, five-float tandem designed and built by Blaine Kern Artists.

Commercializing Carnival

The City of New Orleans rejected several attempts to turn Mardi Gras parades into commercial billboards for corporate America. When the Krewe of America premiered in 1998, it announced grandiose plans to attract Fortune 500 executives to ride in its parade. America folded three years later.

Jefferson Parish legalized limited sponsorship of parades, but only the Fat Tuesday parade of the Krewe of Argus became blatantly commercial. Driving the need for outside financial help are the increased costs of presenting a parade, coupled with a decrease in funds from bingo games, which many krewes use to finance their operations.

National media continued to shine a light on New Orleans, including MTV and the Playboy Channel, which inaccurately portrayed Bourbon Street raunch as if it were representative of the total Mardi Gras experience. Public nudity and women bearing their breasts in exchange for beads are customs mostly confined to the French Quarter.

Satirical parade themes, once a prominent feature of Mardi Gras, returned when the Krewe of Saturn moved from Jefferson Parish to downtown New Orleans in 1993. Le Krewe d'Etat followed suit when it premiered in 1997. Both became instant hits with the critics and the crowds who loved their whimsical processions.

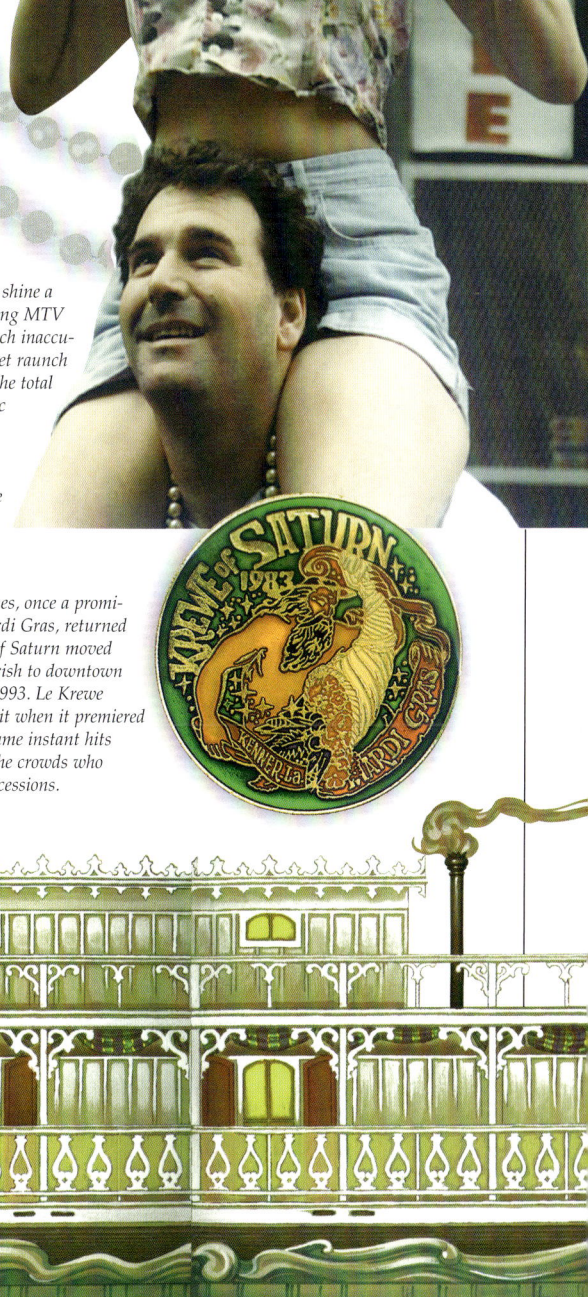

Le Krewe d'Etat quickly became known for its witty themes.

The gas-fueled flambeaux have been a part of Carnival in New Orleans since the first Comus parade rolled in 1857. While once they provided the only source of nighttime illumination, now their use is strictly ornamental. Fewer than ten parades still employ the original torches which date to pre-WWI. In 2002, the Krewe of Orpheus built 50 replicas of the ancient flambeaux.

The Krewe du Vieux was born in 1991 as an outgrowth of the Crewe of Clones, a zany group of marchers whose Carnival activities were sponsored by the Contemporary Arts Center. Du Vieux is an amalgamation of more than a dozen sub-krewes such as Underwear, Space Age Love, Mama Roux, Mystic Inane, Seeds of Decline and K.A.O.S. Because its parade of mule-drawn mini-floats is scheduled before the official 12-day Mardi Gras parade season, it is allowed to roll through the French Quarter, where it annually lampoons politicians and institutions.

Krewe du Vieux

Mardi Gras Indians

The black Mardi Gras Indians are celebrated and cherished in New Orleans. The rich craftsmanship displayed by the men who design their magnificent outfits (called "suits"), has earned worldwide praise. The Mardi Gras Indian tribes date to the 1880s.

Endymion's super float carries 200 riders and is named after the club's founder and captain, Ed Muniz.

Mardi Gras on Display

In 1994, Jefferson Parish opened its Mardi Gras Museum in Kenner's Rivertown. Six years later, the Louisiana State Museum on Jackson Square in the French Quarter converted the Presbytere into a museum dedicated solely to Carnival in Louisiana.

Mardi Gras is the subject of intense scholarly interest with nearly one dozen books published on the topic since 1990.

The collecting of Mardi Gras memorabilia has become popular, with 19th Century items fetching top dollar at New Orleans auction houses and on eBay.

Kenner's Mardi Gras Museum in Rivertown features hands-on exhibits and video presentations.

Carnival historian Henri Schindler has published a series of four books that detail the history and memorabilia of Mardi Gras in New Orleans.

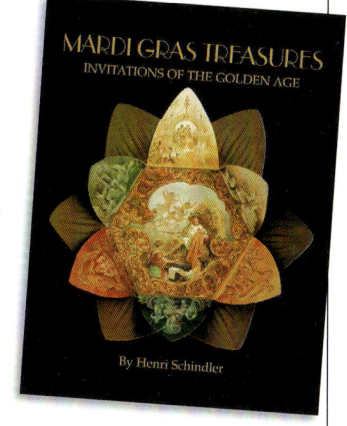

In 2000 the Louisiana State Museum on Jackson Square in the French Quarter converted the historic Presbytere into a multi-faceted exhibit dedicated solely to the celebration of Mardi Gras in Louisiana.

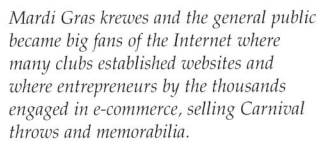

Mardi Gras krewes and the general public became big fans of the Internet where many clubs established websites and where entrepreneurs by the thousands engaged in e-commerce, selling Carnival throws and memorabilia.

81

Muses

Not since the inaugural parade of Orpheus in 1994, has a new krewe made a greater impact than the Krewe of Muses. The 600 member krewe, made up of professional women, quickly became popular for their sassy themes, their spirit, and their innovative throws — some designed by school children. In their second year, the women won the Best Parade award from local weekly newspaper *Gambit*.

After nearly seventy years, the Krewe of Mid City moved its parade from the neighborhood for which it was named and adopted the popular uptown parade route in 2002.

Gay Pride

The number and size of gay Carnival clubs declined in the 1990s, largely due to AIDS, and because members now enjoy a cultural acceptance making secret membership in gay Carnival krewes largely unnecessary.

Chaos Reigns

The Knights of Chaos, named after the mythological father of Momus, paraded first in 2001 on floats purchased from the Knights of Momus. The genealogical connection is reinforced by the parade's mimicry of Momus' satirical style and by the fact that it rolls on "Momus Thursday."

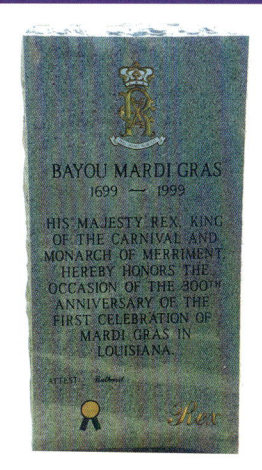

Rex Marks the Spot

In 1999 Rex celebrated the 300th anniversary of Mardi Gras in North America by erecting a plaque near the site where French Canadian explorer Iberville had landed in 1699 and had named the spot, *Pointe Du Mardi Gras*.

After an absence of several years, the televised meeting of the courts of Rex and Comus on Mardi Gras evening returned, courtesy of local PBS affiliate, WYES.

In 2000 the mayor of New Orleans, Marc Morial, personally welcomed the Krewe of Proteus back to the streets of New Orleans after a seven-year absence. The krewe became the first to parade in three separate centuries.

Mardi Gras Marches On

Through the years, Carnival has survived calamities of both man and nature. Having started with a single procession in 1857, it has grown to include nearly 60 parades and more than 100 balls in the metro area as New Orleans. Opportunities to participate in a Carnival club are open to virtually anyone. For more than a million people who annually gather on the streets, it is a cost-free entertainment outlet unmatched by any other event.

An entire industry has grown up around the festivities. According to a study by professor Dr. James McLain, the economic impact of the festivities topped the one billion dollar mark in 2000.

The celebration, however, provides far more than money. Carnival defines the soul of the Crescent City. It is essential to the culture and the spirit of its people.

Bawdy and beautiful, Mardi Gras is New Orleans.

The battle to create innovative throws and favors remains fierce, with lighted beads, float specific medallions, and bobbing head dolls among the most popular items of the young century. Posters issued by parading krewes hit the high-water mark in 2002 when Leroy Neiman designed the Rex proclamation and blue-dog artist George Rodrigue produced the Argus poster. In 2003 Rex reinstituted the annual tradition of publishing Carnival Bulletins that depict each float in its parade.

The end — the clearing of Bourbon Street at midnight, Mardi Gras evening — is the last official act of the Carnival season.

MARDI GRAS REFERENCE GUIDE

This section contains essential information about Carnival in the Crescent City, as well as statistical data on some 550 krewes. Themes for 2,300 parades are listed, along with the names of more than 5,000 kings and queens. More than three dozen categories of information are also presented.

Mardi Gras Dictionary

Ball (*bal masque*, tableau ball) — a masked ball in which scenes representing a specific theme are enacted for the entertainment of the club members and their guests; krewe "royalty" is traditionally presented during the ball.

Boeuf Gras (French) — the fatted bull, the ancient symbol of the last meat eaten before the Lenten season of fasting; a live version was presented in the Rex parade until 1909; a papier maché version appeared in 1959 and continues as one of Carnival's most recognizable symbols.

Captain — the absolute leader of each Carnival organization.

Carnival — from the Latin *carnivale*, loosely translated as "farewell to flesh;" the season of merriment in New Orleans which begins annually on Jan. 6, the Twelfth Night (the feast of the Epiphany), and ends at midnight on Fat Tuesday; the Carnival season leads up to the penitential season of Lent in which fasting replaces feasting.

Court — the king, queen, maids and dukes of a Carnival organization.

Den — a large warehouse where floats are built and stored.

Doubloons — aluminum coin-like objects bearing the krewe's insignia on one side and the parade's theme on the reverse; first introduced by Rex in 1960 and created by New Orleans artist H. Alvin Sharpe; doubloons are also minted and sold in .999 silver, bronze and cloisonne.

Favor — a souvenir, given by a krewe member to friend attending the ball, normally bearing the organization's insignia, name and year of issue.

Flambeaux (plural) — Naphtha-fueled torches, traditionally carried by white-robed black men; in the 19th Century, flambeaux provided the only source of nighttime parade illumination.

Invitation — a printed request for attendance at a Carnival ball; in the 19th Century, many invitations were die-cut and printed in Paris; today, most are printed in New Orleans; invitations are non-transferable, and it is improper to ever refer to them as "tickets."

King Cake — an oval, sugared pastry that contains a plastic doll hidden inside; the person who finds the doll is crowned "king" and buys the next cake or throws the next party; the king cake season opens on King's Day, Jan. 6, the feast of the Epiphany. More than 750,000 king cakes are annually baked in metro New Orleans during the Carnival season.

Krewe — the generic term for all Carnival organizations in New Orleans; first used by the Mistick Krewe of Comus, which coined the word in 1857 to give its club's name an Old English flavor.

Lundi Gras — French for Fat Monday; from 1874 to 1917, the day before Mardi Gras was celebrated by the arrival of Rex aboard a steamboat. The custom was revived in 1987, and Lundi Gras now includes Carnival activities staged by Zulu and Rex.

Mardi Gras — French for Fat Tuesday, the single-day culmination of the Carnival season which annually begins on January 6.

Throws — trinkets tossed from floats by costumed and masked krewe members; among the more popular items are krewe-emblemed aluminum doubloons, plastic cups and white pearl necklaces. Throws are tossed in response to the cry, "Throw me something, mister!"

Mardi Gras Q&A

How Big Is Mardi Gras?
Very big. The latest economic impact report (2000) indicates that Mardi Gras generates more than one billion dollars in annual spending. The 2001 Carnival season included 53 parades in a three-parish (county) area and featured a total of 1,061 floats, 588 marching bands, 3,750 total parade units, and more than 135,000 participants. The combined parade routes covered 301 miles and the processions were on the street for 204 hours.

Is Mardi Gras Really X-rated?
No, it is not. Unfortunately, the wild antics of visiting coeds on Bourbon Street in the French Quarter have gained such publicity that they have become the national image of Mardi Gras. Mardi Gras is generally a safe, G-rated event enjoyed by families. The festivities provide an opportunity for adults to act like kids again.

What Makes Mardi Gras Parades Different?
Throws! Baubles tossed from floats turn New Orleans parades into crowd participation events. It is not uncommon for a float rider to spend $500 or more on beads, cups, and doubloons, which are freely thrown to parade viewers.

Is Mardi Gras Staged For Visitors?
Not really. While the "greatest free show on earth" draws hundreds of thousands of visitors, that is not its purpose. Mardi Gras is a party the city throws for itself. It has developed into a world-class tourist attraction, yet the City of New Orleans doesn't spend a cent promoting it.

What Companies Sponsor Mardi Gras?
They don't. Mardi Gras is the only entertainment venue in the world where the stars foot the bill and the audience gets a free ride. By tradition and by law, Mardi Gras parades in New Orleans may not be corporately sponsored. Carnival clubs are chartered as non-profit organizations. They are financed by dues, by the sale of krewe-emblemed merchandise to the members, and by fund-raising projects such as bingos.

Why Can't I Buy An Official Mardi Gras Poster?
There is no such thing. Unlike the Olympics or the SuperBowl, there is no governing authority to license products. Mardi Gras is like Christmas and Halloween — it belongs to everyone. Beware of any item that bears the title "official." The claim (and the product?) are bogus. Free enterprise reigns supreme over Mardi Gras, making it a virtual paradise for entrepreneurs who compete for counter space and the attention of the public.

Who Coordinates Mardi Gras?
No one. While city governments issue parade permits, there is no overall authority that coordinates the five dozen parades held in the metro area during the 12 days that precede Fat Tuesday. Each parading organization is completely autonomous.

Why Are There No Parades In The French Quarter?
For 117 years, virtually every New Orleans Mardi Gras parade rolled through the French Quarter. In 1973 the fire and police departments felt that the increased size of parade floats, and the crowds that gathered to see them, rendered the narrow streets unsafe so the city issued a ban on parades in that historic area.

What's The Difference Between Carnival And Mardi Gras?
Carnival refers to the season of merriment which always begins on January 6. Mardi Gras (Fat Tuesday) is the single, culminating day of Carnival, and it is always the day before Ash Wednesday.

Mardi Gras Q&A

Is Mardi Gras Really Connected To Religion?
Yes. The Catholic Church licensed Carnival, which means "farewell to flesh," as a period of feasting before the fasting of Lent. The Church also established the set date for the start of the Carnival season — January 6, the Feast of the Epiphany — and the fluctuating date of Mardi Gras.

Why Does The Date Of Mardi Gras Change?
Because it's connected to the moveable date of Easter, which can fall on any Sunday from March 23 to April 25. Mardi Gras is scheduled 47 days preceding Easter and can occur on any Tuesday from February 3 through March 9.

When Was The First Mardi Gras Parade Held In New Orleans?
On February 24, 1857. The Mistick Krewe of Comus, Carnival's first secret society, coined the word "krewe," and was the first to choose a mythological namesake, to present a themed parade with floats, and to follow it with a tableaux ball.

Is It True Mobile Celebrated Mardi Gras Before New Orleans?
Yes and no. New Orleans' first Carnival krewe was founded in 1857 by former members of Mobile's Cowbellian de Rakin Society, which was founded in 1830. However, Mobile's parades were held on New Year's Eve until 1866, when they switched to Fat Tuesday.

Has Mardi Gras Ever Been Canceled?
Yes, but not often. Since 1857, only 13 Fat Tuesdays have been affected. Most cancelations were caused by wars: Civil, WWI, WWII and Korean.

Krewes Are Named After What?
The colorful worlds of Greek, Roman, and Egyptian mythology are the sources of nearly half of the parading krewe names. Other clubs are named after the neighborhoods through which they travel, while some are named after historical figures or places.

What Do The Carnival Colors Mean?
Purple represents justice, green stands for faith, and gold signifies power. Rex, the King of Carnival, selected them in 1872 for his first parade. While they were probably chosen simply because they looked good together, Rex assigned a meaning to each in his 1892 parade, entitled "Symbolism of Colors."

What Are Balls And Why Can't I Go?
Carnival balls are private, formal affairs (tuxedos and long gowns required) and are by invitation only. *Bals Masque* (masked balls) in New Orleans predate the first parade by more than a century. More than 125 private balls are presented each season in the city's Municipal Auditorium and in the grand ballrooms of major hotels. Mock royalty reigns over each ball, where a king, queen, maids and dukes are presented. In the older, society krewes, the court is made up of debutantes. Some clubs stage "tableaux" (theatrical scenes) enacted by krewe members, and favors are given to special guests. Krewes such as Bacchus, Orpheus, Endymion, and Zulu have replaced the traditional ball with extravaganzas presented at the Louisiana Superdome and at the Morial Convention Center. Tickets are sold to these events.

What's The Theme For This Year?
There is no general theme for Mardi Gras, but each individual parade depicts a specific subject. The floats then reflect the krewe's theme for that year. Maskers are costumed in a manner that illustrates the overall parade theme and the individual float title. Among the more popular subjects have been history, children's stories, legends, geography, famous people, entertainment, mythology, and literature.

Do I Have To Mask?
No, but you should, at least on Fat Tuesday, the only day when street masking is legal (from dawn to dusk). Masking, which can be elaborate or makeshift, dates from Roman carnivals when assuming false identifies was a common practice. By law, float riders must be masked at all times.

How Do I Get To Be King?
If you're not a krewe member or a celebrity, you don't. The method of selecting Mardi Gras royalty varies from krewe to krewe. The King of Carnival is chosen by the inner circle of the School of Design, the sponsoring organization for the Rex parade. Some krewes hold random drawings to pick their king or queen. Most clubs charge the selected monarch a fee to reign. In several of the newer krewes, elaborate ceremonies called "coronation balls" are staged to crown their royalty.

Is Secrecy Still A Part Of Carnival?
Yes. While many Carnival clubs are fairly accessible (some even have websites), some maintain the tradition of secrecy that has been a part of Mardi Gras since its earliest days. A unique custom in the older organizations is that the king's name is never made public. An exception is Rex, whose name is revealed the day before his parade. And while many in the media know his identity days in advance, the embargo on publishing it has never been violated.

What About Celebrities?
The Krewe of Bacchus began the tradition of selecting celebrity kings with its first parade in 1969, when Danny Kaye reigned. Endymion and Orpheus also annually invite guest celebrities to ride in their parades. Some of the more popular stars to have appeared are Bob Hope, Dolly Parton, Wayne Newton, John Goodman, Jackie Gleason, Britney Spears, Kirk Douglas, Harry Connick Jr., Nicholas Cage, and the Beach Boys. In most cases visiting stars are not paid to ride, although the krewes do cover their expenses.

Is The Success of Mardi Gras Measured By The Amount Of Trash Collected?
No. Before the age of recycling, the success of Mardi Gras in Orleans Parish was sometimes jokingly measured by the amount of trash collected by the New Orleans Sanitation Department. For several years in the late 1980s, the total for the 12-day parading season topped the 2,000-ton mark

Is Mardi Gras Elitist?
Not any more. While wealthy white males once controlled Carnival (and most of America), Mardi Gras is one of the nation's most diverse institutions, and offers a rich cultural experience to participants and spectators.

How Are Parades Structured?
Almost all Carnival parades follow a standard parade format, normally with the captain appearing at the head of the procession, either on a special float, in a convertible or on horseback. Next come the officers, the king or queen, and in some parades, the maids and dukes, followed by the title float and the floats that carry riding members. An 18-float procession of a 200-member krewe may feature more than 75 units. When band members, dance groups, posses, clown units and motorcycle squadrons are all added up, it is not uncommon for the number of participants to total more than 3,000.

Is There An Official Parade Season?
While several "pre-season" parades have become quite grand in scale, local parish ordinances dictate that the New Orleans Mardi Gras parade season officially begins on the second Friday before Fat Tuesday. During the 12-day period leading up to Mardi Gras, nearly 60 parades are held in the four-parish area of Orleans, Jefferson, St. Bernard and St. Tammany.

Where Do Floats Come From?
Less than a dozen Carnival clubs build their own original floats each year. Since their floats will be used only once, these krewes have greater flexibility with the subject matter their parades portray. Float designs are quite faithful to the parade theme. Most other krewes select from a pool of rental floats, and their themes tend to be generic in nature. Thus, the "Sherwood Forest" float from a parade entitled *Robin Hood* might show up two days later as lead unit in another parade whose subject is *All-Time Favorite Mythical Characters*. In Orleans Parish, a city ordinance prohibits the use of the same float more than twice in the Central Business District during a single parade season.

Active Parading Krewes

The following section includes available information on the 50 parading krewes that were active during the 2003 parade season. In all, data on more than 1,900 parades is presented. Parade themes and royalty names are given for the years that each group paraded, which, in some cases, does not correspond to the club's founding date. Because of space limitations, some names and themes are abbreviated.

While the Knights of Momus and the Mistick Krewe of Comus no longer parade, they are included out of respect for their historical contributions and in the hope that their processions will one day again brighten the streets of New Orleans.

ADONIS

In Greek mythology, Adonis was an extremely handsome young man whose physical beauty was comparable to that of Endymion. This male and female club was founded in 1999 and parades in the West Bank Jefferson Parish City of Gretna. The Mystic Knights of Adonis is not affiliated with the Mystic Krewe of Adonis which paraded in New Orleans from 1949 to 1964.

YEAR	THEME	KING	QUEEN
1999	Adonis Salutes Great Lovers	Gregory L. Dimak	Laura L. Grandquest
2000	Salutes Holidays Of The Millennium	August A. Creppel	Ann H. Blackburn
2001	Adonis . . . Goldbricking In Gretna	Jules J. Yambra Jr.	Mary B. Dufresne
2002	Myths And Legends	Paul J. Bourg	Denise H. Bourg
2003	Adonis Relives Louisiana	Jimmie B. Bourg	Christie C. Bourg

ALADDIN

This Carnival organization, named after a character from *A Thousand and One Arabian Nights*, is comprised of veterans from several other parading krewes. In the rich world of Arabian mythology, Aladdin was the son of a poor widow. He gained fame and fortune when he discovered a magic lamp. Aladdin's first parade was held in 2000, and two years later its membership totaled more than 1,000 men, women, and children. Aladdin's queen is named Jasmine.

YEAR	THEME	ALADDIN	JASMINE
2000	Aladdin Travels The World	Stanley J. LeBlanc Jr.	Annette Marie Aguilar
2001	Louisiana Favorites	Robert F. Galmiche Jr.	Fonnie Galmiche
2002	Movies Of The 20th Century	Lynwood G. Trasks Jr.	Sherri Bridges Trask
2003	Aladdin Says, "Name That Tune"	Troy A. Hoffpauir	Sharon Gayla Hirsch

ALLA

Carnival's fourth oldest parading group was founded by the Westside Social and Carnival Club, and presented its inaugural parade with a single float on Fat Tuesday, 1933. The all-male krewe takes its name from an abbreviation of Algiers, Louisiana — the New Orleans West Bank community through which it travels. Alla staged 10 river parades and nearly 30 tableau balls at the Municipal Auditorium before reorganizing under the auspices of the Golden Gryphon Society in 1978. Alla's king and queen are called the Maharajah and the Maharanee. Alla traditionally presents the largest parade on the West Bank.

YEAR	THEME	KING	QUEEN
1933	Liberty	George Mastainich	Mary Rosamano
1934	Mardi Gras	Joseph Rosamano	Henrietta Hammer
1935	History Makers	Frank Braai	Mrs. George Mastainich
1936	The Dancers	Edward C. O'Hara	Hilda Mae Fleming
1937	Goddess Of Spring	McKinley Vezien	Geraldine Thomas
1938	The Arrival Of Spring	Charles Rantz	Catherine Kerner
1939	Memoirs Of Johann Strauss	Dr. Henry A. LaRocca	Nellie Spahr
1940	Clouds	George Rittner	Catherine O'Hara
1941	Legends Of Old Greece	Sov C. Clements	Doris Curren
1942	Farewell To Carnival	Erwin Salathe Sr.	Dorothy Salathe
1943 - 45	NO PARADES — WWII		
1946	Return Of Alla	Earl Angelo	June Moore
1947	The Jewels Of Cordova	Joseph Lusk	Loyola Mae Donnelly
1948	Great Lovers Of History	Vincent Rosamano	Jean Trupiano
1949	Jean Lafitte, Buccaneer	Herman Soulant	Flora Belle Berthaut
1950	A Cinderella Story	Dr. M. O. Carey	Joan Elaine Chauvin
1951	A Letter To My Darling	John Sprada	Marianne Bragg
1952	Laguna, White Goddess Of The Moon	Joseph B. Sunseri	Eleanor Mary Darcy
1953	Love's Old Story	Dr. Phillip Sunseri	Sylvia Ann Parr
1954	Sheba The Queen	Walter S. Meteye	Marilyn Ann Ruiz
1955	The Meeting Of Antony & Cleopatra	Buster Hughes	Ione Cecile Calzada
1956	Sleeping Beauty	Dr. M. O. Carey Sr.	Jo Anne Mary LaRocca
1957	Our Silver Anniversary Party	Elwood Bozzelle	Kathleen Theresa Darcy
1958	Music Around The World	Gerald (Jerry) Mine	None
1959	A Trip To The Moon	Dr. Floyd Hindelang	Geraldine M. Fitzgerald
1960	King Kong	Bennie Guthrie	Lynn Rose Cemiglia
1961	The Fabulous Marco Polo	Frank Lawson	Betty Lee Whittington
1962	20,000 Leagues Under The Sea	Harry Rosenthal	Carol Anne Thibodaux
1963	Alice In Wonderland	Al Reany	Bonnie Ann Bays
1964	The Great Toy Robbery	Gilbert J. Manson	Mary Francis Henricks
1965	Circus	Dr. Salvador Canale	Connie E. Brechtel
1966	Land Of Oz	John Beninate	Sylvia Ann Hindelang
1967	The Time Machine	Hugh Humphrey Sr.	Elizabeth M. Humphrey
1968	Monster Mania	Dr. Joseph Gregoratti	Cheryl Lee Gregoratti
1969	History Of The Dance	Melton Garrett	Pamela Ann Sunseri
1970	Dr. Dolittle	Jack Boyce	Nancy Ellen Salathe
1971	People, Places And Times	Larry Kabel	June Marie Humphrey
1972	Alphabet Soup	John Ales	Amelia Ann Ales
1973	Little Nemo In Slumberland	Wayne Mayberry	Connie Francis Albaral
1974	Childhood Adventures	Paul Becnel	Anne Ward
1975	Louisiana Festivals	Joe Guidry	Jan Ellen Henderson
1976	America On The Water	Nick Cioll	Naomi Ellen Schultz
1977	Alla's Library	Pat Jordan	Artye Marie Burmaster

YEAR	THEME	MAHARAJAH	MAHARANEE
1978	Alla's Oriental Adventures	Nat B. Knight	Janice Humphrey
1979	A Tribute To Jules Verne	Charles W. Wall Sr.	Lizbeth Jeri Ledet
1980	Once Upon A Time	Mitchell Lulich	Angela Maria Christiana
1981	There Were Giants In The Earth In Those Days	James W. Smith	Deborah Ann Sinclair
1982	Fifty Years Of Alla	Otto Candies	Wendy Sancho
1983	Alla In Movieland	Claude Autin	Kimberly Ann Beninate
1984	Louisiana Jambalaya	Floyd Sinclair	Gina Lisa Giacona
1985	Beauty And The Beast	Blaine Kern	Blainey Kern
1986	In The Beginning	Jack McClanahan	Kelly McClanahan
1987	We The People	Bob Evans	Kasey Elizabeth Olsen
1988	Alla's Cartoon And Comic Festival	Louis Wilson Jr.	Theresa Dries Wilson
1989	The Greatest Show On Earth	John Schwegmann	Mary Jo Kass
1990	Don't Touch That Dial	Corrado Giacona	Susan Dupont
1991	Alla's Aquatic Adventure	Michael C. Sport	Sheri Lynn Sport & Deborah Ann Sport
1992	Alla — 60 Years Young	Harry Lee	Elizabeth Ward
1993	Love Makes The World Go 'Round	Lyle Stockstill	Stephanie Marie Stone
1994	Lasting Legends	Frank Christiana	Michelle Bodenger
1995	Alla's Sound Of Music	Lawrence E. Chehardy	Kelly Sutherland
1996	Fantasy, Fiction And Folklore	George R. Young	Lylyn Stockstill
1997	A Moment In Time	Dr. Natchez Morice	Melissa Bodenger
1998	Doing New Orleans	Michael Blake	Alisa Blake
1999	Tales Of King Arthur	Michael Blake	Alisa Blake
2000	It's All Greek To Me	Dr. J. Giambelluca	Erin Sutherland
2001	Classic Civilizations	John A. Beninate II	Alanna Carr
2002	Alla's In Wonderland	Danny Hughes	Danyael Hughes
2003	Robert E. Nims' Jazz Walk Of Fame	William Nungesser Jr.	Carrie Anne Williams

ANCIENT DRUIDS

Comprised of Carnival veterans from several other Orleans Parish parading organizations, the Ancient Druids wanted to fill an empty slot on the parade calendar, providing New Orleanians and visitors with a first-class parade one week before Fat Tuesday. The Ancient Druids was organized in 1998 and is not related to the Mystic Krewe of Druids, whose parades followed the Rex processions from 1922 to 1935. The all-male club is distinctive in that it does not stage a ball or feature a queen or court. Its king is known as the Arch Druid and he is accompanied on the king's float by a jester. Druids' 200 men are dressed in priest-like robes.

YEAR	THEME	ARCH DRUID	QUEEN
1999	Druid Travels	Secret	None
2000	Druid Leaps	Secret	None
2001	Druid Fluids	Secret	None
2002	Druid Tails	Secret	None
2003	Druid V's	Secret	None

APHRODITE

This St. Bernard Parish women's krewe was founded in 1985. The Greek goddess Aphrodite's birth is based on two different legends. Some historians of mythology claim that she was created out of the foam from the sea. (Aphros is Greek for foam.) In Homer's *Iliad*, Aphrodite was the daughter of Dione and Zeus. In all cases, she was the goddess of fruitfulness, and she personified the virtue of pure love. The Romans called her Venus. Both the Greek and Roman figures of Aphrodite represented the epitome of feminine beauty, and for that reason she was worshipped as the ideal female. In 1996, Aphrodite moved its parade from Tuesday to the Friday before Fat Tuesday.

YEAR	THEME	KING	QUEEN
1986	To The Ladies	S. Joe Griffith	Janis R. Carollo
1987	Aphrodite's Literary Wonderland	Mickey C. Prattini	Angie W. Gary
1988	Daze Of Holidays	Raymond Chenevert	Melanie A. Chenevert
1989	Aphrodite's Nature Book	Adolfo Bello Jr.	Jill W. Dolese
1990	Musical Memories	Peter Ajan Jr.	Lezlie Dolese Nunez
1991	Aphrodite's Tropical Paradise	Douglas J. Carlos	Pamela Lapara
1992	Aphrodite's Royal Feast	Charles Franks Sr.	Barbara Landry Kellum
1993	Cinema Classics	Leon Borja	Lee Falgout Ajan
1994	Childhood Memories	Robert L. Treadway	Gloria G. Sturlz
1995	Aphrodite Celebrates 10 Years	Stephen W. Bruno	Mabel B. Mangano
1996	Aphrodite's Dream Vacation	Joseph W. Browning	Louise E. Browning
1997	What A Way To Go	Richard Louis Pouey	Tracy Petruccelli Pouey
1998	Creature Feature	Jack C. Camhout	Beverly C. Kostopoulos
1999	Aphrodite's Famous Festivals	David Patrick Brousse	Millie M. Munsch
2000	Landmarks In Time	Scott M. Carollo	Christine P. Faust
2001	Cooking With Aphrodite	Patrick Senko Jr.	Michelle Vanbenschoten
2002	Aphrodite's Travel Channel	Ricky Hartman	Ricci Parker
2003	Back To Nature	Louis F. Roubion	Lisa L. Adler

AQUILA

Sponsored by the Eagle's Nest, Inc. (Aquila is Latin for eagle), this popular Metairie group was founded in 1976. This couples and singles krewe adheres to one of the primary customs of 19th Century Carnival clubs — the theme of the parade remains secret until the night of the ball. Since its founding, Aquila has been most active in the tourist and convention business, having restaged its tableau ball for visitors nearly 600 times.

Active Parading Krewes

Royal mini-floats transport the maids and dukes in this parade that features exquisite costumes and elaborate headpieces and collars as its trademarks. The club's motto is "Metairie's Finest." In 2000, Aquila moved its parade from Thursday to the Friday before Fat Tuesday.

YEAR	THEME	KING	QUEEN
1977	A Man And His Dream	Anthony Alessandra	Mildred W. Basile
1978	Ancient And Mythical Kingdoms	Charles E. Wingerter	Mrs. Philip S. Nitse
1979	A Kaleidoscope Of Fantasy	Paul C. Perret	Mrs. Paul C. Perret
1980	Hallelujah Hollywood	Capt. Robert H. Wilson	Mrs. Robert H. Wilson
1981	America Is A Lady	Donald Earl Raziano	Diana Lynn Mehn
1982	With These Hands	Carl R. Livermore Sr.	Edna Livermore
1983	Somewhere In Time	Al Russell Jr.	Diane Lynn Barrilleaux
1984	One Step Beyond	Adam Mehn III	Brenda K. Chetta
1985	Man's Reflections Of A Woman	Richard A. Pelanne Sr.	Jeanne S. Heikamp
1986	Thrill Of Victory Agony of Defeat	Gregory Reyer Caire	Dinya Toledo Lynch
1987	Shall We Dance	Lynn J. Drury	Angela Lynne Drury
1988	A Festival Of Celebrations	Leonard B. Hebert Jr.	Yvette Ann Hebert
1989	Childhood Remembrances	Barnette H. Mahler Jr.	Joyce Hoffmann
1990	This Land Is Your Land	Wilbur P. Daigle Jr.	Karen Ann Cashio
1991	Let Us Entertain You	Dr. Richie Thomas	Ethelyn F. Daigle
1992	With Pen In Hand	Victor D. DiGiorgio	Cherri A. Desporte
1993	Destination And Methods Unlimited	Frederick A. Belou	Mary Lou Belou
1994	Once Upon A Time	Matthew J. Hedrick Jr.	Sally Bernard Hedrick
1995	That's All Right Mama	Robert E. Morrill	Linda Wimprine Boesch
1996	Give My Regards	Timothy Bourgeois Sr.	Joyce Wingerter Cronin
1997	Let The Games Begin	James C. Oncale	Carolyn Landry
1998	Heroes Of Fact And Fiction	Peter A. Marx	Sarah Katherine Krekel
1999	Don't Touch That Dial	Larry Sharer	F. Diane Pickett
2000	From Aquila, With Love	Sidney J. Dantin	Kim M. Toups
2001	The Golden Dream	James C. Oncale	Carolyn Landry
2002	Rhythm Of The Islands	David Michael Aranda	Sandra Guarisco
2003	Spirit Of Louisiana	David Michael Aranda	Jeanne Marie Garner

ARGUS

The peacock-emblemed Krewe of Argus is named after the mythological, 100-eyed Greek guardian of Io. Argus presented Metairie with its first Fat Tuesday parade in 1974. For the next decade, entertainment celebrities such as Barbara Eden, Shari Lewis, Phyllis Diller, and Loretta Swit reigned as Empresses of Argus. In 1985, with a male and female membership that had tripled since 1982, a new custom of selecting royalty from within its own ranks began. The club allows commercial sponsorship of its floats.

YEAR	THEME	KING	QUEEN
1974	Aesop's Fables	George J. Ackel	None
1975	Argus Salutes Jefferson Parish	None	Barbara Eden
1976	Argus' Song Book	None	Kay Starr
1977	Argus' Aquatic Adventures	None	Phyllis Diller
1978	The Kingdom Of Tut	None	Shirley Jones
1979	Argus' Movie Awards	None	Cathy Lee Crosby
1980	Argus' Library	None	Connie Stevens
1981	Creatures Of The Imagination	None	Loretta Swit
1982	Argus On Vacation	None	Dianne Ladd
1983	10 Years Of Mardi Gras In Jefferson	None	Shari Lewis
1984	Remember When . . .	None	Lee Meredith
1985	Famous American Festivals	Herb Cammatte	Michele Shane Bandi
1986	Creatures Great And Small	Vincent Impastato	Gena Pausina-Cherry
1987	Characters Of Fantasy And Fact	Charles J. Nelson	Stacey Shane-Schott
1988	The Argus Sports Page	Carol V. Charvet	N. Cammatte-Wilder
1989	Jefferson Parish Salutes Louisiana	Jerry Crawford	Janet L. Allen-Ritzmann
1990	Men Of Distinction	Joseph Sexton	G. Allen-Choojitarom
1991	The Good Earth	Ken Hollis	J. Artigues-Ingram
1992	Life's Pleasures	Lawrence Chehardy	Lauren Teresa Berner
1993	Unexplained Mysteries	Patrick T. Bossetta	Amy E. Alexander
1994	Argus Switches Cable Channels	J. F. Allen Jr.	Janet L. Allen-Ritzmann
1995	Argus Celebrates	Drago Cvitanovich	Melissa Jean Bossetta
1996	Argus' Eyes	Frederick R. Heebe	Neille Bernard-Kelly
1997	Argus Celebrates 25 Years	John Persson Jr.	Jacqueline N. Webre
1998	Festivals Of The World	Dr. G. A. Cvitanovich	Amy K. Passons
1999	Extra, Extra, Read All About It	Aaron F. Broussard	Jennifer M. Massey
2000	It's About Time	Salvador Anzelmo	Lacey Anne Blalock
2001	Proverbs	Michael Flower	Shannon Marie Fay
2002	Oldie But Goodies	Michael Roppolo	Ashliegh Gilley
2003	Colours	Rep. Danny Martiny	Alana Lincoln

ATLAS

The celebrated strongman made famous in the mythology of ancient Greece is the namesake of this Jefferson Parish krewe, which was founded in 1969. Each year Atlas enjoys the distinction of opening the Metairie Mardi Gras parade calendar. The Krewe of Atlas is unique in that it is overseen by a 10-member board of directors and a captain. The innovative male and female organization is credited with many firsts, including being the first to roll over the standardized Jefferson Parish Veterans Boulevard parade route now shared by more than a dozen other Carnival clubs.

YEAR	THEME	KING	QUEEN
1970	The Countries Of Atlas	Harold J. Toca	Doris Moulliet
1971	Great Discoveries And Inventions	Thomas F. Ridgley	Sandra C. Martina
1972	Music Of Famous Rivers	James P. Balser	Shirley Schwebel
1973	A Visit To The Zoo	Thomas A. Baroni	Wanda Tapie
1974	Let's Mask For Mardi Gras	Elroy Schwebel	Judy Brunner
1975	World Of Make Believe	John Dedebant	Bertha M. Albright
1976	Great Moments In American History	Joseph D. Smith	Rickie T. Brandt
1977	Movie Madness	Jules Greenberg	Cynthia B. Hebert
1978	Classics Of Literature	Peter G. Pauli	Barbara B. Roth
1979	Our First Decade	Ernest J. Autin Jr.	Claudia D. Ballantyne
1980	Voyage To The Bottom Of The Sea	Farrell A. Tapie	Georgiana L. Balser
1981	Stories Of Enchantment	John D. Mitchell Sr.	Carolyn Jean Johnson
1982	Americans All	Maurice E. Roques	Patricia L. Clotworthy
1983	Our Planet Earth	Jake A. Terranova	Michelle C. Labiche
1984	When The World Was Young	Charles H. Clotworthy	Darlene A. Larroque
1985	The Famous And The Infamous	Thomas E. Cambre	Rickie Tapie Brandt
1986	The Best Days Of Our Lives	David L. Carrick Sr.	Mary Lynn Shannon
1987	And the Melody Lingers On	Robert Palestina	Sandra Pauli Gulley
1988	A Momentous Occasion	Rudolph Mustereifel Jr.	Kathleen M. Tapie
1989	Atlas 20 Years Later	Elward J. Myers Sr.	Joan F. Montecino
1990	Lifestyles Of the Rich And Famous	Helaire J. Bordelon Jr.	Nicole Olson Palestina
1991	History Of the World	Dominick J. Scandurro	Ronnie I. Myers
1992	Atlas Studies The Universe	John W. Richey	Dianne M. Raphael
1993	Atlas On the Move	Clarence L. Unger Jr.	Rita D. Bezou
1994	Silver Memories	Anthony J. Militello Sr.	Anne Scott Brown
1995	Atlas' Cinema Classics	Louis A. Hosch Jr.	Susan D. Rushing
1996	Havin' A Party	Scott A. Cipriano	Dana Jones Poche
1997	Literary Masterpieces	Robert D. Brown	Melinda J. Murray
1998	Freaky Friday	George M. Bezou Jr.	Rita D. Bezou
1999	30 Years Of Atlas	Louis A. Hosch Jr.	Susan D. Rushing
2000	Atlas' International Celebration	Eric R. Phillpott Jr.	Erin P. Growden
2001	Way Down Yonder	Roy D. Acord	Karen M. Acord
2002	The Atlas Atlas	Rondel P. Frank	Susan E. Buckel
2003	Happiness Is	Thomas D. Ignelzi	Hope S. Ignelzi

BABYLON

Babylon was an important city located on the Euphrates River in southwest Asia. Its namesake Mardi Gras krewe was founded in 1939 in New Orleans. The men call their reigning monarch "Sargon" — the king who was the legendary ruler of the ancient Semitic races. Secrecy is of great significance to the Knights of Babylon, and the identity of their king is never revealed to the general public. The title of Babylon's elaborate parade and ball theme is also undisclosed until the day of the event. Each float depicts a chapter in a continuing story, usually historical, classical, or literary in theme. The parade includes flambeaux and several signature floats, including the "Hanging Gardens of Babylon."

YEAR	THEME	SARGON	QUEEN
1940	Travelogue	Secret	Julia H. Peytral
1941	Capricious Nature	Secret	Claudine McGovern
1942-46	NO PARADES — WWII		
1947	The Arts	Secret	Tereze Bordes Oser
1948	Fancy's Flight	Secret	Joyce Frink
1949	The Sciences	Secret	Rose M. Monjure
1950	The Marches	Secret	Rose Mary Gambino
1951	Historical Highlights	Secret	Mary Ann Leggio
1952	Contributions To Civilizations	Secret	Patricia Ann Delaney
1953	Fabulous Festivals	Secret	Edna Raphael
1954	Tales Old, Ever New	Secret	Lyrleen Regina Gaudet
1955	Masks	Secret	Lynn Marie LeBoeuf
1956	The Theatre	Secret	Diane Olive Gruber
1957	Makers Of History	Secret	Jeannine Lee Monte
1958	Scenes From The Operas	Secret	Mary Andrea LaRocca
1959	Art Through The Ages	Secret	Jean Bonnar Thompson
1960	Alice In Wonderland	Secret	Charlene Diane Mary
1961	Rogues And Renegades	Secret	Gwendolyn F. Burk
1962	The Musical Theatre	Secret	Marilynn Marie Meyer
1963	Hans C. Anderson's Fairy Tales	Secret	Mary Edna Miller
1964	Le Ballet	Secret	Marie Therese Martin
1965	Poems Of Youth	Secret	Margaret Ann Martin
1966	The Life Of Benjamin Franklin	Secret	Sydney Elaine Jones
1967	Behind The Golden Curtain	Secret	Adrienne Manette Giroir
1968	Gone Are The Days	Secret	Cheryl Gregoratti
1969	Don Quixote	Secret	Carol Lynn Waszkowski
1970	Around The World In Eighty Days	Secret	Judy Garwood Wolff
1971	The Student Prince	Secret	Lisa Ann Hebert
1972	Peer Gynt	Secret	Helen Frances Rogers
1973	Aida	Secret	Karen Elizabeth Anticich
1974	Anna And The King Of Siam	Secret	Kathleen Patricia Verges
1975	Robin Hood	Secret	Andrea Marie Kambur
1976	Commodore Matthew Calbreath Perry	Secret	Beatrice Ann Flair
1977	The Little Glass Slipper	Secret	Deborah Joyce Verges
1978	Mozart	Secret	Diana Lizabeth Davis
1979	NO PARADE — POLICE STRIKE	Secret	Karen Patrice Mintz
1980	Babes In Toyland	Secret	Donna Claire Persich
1981	Tevye's Tale	Secret	Carol Ann Leingang
1982	Snow White	Secret	Diane Mary Sinclair
1983	Kismet	Secret	Virginia Claire Davis
1984	Once And Future King	Secret	Margaret Mary Persich
1985	Desert Song	Secret	Afton Lenora Richard
1986	The Matchmaker	Secret	Robin Lael Cooper
1987	Oklahoma	Secret	Priscilla Jone Piker
1988	The Trapp Family Singers	Secret	Charlotte Claire Mary
1989	The Golden Years	Secret	Janette Andra Carden
1990	Pygmalion	Secret	Joann Olga Wax
1991	Oliver Twist	Secret	Mignonne Cecile Mary
1992	Carmen	Secret	Heather Marie Jones
1993	Naughty Marietta	Secret	Suzanne B. Cooper
1994	New Moon	Secret	Angelique M. Guidry
1995	Music Man	Secret	Julie Jaye Jacob
1996	Gigi	Secret	Carra Adelea Sinclair

1997	South Pacific	Secret	Jessica Nora De John
1998	Yankee Doodle Boy	Secret	Danielle E. Derbes
1999	For The Love Of Opera	Secret	Therese Marie Wax
2000	L'histoire de Notre Heritage Francais	Secret	Anupama Kewalramani
2001	The Works Of L. Frank Baum (OZ)	Secret	Ashley Erin Capdepon
2002	Guys And Dolls	Secret	Diana Elizabeth Macera
2003	Sauntering Through Sondheim	Secret	Jamie Kay Orth

BACCHUS

Twelve businessmen met in 1968 to explore new directions for Carnival clubs in New Orleans. From that gathering emerged Bacchus, the most innovative and imitated krewe founded during the 20th Century. The largest floats ever assembled, the transformation of the tableau ball into a massive supper dance with Las Vegas-style entertainment, and the choice of a national celebrity as its monarch are a few of the tradition-breaking moves made by the Bacchus organization. The Greek god of wine parades with more than 1,000 men on the Sunday evening preceding Fat Tuesday.

YEAR	THEME	BACCHUS	QUEEN
1969	The Best Things In Life	Danny Kaye	None
1970	Remember When . . .	Raymond Burr	None
1971	Bacchus Salutes Mardi Gras	Jim Nabors	None
1972	The Bacchus Book Of Horrors	Phil Harris	None
1973	Bacchus Goes To The Movies	Bob Hope	None
1974	Bacchus Reads The Comics	Glen Campbell	None
1975	Bacchus' Circus Parade	Jackie Gleason	None
1976	Spirit Of '76	Perry Como	None
1977	Happily Ever After	Henry Winkler	None
1978	Monarchs And Memories	Ed McMahon	None
1979	*NO PARADE — POLICE STRIKE*	Ron Howard	None
1980	The Undersea World Of Bac-chu-steau	Pete Fountain	None
1981	The Old Testament	Sgt. John McKeel Jr.	None
1982	American Heroes And Heroines	Dom DeLuise	None
1983	Jewels Of The Zodiac	Charlton Heston	None
1984	Rivers Of The World	Kirk Douglas	None
1985	In Vino Veritas	Lorne Green	None
1986	New Orleans, We Love You	John Ritter	None
1987	Bacchanal	William Shatner	None
1988	20 Years Of Bacchus	Alan Thicke	None
1989	Sing Along With Bacchus	Billy Crystal	None
1990	Our Planet Earth	Dennis Quaid	None
1991	The Bacchus Gallery Of Art	Steve Guttenburg	None
1992	What A Way To Go	Gerald McRaney	None
1993	Silver Jubilee	Harry Connick Jr.	None
1994	I'm Sending You A Bouquet Of Roses	Jean-Claude V. Damme	None
1995	Color My World	John Larroquette	None
1996	Games People Play	Dick Clark	None
1997	Bacchus' Comic Book Heroes	Tom Arnold	None
1998	Where Y'at Dawlin?	Drew Carey	None
1999	A Tribute To Jules Verne	Jim Belushi	None
2000	Milestone To The Millennium	Luke Perry	None
2001	Denizens Of The Deep	Larry King	None
2002	Bacchus Journeys Through Africa	Nicolas Cage	None
2003	Bacchus' Fantasy Whirl	Jon Lovitz	None

BARDS OF BOHEMIA

Formed in 1933, the Bards of Bohemia has a rich tradition in New Orleans Carnival history. Its members were instrumental in the organization of two other parading clubs, Hermes and Babylon. Bards enjoyed a reputation for staging elaborate *bals masque* for nearly 50 years before it began a new tradition in 1981, a before-the-ball party in Armstrong Park. In 1988, the Bards joined the official Carnival calendar as a regular parading krewe. Many of Bards' male and female members are attorneys. Bards annually honors local celebrities and also selects a "Great American." Rudy Valee, Nancy Sinatra, Dr. Joyce Brothers, Carol Conners and Ben Vareen are among those so honored.

YEAR	THEME	KING	QUEEN
1988	Let's Celebrate	Frank L. Branson	Jennifer Ann Branson
1989	My Favorite Fantasy	Henry Witter	Evangeline Ann Vavrick
1990	History's Heroes	Douglas O. Foote	Evangeline Ann Vavrick
1991	Wonders Of The World	Paul Eugene Mann	Misty Lynn Berg
1992	Great Americans All	Howard L. Nations	Sherry Nations
1993	Famous Lovers	Samuel Solomon	Bonnie G. Seidler
1994	New Orleans, We Love You	Thomas Durel	Rhonda Shear
1995	Bards' Tales Of Horror	Gary Dennis Hughes	Tracy Heil King
1996	Music Through The Ages	Paul O'Connor	Elizabeth O'Connor
1997	The World Of Entertainment	Harry Blackstone Jr.	Bellammie Blackstone
1998	The Bards Classics	Bruce Calamari	Barbara Capone
1999	Phiends, Phantoms And Phantasy	Jay Weil	Catherine Weil
2000	The Captain's Silver Anniversary	Peter Brechtel III	Christine R. Brechtel
2001	2001 A Bards' Odyssey	Dr. Samuel H. Mehr	Christine Ann Mehr
2002	*NO PARADE*		
2003	70 Years Of Tradition	James Blache	Judith Blache

CAESAR

Rather than tap the rich mythological world that provides the source names for many Mardi Gras clubs, this Jefferson Parish organization named itself after Rome's most famous real-life citizen. From Caesar's elaborate Coronation Ball to the shape of the multi-colored cloisonné doubloons, every aspect of the krewe's activities carries the Roman motif. "Royal barges" transport Caesar's maids, and along with the captain, empress, and emperor, their elaborate costumes and neon lighted headpieces are among the most exquisite in all of Mardi Gras. Caesar's all male membership tops 700. The krewe includes characters that appeal to children. Past groups have included Snoopy & Peanuts, Power Rangers, Rug Rats, and Mickey and Minnie Mouse. Caesar annually restages part of its parade in Disneyworld.

YEAR	THEME	EMPEROR	EMPRESS
1980	Hail To The Heroes	Vincent Maenza	Roslyn Kracke
1981	Circus Maximus	Lionel Gerstner	Loria Breaux
1982	Seven Seas Of Caesar	Chester A. Hingle	Linda Fuller Kern
1983	Happily Ever After	Gary A. Bisso	Alana Hailey
1984	Great Ages Of Man	Roger Russell	Deborah Schlumbrecht
1985	Tell Me A Story	Anthony Herrle	Erin Pisciotta
1986	I Write The Songs	Oscar Paysse Jr.	Anna Marie Daniels
1987	Caesar's Cinema Classics	Henry Smith	July Sapir
1988	Come Fly With Me	Dr. Don Ray Guzzetta	Kathy Rohr Meehan
1989	Caesar's Main Street Parade	Autry Glenn Sandlin	Nancy Powell
1990	Extra, Extra, Read All About It	Harry J. Glidden	Kelly Mayeur Feraud
1991	Give My Regards To Broadway	Shelby F. Powell	Kerri Hardin
1992	Just For Kids	Robert B. Bland Jr.	Michelle Newfield
1993	Caesar's Library	Robert S. Bland	Christine Ross
1994	Walt's Wonderful World Of Animation	Robert G. Stanley	Robyn Carnesi
1995	Great Caesar's Ghost	Greg Kleinpeter	Michelle Falgout
1996	Caesar's TV Focus	John Economy	Kerri Tedesco
1997	Child's Play	Michael Pitman	Kathleen Ruppert
1998	Let Us Entertain You	Richard J. Landry	Erin Marie Duffy
1999	Caesar Celebrates	Conrad Jules Baker Jr.	Ginger Lynn Guzzetta
2000	Viva Las Vegas — 2000	C. T. Burkenstock Jr.	Melissa Ann Ericksen
2001	From Alpha To Omega	A. Allan Hailey	Jessica Elizabeth Carvin
2002	Caesar's Tribute To The Arts	David C. DeVun	Aimee Michelle Trosclair
2003	Do You Believe?	James Friedman	Ashley Michelle Morel

CARROLLTON

The uptown neighborhood of Carrollton was once a small township located on the edge of Orleans and Jefferson Parishes. This parading krewe was founded in 1924 when the Seventh District Carnival and Social Club began staging the annual "Carrollton Carnival" on Fat Tuesday. When rain washed out most of Mardi Gras in 1933, the men staged the only daytime parade of the season. A fire that destroyed its den (and the outbreak of World War II) caused the club to fall into abeyance in 1942, but the group reorganized, staged a colorful 12-float parade in 1947, and has been a popular fixture ever since. The all-male krewe includes more than 250 members.

YEAR	THEME	KING	QUEEN
1924 - 41	7th District Carnival and Pleasure Club		
1942 - 46	*NO PARADES — WWII*		
1947	A Fantasy Of Fairy Tales	John C. Ackermann	Ada Ruth Rebaudo
1948	Favorite Songs Of The American Past	Adrian A. Arnaud	Mary Elise Exnicios
1949	Holidays Around The World	Everett Marks	Beth O'Neill
1950	Rise And Fall Of King Winter	Lucien Rolland	Mildred Mary Long
1951	Scenes Of Beauty	Salvador F. Centanni Sr.	Myra Centanni
1952	Nature's Colorful Realm	Dennis Rufin	Joy Ann Scheuring
1953	Wedding Anniversaries	John Mailhes	Yvette Anne Guillot
1954	Between The Bookends	Joseph B. Exnicios	Rose Mary Gambino
1955	Toyland After Midnight	William A. Long Sr.	Joy Anne Cuoco
1956	Bluebird	Frank C. Saporito	Barbara Mae Braud
1957	Best Loved Poems	Manuel B. Zabala	Lorraine Centanni
1958	The Glittering Festival	Fred Husser	Shirlee Gagliano
1959	Fantasy Land	Russell Leonard Cuoco	Carole Andree Cuoco
1960	The Nutcracker	John Joseph Matranga	Jeannine C. Matranga
1961	Memories Of A Concert Hall	Earl A. Noble Sr.	Linda Lee Normand
1962	Immortal Works Of Victor Herbert	William B. Gatipon Sr.	Melba Martin
1963	Myths And Legends	Martin J. Paul Jr.	Karen Kaye Smith
1964	Romantic Melodies	Carroll D.Van Geffen Sr.	Margaret Donna Paul
1965	The Eternal Cycle	Louis D. Haeuser	Lurline Linda Watts
1966	Reveries Over A Scrapbook	Walter Gemeinhardt	Marie Margaret Mouton
1967	Highlights Of American History	William James Lee Jr.	Karen Ruth Richard
1968	Saga Of The Mississippi	Joseph P. Aucoin	Bonnie Lee Tunstall
1969	The Sciences	Anthony A. Campo	Jo Ann Campo
1970	Tales Of History And Legend	Edward John Ziegler	Shelley A. Van Geffen
1971	Silver Memories	Forrest R. Singer	Bridget Anita Heaton
1972	Songs To Remember	George Van Geffen	Rebecca Hazel Heaton
1973	The Golden Years Of Broadway	John Minor	Kim E. Van Geffen
1974	It's 50 Years	Percy Chatelain	Kathleen T. Van Geffen
1975	Theatre Tunes, Ladies And Lovers	Merrith Karl	Gia Marie Rabito
1976	We The People	O. J. Viviano	Renee Elise Van Geffen
1977	Toys	Vincent Arena	Lisa Frances Restivo
1978	The Four Seasons	John Francis Karl	Marlene Ann Caldarera
1979	A Tribute To The Sunbelt States	Joseph D.Catalano Sr.	Darni Dale Jordan
1980	Holidays	James C. Farrelly	Lisa Marie Fitzmorris
1981	Around The World With Songs	Salvadore Centanni Jr.	Francesca Marie Cuccia
1982	Wonders Of The Sea	John J. Sehrt Jr.	Pamela Ann Van Geffen
1983	Cinema Classics	Emile P. Miller	Pamela Mary Villarrubia
1984	As Time Goes By	Richard Hamilton Sr.	Lydia Ann Bailey
1985	Magical Moments In Music	Michael J. Bowler	Julie Beth Van Geffen
1986	The Best Of Everything	Edward L. Crochet Jr.	Shannon M. Fitzmorris
1987	Truly American	Baptiste DeBroy	Rebecca Ruth Plaisance
1988	Cities & Parishes Of South Louisiana	Allen I. Boudreaux	None
1989	Festivals Of North Louisiana	Joseph Scott Knecht	Rachelle H. Livaudais
1990	Memories	Joseph M. Livaudais	Paula Ruth Foote
1991	Follow Your Dreams	Frank J. Knecht III	Ramona D. Williamson
1992	Know What It Means To Miss N.O.?	Warren W. Wingerter Jr.	Aline Marie Williams
1993	Famous Fairy Tales	Raymond A. Melan	Amanda A. Livaudais
1994	Seventy Years Of Nostalgia	Willis John Williams Jr.	Erin Martin Bruce
1995	Carrollton Travels To USA	Wayne Michael Lee	Lena Marie Nuccio
1996	Carrollton Salutes Famous Americans	Wm. M. Lagrange Sr.	Lori Angela Carroll
1997	Believe It Or Not	Albert Peter Bode Jr.	Alison Marie Bode

Active Parading Krewes

1998	Carrollton Shoots The Movies	Clement J. Buckman	Catherine Steele Dunn
1999	Through The Years	Capt. John S. White	Leslie Jeanne Slaton
2000	A Family Affair	Gregory John Bruce	Maurina Ann LaRocca
2001	2001: A Musical Odyssey	James M. Falter	Carol Keene Romaguera
2002	Splendors Of Nature	Morris Daniels	Ashley Elaine Schiavi
2003	Childhood Memories	Dr. Ronald Aslett	Laura Ashley Cotaya

CENTURIONS

The fabled Roman armies were led into battle by a dedicated group of soldiers known as the Centurions. The 350-member, all-male krewe is named after those noble warriors and was founded in 1979 by a group of Harahan-River Ridge businessmen. The club presented its first two parades on Jefferson Highway. In 1983, the men switched to the standard Veterans Memorial Boulevard route. In 1988, the group changed its parade night from Tuesday to the second Sunday before Mardi Gras. Centurions designs its parade theme around subjects that will entertain children. Members are also active in community fund-raising projects.

YEAR	THEME	KING	QUEEN
1981	Games Children Play	John Hope	Julie Blanchard
1982	Follow The Yellow Brick Road	Jerry Himel	Lori Merritt
1983	Centurions' Sweet Shop	Ronnie de St. Germain	Angela Olivier
1984	They All Ask For You	Rodney Riviere	Cheryl Riviere
1985	Centurions Children's Matinee	Tony Catalano	Robin Broussard
1986	Disney Rides Again	Philip DeSalvo	Karen Pflueger
1987	Born In The USA	Richard Stevens	Julie Rosen
1988	Broadway At The Saenger	Joseph David	Kellie Hope
1989	And Baby Makes Ten	John Pankratz	Kim Granier
1990	Did You Ever Wish Or Dream?	Karl Keller	Natalie Deffner
1991	And That's Entertainment	Val Pitre	Dawn Deffner
1992	The Genius Of It All	Bruce Ponthieu	Jennifer Meisner
1993	Treasures Of Our Years	Carl Henderson	Carolyn Walker
1994	Dad's Hat I'll Wear	Steven Rosen	Paige Busch
1995	Greatest Teams, For Love Or Victory	Dennis Van Dyke	Stephanie Bryant
1996	Remembers Words Of Wisdom	Michael Olivier	Aimee Castellon
1997	Home Sweet Home	Darryl Schmitt	Christine Bernard
1998	The Sounds Of Music	Leonard Kinler	Cathy Castellon
1999	Louisiana How Living Is Easy	Allen E. Deffner	Catherine L. Breslin
2000	Centurions Enjoy The Classics	Dennis McCrory	Olivia Elizabeth Moran
2001	Centurions' Great Inventions	George Ferris Breedy	Julia Ann Howell Breslin
2002	Here They Come — Two By Two	Roy Jospeh Campise	Tiffany Ann Campisi
2003	Join Centurions Under The Sea	Matthew Plunkett Sr.	Victoria Maria Castellon

CHAOS

The Knights of Chaos was organized during the summer of 2000. The group is made up of veterans of other parading and non-parading Carnival krewes. The club utilizes Momus floats and presents a satirical parade in the Momus tradition. Chaos also parades on the Thursday before Fat Tuesday, a night that for more than a century had been known as "Momus Thursday." (The Knights of Momus departed the parade calendar in 1992, but continue to stage balls).

YEAR	THEME	KING	QUEEN
2001	Causin' Chaos	Secret	None
2002	Chaos Goes Fishing	Secret	None
2003	Chaos Goes To Sunday School	Secret	None

CHOCTAW

The Krewe of Choctaw traces its origin to State Representative Leonard Santos, a member of the Old Regular Democratic Organization, which named the krewe more than six decades ago. The inspiration for the group's motif was a wooden Indian, a favorite figure housed at the political association's headquarters on St. Charles Avenue. Formerly under the sponsorship of the Old Reliable Pleasure Club, the influence of the early settlers of Louisiana is obvious. The krewe's annual ball is named the "Big Pow Wow," and Choctaw calls its king, queen, pages, and ladies-in-waiting its chief, princess, papooses and Indian maidens.

YEAR	THEME	CHIEF	PRINCESS
1939	Parade Had No Theme	Leonard Santos	None
1940	NA From Krewe	William Dubret	None
1941	The Gold Rush Of 49	A. P. Gary	June Barnett Lawson
1942-1945	NO PARADES — WWII		
1946	Pioneer Days	John Beninate	Geraldine Hunt Mull
1947	Marine Scenes	Louis Zinc	Joyce Buhler Callahan
1948	Dreams Of Art	Capt. Charles Henly	Dolores Henly
1949	Fairy Tales And Fantasy	Henry H. Klink	Gloria Panepinto Hebert
1950	Say It With Love	Louis J. Panuski	Edmae Clabert Landry
1951	Great Explorers	John Goodwyne	Joan Lawson Lilly
1952	Early Americans	Nick Christiana	Doris Bertoniere Oser
1953	Foreign Travelers	Sidney Bayard Sr.	Carolyn H. Greene
1954	The Legend Of The Star Maiden	J. C. Standridge	Florita Joia Hinchey
1955	Americana	Thomas Kelly	Frances S. Tingstrom
1956	The Legend Of Davy Crockett	Charles Murley	Dolores Ruiz Plaisance
1957	Holidays	Earl James Zinc	Susie Stuntz Newberry
1958	Children's Stories And Rhymes	Herman Fabian	Thais Suterland Favrot
1959	Great Lovers	Benny Samanie	Catherine A. Hardouin
1960	Indian Tribes	Joe Caimi	Gerald Lynn Concrey
1961	Cortez At The Court Of Montezuma	H. P. Rosenthal	Shirley Bertoniere
1962	The Legend Of Jean Lafitte	B. B. Johnson	Helena M. Bieber Mollo
1963	Michoud To The Moon	Capt. B. A. Rousselle Jr.	Suzanne S. Ochello
1964	Favorite T.V. Programs	Louis J. Kennedy	Charlene M. Zibilich
1965	New Year's Festival	Arthur S. Lawson	Betty Keener Dupont
1966	Bienvenidos	Emile T. Weathers	Wandolyn Thomassie
1967	Sojourn To Other Nations	Stanley L. Sutherland	Pamela M. Simmons
1968	New Orleans 250 Anniversary	Ernest F. Burmaster Sr.	Anita Louise Spahr
1969	When You Wish Upon A Star	Charles W. Wall	Bonnie R. Wall
1970	Moonlight On The Ganges	Gerald J. Lege Jr.	Karen Ann Murphy
1971	Vacation Land USA	Walter M. Ruiz	Celeste L.Sisung
1972	Movie Magic And Madness	Charles G. Jones	Sylvana M. Gregg
1973	Among Our Souvenirs	Alvin F. Alonzo Sr.	May M. McMahon
1974	Unforgettable Rhymes Mother Goose	Vincente E. Radosta Jr.	Peggy RoszinaPrice
1975	The Great Tribal Reunion	Ernest Burmaster Jr.	Barbara Dowdy Harris
1976	Great Events Of American History	Michel A. Hardouin Sr.	Eileen A. De Stefano
1977	Sing Along With Choctaw	George O'Dowd	Antoinette A. Beninate
1978	Happiness Is	Peter F. Algero	Cara Mothe Neel
1979	Under The Big Top	John E. Plaisance	Denise Mary Ditcharo
1980	Choctaw Reads The Comics	John E. Cassreino Jr.	Vickie Smith Hano
1981	Famous Faces Of Fact And Fiction	Ernesto A. Sanchez Jr.	Angele Ruiz Stenger
1982	Color Me Happy	Nicholas J. Beninate Jr.	Elizabeth Alice Brown
1983	Choctaw Turns The Pages Of History	Darren M. Vincent	Deborah Ann Ducote
1984	The Good Life	Louis A. Roussel	Celyn Mary Novak
1985	50th Anniversary Dreams Of Past	Donald C. Szabo	Fran Charlotte Favrot
1986	Cavalcade Of Sports	Bennie Carl Goings	Gina Elizabeth Goings
1987	Choctaw's Childhood Of Classics	Randolph Olano	Monica Ann Bernard
1988	I Love A Parade	Charles E. Turbeville	Mary Ellen Wattigney
1989	Choctaw's Cartoon Classics	Kelly P. McGovern	Kim Marie Chabert
1990	Coming To America	Gary Lerouge	Colleen E. Shelley
1991	The World Of Entertainment	Kenneth M. Leblanc	Steffanie Gione Pierozzi
1992	A Visit To The Library	Richard G. Hamilton	Michelle Lynn Helmer
1993	Choctaw Sings Colorful Melodies	Thomas Muhoberac Jr.	Patti R. Richey
1994	Flights Of Fantasy	Robert F. Childress	Cynthia Dee Packer
1995	Choctaw's 60th Tribal Reunion	Ricky Bush	Faith Gomez Saragusa
1996	Choctaw . . . On Broadway	Stanley J. LeBlanc Jr.	Katherine Arris Moreau
1997	Choctaw Entertains Children	Rody Landry	Ginger Zatarain
1998	Favorite Classics	Donald M. Herbert	Dale Marie Simon
1999	The Stuff That Dreams Are Made Of	Charles Moise Favrot	Candice Grace Sisung
2000-2002	NO PARADES		
2003	Choctaw Loves Mardi Gras	Charles Moise Favrot	Candice Grace Sisung

CLEOPATRA

The Krewe of Cleopatra was founded in 1972 as the first Carnival club for women on the Mississippi River's West Bank. Cleopatra officially opens the metro parade calendar that culminates on Fat Tuesday. The Egyptian Queen of the Nile, who ruled for nearly two decades, was an actual person, not a mythological figure like the namesakes of many other krewes. As her motto proclaims, "Her Beauty is Timeless, Her Age is Now — Forever." The Egyptian motif is expertly executed by the parade's floats. Cleopatra rides with more than 500 women.

YEAR	THEME	KING	QUEEN
1973	Queens And Enchantresses	None	Evelyn Hilderbrand
1974	Gifts To Caesar	None	Denise Guidry
1975	Cleopatra's Dreams Of Conquest	None	Elizabeth Schwarz
1976	Feasts, Festivals And Celebrations	None	Vicki O'Brien
1977	Great Moments In Grand Opera	None	Elizabeth Martin
1978	Gardens Of Grandeur	None	Dottie Daigle
1979	Circuses Of The World Entertain Cleo	None	Sharon Arnold
1980	Cleopatra's Vanity Of Fragrances	None	Gail Williams
1981	Cleopatra Visits Camelot	None	Jan Esther Cogan
1982	Cleopatra Lights Up Broadway	None	Glenda Ledet
1983	Cleopatra Visits The Heavenly Bodies	None	Lorraine Ott
1984	Cleopatra Heralds The World's Fair	None	Nicki Fischer
1985	Cleopatra's Sweet Smell Of Success	None	Frances S. Tingstrom
1986	A Pretty Girl Is Like A Melody	None	Eileen Adams
1987	Waltzing Down Memory Lane	None	Norma W. Kouri
1988	Oh! You Beautiful Doll	None	Norma Glynn
1989	Fantasies In Feathers	None	Terri Laird
1990	Let Us Entertain You	None	Laura Disimone
1991	Way Down Yonder In New Orleans	None	Pamela Dow
1992	Our Precious Moments	None	Linda Girouard
1993	A World Of Fashion	None	Constance Cain Rector
1994	The Many Lives Of Cleopatra	None	Emma Lois Plaisance
1995	If I Ruled The World	None	Dolores "Lola" Buras
1996	A Few Of My Favorite Things	None	Kim Benoit Cappiello
1997	Silver Cheers — It's 25 Years	None	Terry Adams Rittiner
1998	Isn't It Romantic	None	Lizette Chinn-Christiana
1999	It's Only Make Believe	None	Jackie Miljak Slyvest
2000	I'll See You In My Dreams	None	Sherry Adams Buras
2001	Some Enchanted Evening	None	Alison L. Zellar
2002	A World Of Pearls	None	Barbara Duplantis
2003	Takes A Walk On The Wild Side	None	Linda L. Middleton

COMUS

Mardi Gras' very first organization chose its name from the Greek *komos*, meaning "revelers," when it first formed in 1857. The historic group not only saved the institution of Carnival, which had fallen into near fatal abuses in the 1850s, but Comus also established the patterns for all future organizations — Comus coined the term "krewe," was the first to form a secret Carnival society, to choose a mythological namesake, and to present a themed parade with floats and follow it with a ball. Comus stopped parading after its 1991 presentation, but continues to stage a ball on Mardi Gras evening.

YEAR	THEME	COMUS	QUEEN
1857	Demon Actors Milton's Paradise Lost	Secret	None
1858	Mythology	Secret	None

Active Parading Krewes

Year	Theme	King	Queen
1859	The English Holidays	Secret	None
1860	History Of America	Secret	None
1861	The Four Ages Of Life	Secret	None
1862-65	NO PARADES — CIVIL WAR		
1866	The Past, The Present, The Future	Secret	None
1867	The Feast Of Epicurus	Secret	None
1868	Departure Of Lalla Rookh From Delhi	Secret	None
1869	The Five Senses	Secret	None
1870	The History Of Louisiana	Secret	None
1871	Spencer's Faerie Queen	Secret	None
1872	Dreams Of Homer	Secret	None
1873	The Missing Links To Darwin's Origins Of The Species	Secret	None
1874	Comus' Greeting To The Nations	Secret	None
1875	NO PARADE — CIVIL UNREST		
1876	4,000 Years Of Sacred History	Secret	None
1877	The Aryan Race	Secret	None
1878	The Metamorphoses Of Ovid	Secret	None
1879	NO PARADE — YELLOW FEVER		
1880	Aztecs And Their Conquest By Cortez	Secret	None
1881	The Myths Of Nordland	Secret	None
1882	The World's Worships	Secret	None
1883	NO PARADE		
1884	The History Of Ireland	Secret	Mildred Lee
1885 - 89	NO PARADES — INACTIVE		
1890	Palingenesis Of The Mistick Krewe	Secret	Katherine Buckner
1891	Demonology	Secret	Cora Jennings
1892	Nippon, The Land Of The Rising Sun	Secret	Winnie Davis
1893	Salammbo	Secret	Josephine Maginnis
1894	Once Upon A Time	Secret	Mathilde Levert
1895	The Songs Of Long Ago	Secret	Emily Poitevent
1896	The Seasons	Secret	Emma Kruttschnitt
1897	Homer's Odyssey	Secret	May Schmidt
1898	Scenes From Shakespeare	Secret	Isabel Hardie
1899	Josephus	Secret	Robbie Giffen
1900	The Golden Age	Secret	Marietta Laroussini
1901	Selections From The Operas	Secret	Margaret Richardson
1902	The Fairy Kingdom	Secret	Adele Brittin
1903	Mahabharata	Secret	Myrthe Stauffer
1904	Izdubar	Secret	Baylissa Myles
1905	The Lost Pleiad	Secret	Helen Rainey
1906	The Masque Of Comus	Secret	Celeste Janvier
1907	Tennyson	Secret	Adele Penrose
1908	Gods And Goddesses	Secret	Myra Walmsley
1909	Flights of Fancy	Secret	Edna May Hart
1910	Mahomet	Secret	Ruth Bush
1911	Familiar Quotations	Secret	Kate Nott
1912	Tales From Cathay	Secret	Marie Celeste Stauffer
1913	Time's Mysteries	Secret	Marie Elise Whitney
1914	Tales From Chaucer	Secret	Mary Orme
1915	Lore And Legends Of Childhood	Secret	Dorothy Spencer
1916	Glimpses Of Modern World Of Art	Secret	Mildred Post
1917	Romantic Legends	Secret	Elise Mason Smith
1918 - 23	NO PARADES — WWI		
1924	God Of Mirth Greets Ye Once Again	Secret	Virginia Claiborne
1925	The Realms Of Fantasy	Secret	Emily Hayne
1926	The Garden Of Cashmere	Secret	Jean Fenner
1927	Arabesques	Secret	Frances Kittredge
1928	Travels Of Marco Polo	Secret	Betty Hardie
1929	Gleanings Of The Past	Secret	Ormonde Butler
1930	The Legend Of Faust	Secret	Louise Carroll
1931	Jewels From Byron	Secret	Adele T. Jahncke
1932	Fairyland Of Flowers	Secret	Lucille Williams
1933	Feathered Fantasies	Secret	Mettha Westfeldt
1934	The Realm Of Neptune	Secret	Marigayle Hopkins
1935	Insect Life	Secret	Lily McCall
1936	The Beautiful	Secret	Augusta Walmsley
1937	From Nature's Paint Pot	Secret	Susan Olga Buck
1938	Comus Visits The States	Secret	Kathleen Eshleman
1939	Animals Of Fact And Fable	Secret	Veva Penick Miller
1940	Picturesque Passages From The Poets	Secret	Adele Williams
1941	Nature's Moods	Secret	Gladys Lodoiska Gay
1942 - 45	NO PARADES — WWII	Secret (1942)	Elaine Leverich (1942)
1946	Famous Gifts Of Facts And Fancy	Secret	Harriott Phelps
1947	Quests Of History And Legend	Secret	Anne Cameron Kock
1948	Medley Of Childhood Memories	Secret	Patricia Tobin
1949	Familiar Facts And Fancies	Secret	Elizabeth Kennard
1950	Priceless Products	Secret	Constance Ivy Burke
1951	NO PARADE — KOREAN WAR		Margaret Ann Williams
1952	Bible Stories We All Know	Secret	Grace Phillips Parker
1953	The States Of The Louisiana Purchase	Secret	Marie Louise Provosty
1954	The Garland Of Comus	Secret	Marguerite E. Howard
1955	Our Latin American Neighbors	Secret	Ruth Milliken Nairne
1956	Our Early Contemporaries	Secret	Moyna Blair Monroe
1957	Famous Gardens Of The World	Secret	Elizabeth Montgomery
1958	Famous Gems & Jewels Of The World	Secret	Nellie May Kelleher
1959	Poetry Of The American Scene	Secret	Harriett McCall Davis
1960	The Lore And Lure Of Legend	Secret	Kathleen M. Wisdom
1961	Selected Letters From A-L-P-H-A-B-E-TSecret		Ruth H. Whitney
1962	Nature, The Master Artist	Secret	Jessie Wing Sinnott
1963	The World Of Mark Twain	Secret	Elizabeth P. Strachan
1964	Fantastic Voyages	Secret	Nancy Leigh Henderson
1965	The Lure And Lore Of Gold	Secret	Carolyn Stauffer Crusel
1966	Monsters And Metamorphoses	Secret	Catherine Jane Maunsell
1967	Music Hath Charms	Secret	Charlotte S. Smither
1968	Highlights In The History Of N. O.	Secret	Martha Milliken Farwell
1969	Famous Gardens Of The World	Secret	Wendell Logan Simpson
1970	Cities Of Destiny	Secret	Carolyn N. Howard
1971	Feasts And Festivals	Secret	Louise W. McIhenny
1972	Fabled Islands	Secret	Mary Rushton Kock
1973	Adventures Of Perseus	Secret	Clara Pollard Walmsley
1974	Visions Of Valhalla	Secret	Gayle Stocker Denegre
1975	Comus' Constellations	Secret	Emilie A. Montgomery
1976	Coin Of The Realm	Secret	Ellen Fisher Simmons
1977	Winged Wonders	Secret	Marian Gayle Hopkins
1978	Sorcery	Secret	Miriam W. Wadick
1979	NO PARADE — POLICE STRIKE	Secret	Elaine Stokes Reily
1980	The Enchanted Arts	Secret	Joanne Carter Fenner
1981	Idolatry	Secret	Elizabeth M. Grace
1982	Ophidian Lore	Secret	Deidre Marie Provosty
1983	Gilgamesh	Secret	Ethelyn Dunbar
1984	Cataclysms	Secret	Margaret Lee Winston
1985	Masks Of Comus	Secret	Allison Wood White
1986	Deities	Secret	Carolyn Burton Crusel
1987	Gardens Of Antiquity	Secret	Elizabeth F. Kennan
1988	Feathered Fantasies	Secret	Allison Blanc Lewis
1989	Visions Of The Sun	Secret	Nina Pratt Gensler
1990	The Bowers Of Comus	Secret	Virginia Scott Freeman
1991	The Entomological Empire	Secret	Helen Hardie Nalty

Balls Only

Year	Theme	King	Queen
1992	Enchantments And Metamorphoses	Secret	Rosemary McIhenny
1993	Meanwhile ,Welcome Joy And Feast	Secret	Caroline A. Monsted
1994	Reveries Of Comus	Secret	Anne Dunklin Phillips
1995	Prophecies Of Comus	Secret	Sara Evans Schmidt
1996	The Starry Quire	Secret	Anne Wing Monsted
1997	Sic Volo Sic Jubeo	Secret	Katherine F. Dickson
1998	Vineyards Of Parnassus	Secret	Alston Walker McCall
1999	Gifts Of Comus	Secret	Mary-Frances Labouisse
2000	To The Glorious Future	Secret	Caroline D. Stewart
2001	Butterflies of Winter	Secret	Charlotte H. Haygood
2002	Grotto of Calypso	Secret	Lindsey Ewing Powell
2003	Songs of Comus	Secret	Dorothy Davis Ball

D'ETAT

Le Krewe D'Etat was founded in 1996 to help resurrect the traditional, satirical style of Mardi Gras parades. The club's first appearance in 1998 was very well received by parade critics and by the general public. In keeping with its name's meaning, the "Dictator" reigns over the streets in the place of a traditional monarch. Secrecy is of great importance to the krewe, and the identity of its ruler is never made public.

YEAR	THEME	DICTATOR	QUEEN
1997	Live To Ride, Ride To Live	Secret	None
1998	Looziana: Scandals And Scoundrels	Secret	None
1999	The Dictator's Circus	Secret	None
2000	Cinema D'Etat	Secret	None
2001	D'Etat.Com	Secret	None
2002	Rock Around D'Etat	Secret	None
2003	Bard D'Etat — Tales Told By Idiots	Secret	None

ENDYMION

The largest krewe in Mardi Gras history was founded in 1967 and is named for the Olympian god of fertility and eternal youth. It began as a small neighborhood venture in the Bayou St. John-Gentilly area. By 1974, Endymion had grown into a super club. The krewe annually selects celebrity grand marshals, such as Dolly Parton, Chicago, and the Beach Boys, who both thrill the parade spectators and entertain members and their guests at the Extravaganza held in the Louisiana Superdome immediately following the parade. By 2000, the club's all-male membership topped 2,000, and attendance at its after-parade party totaled more than 15,000.

YEAR	THEME	KING	QUEEN
1967	Take Me Out To The Ball Game	Harry P. Rosenthal	Mrs. Harry P. Rosenthal
1968	Highlights Of The Silver Screen	Henry P. Lusse	Janice Marie Assunto
1969	Music . . . And That Reminds Me	Salvatore Caserta	Beverly Mary Christina
1970	Kingdoms Revisited	Lawrence J. Rouse	Diana Lee Bordelon
1971	N.O., America's Most Interesting City	Alphonse Maenza	Lucille Ann Surgi
1972	Fables And Folklore	John A. Gereighty	Joni Leigh Centanni
1973	Golden Reflections	Roland Dobson	Lucy Ellen Vesich
1974	Endymion Salutes The Ladies	William Kent Dupre	Judy Lee Behler
1975	America Celebrates	William R. Nichols	Cheryl M. Pendergast
1976	Hail To The Chiefs	Irving Wallace	Lisa Anne Phillips
1977	It's A Small World	Edward J. Corcoran	Rhonda Shear
1978	The Superstars	Frank D'Amico	Tianne Dimitri
1979	Endymion, A Thing Of Beauty	Tom Delatte	Sandy Rita Brett
1980	Broadway On Parade	Salvadore Pardo	Rhonda Ann Fox
1981	Heartbeat Of America	George Hesni	Robyn Mary Orgeron
1982	Literary Treasures	Philip Accardo	Sandy Dimitri
1983	Myths And Legends	Stanford Rankins Jr.	Bonnie Brett
1984	It Was A Very Good Year	Joseph D. Medina Jr.	Mary Elizabeth Muniz
1985	Come To The Mardi Gras	Edward L. Martina Jr.	Kelly Quaid Flick
1986	What Might Have Been	Frank Meduna III	Michelle Louise Muniz
1987	I'd Rather Be . . .	Burton Himbert Jr.	Leanne Quaid Flick
1988	New Orleans, This Is Your Life	Lawrence R. Holmes	Phyllis Anne Accardo
1989	They Changed The World	Donald Broussard	Dina Ann Dimitri
1990	Saturday Night At The Movies	David C. Johnson	Maria Ktistakis
1991	Silver Memories	Robert T. Reynolds	Margie Muniz
1992	The World's Greatest Mysteries	Dr. Jeff T. Jones	Kimberly Ann Ello
1993	Flights Of Fantasy	Bradley W. Butler	Cynthia Alana Benbow
1994	Endymion's Rockumentary	Vern Cavalier	Shannon Kelly

Active Parading Krewes

1995	Creature Features	William Robinson	Danica Colleen Benbow
1996	Master Storytellers	Roy Cascio	Kristi Lamarque
1997	Les Festivals Internationale	Nathan J. Galliano	Catherine M. O'Gorman
1998	Biographies	Thomas L. Tompson	Katherine M. Kleinpeter
1999	Mardi Gras From The Beginning	Robert Guillot	Emily Lee McMakin
2000	At Home In The Dome	Howard Raymond	Bridget C. Loehen
2001	2001: A Space Odyssey — Mankind's Journey Into Space	Joseph A. Marino III	Elise Marie McDonald
2002	Masquerade	Alfredo Padilla	Katrina Ann Clarkson
2003	New Orleans From A To Z	Patrick Nunez	Kathryn E. Rittner

EXCALIBUR

Named after the legendary sword of King Arthur, the male and female Krewe of Excalibur was the first Jefferson Parish krewe to be founded in the new millennium. The Metairie-based organization quickly estalished a reputation for their exquisite court costumes.

YEAR	THEME	KING	QUEEN
2002	A Knight At The Movies	Lawrence Chehardy	Micki Chehardy
2003	Louisiana Buy Centennial	William E. Woodward	Mrs. Lynn J. Drury

GLADIATORS

Since 1973, St. Bernard Parish's first parade of the Mardi Gras season has been presented by the Gladiators, an organization that was formed by professional and business men. The Parish's only all-male parading krewe is named for the ancient Romans famous for their strength and bravery. Gladiators has selected national sports celebrities to portray their leader, whom they call Caesar.

YEAR	THEME	CAESAR	EMPRESS
1974	Gladiators Then And Now	George Blanda	Sherie Columbo
1975	Rogues, Famous And Infamous	Ken Stabler	Carolyn Natal
1976	Louisiana Lagniappe	Johnny Bench	Nora Egan
1977	Wonderful World Of Sports	Bert Jones	Antoinette Abadie
1978	World Of The Gladiators	Joe Ferguson	Linda Van Gilder
1979	Gladiators Salutes Mon. Night Football	Ray Guy	Cathy Bourgeois
1980	Olympics	Norris Weese	Edna Johnson
1981	Gladiators Salutes the Gods	Billy Kilmer	Norma Cochran
1982	Carnival Time	Sonny Jurgenson	Beverly McDougall
1983	Ten Years Of Memories & Happiness	Danny Abramowicz	Karen Battaglia
1984	Oscar Winners	Archie Manning	Delores Long
1985	Gladiators Salute Great Americans	Richard Todd	Connie Thompson
1986	Broadway Musicals	Brian Hansen	Joann Suarez
1987	Great American Sportsmen	Morten Anderson	Audrey Bello
1988	15th Anniversary	Leon Borja	Diane Caire
1989	Festivals Of Louisiana	Cola Long	April LeBlanc
1990	Famous Louisianians	Paul Dugas	Denise Labella
1991	Music, The International Language	Gill Fenerty	Mitzi Sauvage Botsay
1992	Salute To A Child's Wish	John Tice	Jennifer Esposito
1993	20 Years Of Memories	Tommy Barnhardt	Melanie A. Chehevert
1994	Magical Creatures Of The World	Rich Mauti	Stacey Kamlade
1995	Comics On Parade	Jerry Pellegrini	Cheryl Hoselle Hurstell
1996	Our Musical Heritage	Tom Dempsey	Natasha M. Cuccia
1997	Young At Heart	Bobby April	Jill W. Dolese
1998	Cinema Treasures	Brett Bech	Christina Denise Botsay
1999	Phiends, Phantoms And Phantasy	John Fauquar	Claudette S. Ponstein
2000	Children Of All Ages	Ron Swoboda	Jeri Kaupp Barron
2001	Gladiators Celebrates Festivals	Jim Henderson	Jennifer Dupas
2002	Events In Time	None	Cheryl R. Georgusis
2003	Gladiators-30 Years-Louisiaia 200 Yrs.	None	Kelli Patricia Egan

GRELA

The Krewe of Grela's name is derived from the first three letters of Gretna, the West Bank community through which it parades, and the abbreviation for Louisiana. Grela staged the first Mardi Gras parade ever held in Jefferson Parish in 1948. Three years later, the organization was the first from that parish to present a *bal masque* at the New Orleans Municipal Auditorium. In 1983, after 37 successful years, the Krewe of Grela switched the day of its parade from Saturday to Fat Tuesday. The move was very popular as West Bank parade-goers cheered the krewe's decision. The male, female, and children's krewe featured Milton Berle as its guest grand marshal in 1998.

YEAR	THEME	KING	QUEEN
1948	Floweramia	Judge Leycester Trauth	Katherine Spahr Ward
1949	Visit Of Marco Polo To Great Khan	Richard Guidry	Rosemary Rotolo
1950	Characters Of Childhood	George Bayhi	Theresa Kerner
1951	NO PARADE — KOREAN WAR	Lynn A. Blanchard	Carol Lee Kerner
1952	NO PARADE		
1953	Fabulous New Orleans	French M. Jordan	Lola French Jordan
1954	El Romance De Mejico	Thomas D. Jenkins	Janis Ruth Jackson
1955	Taj Mahal At Agra	Roy James Guedry	Carol Lee Kennedy
1956	Knighthood For Tristram	G. Robert Murphy	Jo Ann F. Hildebrand
1957	The Mystical Parchment	Peter Taulli	Marian Ann Robin
1958	The Lost Key	William J. White	Mary Louise White
1959	The Center Ring	Arthur Lawson	Grace Marie Jones
1960	Fantasy Beneath The Sea	Louis J. Kennedy Sr.	Cathryn Kass
1961	Our World Elements	Mark G. Hynes	Marjorie Lee Hynes
1962	Themes Of Yesterday	Audrey C. Lands Jr.	Marjorie Lee Hynes
1963	Broadway, Rogers And Hammerstein	Anthony Christians	Prudence Keller
1964	The World Of Make-Believe	Charles Wichers	Prudence Keller
1965	Animal Kingdom	John L. Dulcich Jr.	Prudence Keller
1966	Nursery Rhymes	Ira E. Capdevielle	Laura Gomez
1967	Inventions And Explorations	Louis A. LeBoeuf Jr.	Mary Ann Blanchard
1968	Men Of Fame And Infamy	John D. Murphy	Carolyn L. Lohman
1969	Gretna Baseball In The 1920s	Hugh F. O'Connor Jr.	Janet L. Massey
1970	Stories From The Arabian Nights	Ernest F. Burmaster Sr.	Sharon Ann Burmaster
1971	Oriental Travels	Joseph S. Lauricella	Debra Ann Cambre
1972	Grela's 25th Anniversary	Gary M. Scheffler	Alice Marie Kern
1973	Classics Of Literature	Arthur S. Lawson Jr.	Erin M. Murphy
1974	Daze Of Wine And Romans	Larry Sisung	Cynthia Ann Hartman
1975	Music We Remember	Calvin Kass	Sandra Menge
1976	America's Pleasures And Holidays	George Taix	Kelly Ann Leonard
1977	Grela's Grand Tour	Ernest T. Bellanger	Mary Ann Bellanger
1978	Grela's Journey Into Fantasyland	Robert H. Fray	Pattie Marie Olsen
1979	Grela's Pick Of The Flicks	Michael Badalamenti	Tina Badalamenti
1980	Men of Destiny	Melvin T. Cheramie	Edith Marie Ledet
1981	Grela Reads The Classics	Nelson J. Cantrelle Jr.	Monica L. Carmadelle
1982	Grela On Broadway	Irving W. Scheffler	Catherine Cambre
1983	Legends And Folklore	Vance Weinberger	V. Matherne-Bradford
1984	I Hear a Rhapsody	Edmond H. Feicht Jr.	Jean Ann Jacobsen
1985	Glorious Gems Of Grela	Wayne Dunne	Mary Elizabeth Cambre
1986	Grela Salutes The Circus World	George M. Papale	Michelle Ocman
1987	Grela's Scrapbook	Willie Hinkel	Jena Matherne-Roussel
1988	Louisiana's Heritage	Roy Liner	Jean Marie Kass
1989	Grela's Around The World Tour	Leslie Clark	Kim Dupree
1990	Festivals Of Louisiana	Larry Libert	Jacqueline Feicht
1991	The Game Of Monopoly	Allen Bebee	Mabel Cowart
1992	Hooray For Hollywood	Michael Larousse Sr.	Tracey Larousse
1993	Viva Las Vegas	Robert Wolfe	Bonnie Carruthers
1994	Lovers Around The World	Mark Plaisance	Gloria Larousse
1995	Grela's Cartoon Comics	A. J. Cambre	Dana Maria Pancpinto
1996	Grela's Broadway Musicals	Frank J. Pancpinto Jr.	Angela Panepinto
1997	Grela's 50 Years Of Memories	Kahn Mark Miller	C. Naomi Terrier
1998	Grela's Fictional Heroes Of The World	Steven W. Young	Kelly Coroy
1999	Grela's Television Features	Gilbert Boudreaux III	Candy Willtz Meche
2000	Rolling Into The New Millennium	Eddie Edwards	Kilee Mignon Hoskin
2001	Grela Celebrates Cajun Style	Judge Steve Windhorst	Rhonda Guidry
2002	Grela's World Tour 2002	Johnny Pellegal	Donna Garcia
2003	Dance To The Music	Tim Kerner	Keri Alison Evans

HERMES

During the Great Depression of the 1930s, the Carnival schedule had shrunk to only three parades staged on Mardi Gras Eve and on Fat Tuesday. To offer visitors more days to enjoy the pleasures of the season, a group of businessmen formed the Knights of Hermes in 1937, staging a parade that would bridge the weekend before the arrival of Rex. The founders chose the Greek messenger of the gods, Hermes, as their namesake. A golden statue of the sandaled, winged courier appears at the lead of the procession. Hermes' 1938 introduction of neon lighting as a means of float illumination was a first for Mardi Gras. The all-male krewe is known for its outstanding costumes which are color coordinated to match the floats.

YEAR	THEME	KING	QUEEN
1937	Melodies	Secret	Marjorie Lee Smith
1938	Memories Of Childhood	Secret	Leila Wilkinson
1939	March Of The Year	Secret	Roma de Lucas
1940	Visions	Secret	Denise Freeman
1941	Pages From History	Secret	Audrey Reinhard
1942 - 45	NO PARADES — WWII		
1946	Prose And Poetry	Secret	Irma Mary Oser
1947	World's Operas	Secret	Shirley Mae Groetsch
1948	Famous Rulers Of History	Secret	Beverly Ann Lafaye
1949	Tales From Shakespeare	Secret	Joel Doell
1950	The Life Of Napoleon Bonaparte	Secret	Kathryn Marie Gordon
1951	Figures From Favorite Fables	Secret	Barbara Dee Walther
1952	Royal Romances	Secret	Ethel Elizabeth Seiler
1953	The Superstitions	Secret	Ramona Hattier
1954	Alice In Wonderland	Secret	Jewel David
1955	Prince Valiant	Secret	Dawn Hebert
1956	The Snow Queen	Secret	Marian Miller
1957	The Little Chinese Princess	Secret	Donna Ann Odom
1958	Cinderella	Secret	Sharon Arline Collard
1959	The Forty Thieves	Secret	Beverly Dawn Walther
1960	Isabella Of Spain	Secret	Frances Lenora Stall
1961	Horrors And Supernaturals	Secret	Phyllis Jean Terry
1962	Sleeping Beauty	Secret	Maria Barbara Springer
1963	The Good King Arthur	Secret	Judith Owen Miller
1964	A Chinese Fairy Tale	Secret	Mary Frances Henricks
1965	Mother Goose Fantasia	Secret	Medeline Jude Gabler
1966	Aladdin And The Lamp	Secret	Susan Marie Holmes
1967	Prince Valiant Discovers America	Secret	Marilyn Ann Springer
1968	Chevalier Of The Mississippi	Secret	Patricia Ann Simpson
1969	The Little Mermaid	Secret	Keith Ann Bateman
1970	The Quest Of Hermes	Secret	Emily Louise Barnes
1971	Alexander Of Macedon	Secret	Mary Jean Gabler
1972	The Prince With Donkey's Ears	Secret	Barbara Anita Barnes
1973	Omar The Tentmaker	Secret	Barbara Aline Batt
1974	Dorothy In The Land Of Oz	Secret	Suzanne E. Stewart
1975	A Past To Remember	Secret	Jan Marie Gabler
1976	America's Last King — George III	Secret	Cynthia Anne Coffin
1977	Back To Never Land	Secret	Diana Lizebeth Davis
1978	The Dreamer Of La Mancha	Secret	Barbara B. Monteleone
1979	NO PARADE — POLICE STRIKE	Secret	Erin Mary Burks
1980	Lafitte's Trust Reunited	Secret	Julie Ann Coffin
1981	The Puppet With No Strings	Secret	Mary Patricia Piper
1982	Dream On A Midsummer's Night	Secret	Mari-Ofe Rodriguez

Active Parading Krewes

1983	The Piper's Magic Tunes	Secret	Tessa Mariana Martinez
1984	Return To Sherwood Forest	Secret	Catherine Farnsworth
1985	All For One And One For All	Secret	Virginia Claire Davis
1986	A Yankee Goes To Camelot	Secret	Cathryn Ashley Jackson
1987	Fall Of The Giants	Secret	Michelle Andree Montz
1988	The Kobbled Kat	Secret	Ashley Frances Stumpf
1989	The Count's Revenge	Secret	Michelle Marie Miller
1990	A Golden Yarn	Secret	Lindsey Arden Jackson
1991	A Tale Of Two Kiddies	Secret	Tracy Elizabeth Aron
1992	Return To Treasure Island	Secret	Jennifer Van Vrancken
1993	Beauty Within The Beast	Secret	Rebecca E. Murphy
1994	Phantom Of The Opera	Secret	Marjorie Lynn Miller
1995	The Romance Of Frankenstein	Secret	Stella Mimi LeGardeur
1996	The Mikado's Law	Secret	Erin Patricia Simpson
1997	Love And Death On The Nile	Secret	Christina E. Murphy
1998	The Gift Of The Golden Curse	Secret	Vanessa Van Vrancken
1999	Magical Mystical Dreamcoat	Secret	Allison Aden Berger
2000	The Elusive Pimpernel	Secret	Grace Elizabeth Heslin
2001	The Birth Of Hermes	Secret	Emily Elizabeth Davis
2002	Tribute To Uncle Poseidon	Secret	Adair Smith-Lupo
			Monroe Williams
2003	Hades Lord Of The Underworld	Secret	Diana Dee Winingder

IRIS

In classical Greek mythology, Iris was the goddess of the rainbow and the messenger to the gods. The Krewe of Iris was founded in 1922. Ten years before its inaugural street parade in 1959, the Iris tableau ball became the first such event ever to be televised. One of the more notable gentlemen to serve as king was former New Orleans Mayor and U. S. Ambassador, "Chep" Morrison. The krewe prides itself on strictly following the traditional customs of Carnival — full length masks and white gloves are worn, and beverages are forbidden aboard floats. The club has more than 900 female members.

YEAR	THEME	KING	QUEEN
1959	Say It With Music	John B. Sousa	Lillian Fonseca
1960	Louisiana The Enchanted	Carl J. Delcuzé	Ressie Christopher
1961	Meet Me Tonight In Dreamland	Warren A. Griffith	Lettie Keen
1962	N. O. Gateway To The Americas	deLesseps S. Morrison	Lillian Fonseca
1963	See America First	Frederick C. Sullivan	June Dragon
1964	Champagne Flight To Europe	Hebert R. Van Wyk	Romona Ford
1965	Show Business	Edward H. Levitt	Doris Maurice
1966	Mardi Gras In New Orleans	Richard D. Harwood	Gail Jones
1967	Wonderful World Of Entertainment	Christopher G. Darrell	Lillian Fonseca
1968	That's What I Like About The South	Charles L. Villemeur Jr.	Ruby Wilkinson
1969	Las Vegas, USA	Dr. Robert C. Albrecht	Mary Samson
1970	Music Maestro Please	Frank J. Scariano	Judy Scariano
1971	The World Is Yours — Happy Landing	René B. Serrano	Vivian Lide
1972	Lovely Louisiana Legends	Thomas F. Ellis Jr.	Betty Ellis
1973	Your Hometown Newspaper	Daniel L. Kelly Jr.	Bette Mopsik
1974	Rediscover America	Christopher G. Darrell	Betty Ellis
1975	Era Of The Grand St. Charles Hotel	Nelson Carter Church	Romona Ford
1976	The Vieux Carre, N.O., LA, USA	Forrest R. Singer	Diane Mannina
1977	Reminiscences Of Captain's 25 Years	Roy Charles Young	Virginia Riedel
1978	Come To The Mardi Gras En Masque	Joseph F. Frederick Jr.	Ruth Hingle
1979	The Wonderful World Of Travel	Baptiste H. DeBroy	Jackie Delcuzé
1980	Strike Up The Band	Joseph F. Frederick Jr.	Marilyn Beaupre
1981	Let The Good Times Roll	John J. Charpentier	Fay Dudenhefer
1982	Thirty Years Of Happiness	Cecil M. Kenney	Marie Siguera
1983	Welcome To Our Whirl	Brian David Monie	Cindy Beaupre
1984	When You Wish Upon A Star	Louis J. Drouant Jr.	Sheila Dupepe
1985	A Toast To The Joys Of Living	Cecil M. Keeney	Ruth Keeney
1986	America the Beautiful	Nelson Carter Church	Frances DeBroy
1987	Music, The Universal Language	Randolph M. Howes	Emily Heine
1988	Wonderful World Of Make Believe	Hon. Don J. Dupepe	Fay Dudenhefer
1989	Way Down Yonder In New Orleans	Dr. Onyx P. Garner Jr.	Helen Sorrels
1990	Sitting On Top Of The World	Thomas K. Winingder	Diane C. Winingder
1991	Getting To Know You	Nelson Carter Church	Fran DeBroy Markland
1992	Iris Celebrates 75 Years Of Memories	Bobby S. Roberts	L. Beatrice Abene
1993	Fine Tuned For Fun	Dr. Donald P. Bell	Deborah A. Bell
1994	A Mardi Gras Fantasy	Wayne Citron	Rose Ann Citron
1995	Making Dreams Come True	Richard M. Smith	Dr. Barbara T.Thompson
1996	For The Young At Heart	Edward D. Reynolds	Suzanne E. Brady
1997	A Sentimental Journey Of 80 Years	John F. Meyer Jr.	L. Beatrice Abene
1998	Love Makes The World Go Round	J. Franklin Benjamin	Charleen P. Benjamin
1999	Hollywood Dreamin'	Edward B. Fabacher Jr.	Gloria W. Fabacher
2000	Echoes Of The 20th Century	Ron Domin	Betty Brooks Trosclair
2001	Life Is A Celebration	Raymond H. Gustafson	Fran DeBroy Markland
2002	If I Ruled The World	Thomas D. Sullivan	Melinda K. Richard
2003	Music Transcends Life	Edward D. Campbell Jr.	Sarah Stephens

ISIS

Isis was the mother of Horus and the sister and wife of Osiris in the mythology of ancient Egypt. She was honored as the goddess of the earth and the moon, and was a symbol of motherhood and fertility. Isis was also worshipped in the Greek and Roman empires. She was traditionally represented as a woman wearing a bull's horns with a solar disk between them. In 1973 this all-female organization was chartered in the city of Kenner, and the women held their first seven processions there before adopting the standardized Veterans Memorial Boulevard parade route, which more than a dozen Jefferson krewes share.

YEAR	THEME	KING	QUEEN
1973	Gods And Goddess	Charles Villemeur	Margie Raffo
1974	Famous Ladies In Songs	Rene Paul Richerand	Shirley LeDoux
1975	Festivals Around The World	Salvador M. Grisaffi	Mildred Grisaffi
1976	America's Broadway Heritage	John P. Raffo	Doris Toups
1977	Vamps And Vixens	Gerard S. Plauche	Joyce Plauche
1978	Splendors Of The Seas	Isidore J. Dugas	Joyce Dugas
1979	Viva Mexico	Normand P. Toups	Cheryl Jones
1980	Hawaii Tropical Paradise	Armond J. Blondeau	Mary San Marco
1981	New York — The Big Apple	Stanley M. Bejma	Karen K. Bejma
1982	Majestic Waters Of The World	Peter J. Fernandez	Carmen Fernandez
1983	Literary And Legendary Women	Earnest L. Bauer	Pamela Trocchiano
1984	You've Come A Long Way Lady	Daniel L. Earles Sr.	Rosary Earles
1985	Melody Lingers On	William F. Ross	Sylvia Buttone Ross
1986	America Dances The Blues Away	Charles L. Castaing	Charlene Plauche
1987	Star Performance	Philip Nicholas Chisesi	Charisse Chisesi
1988	Where Life Is A Ball	Russell Amato	Heidi Zimmerman
1989	Journey Into Imagination	William H. Wactor	Glenda Wactor
1990	Isis Salutes The States	Emmanuel Stefanakis	Sherri Shuh Eck
1991	Curtains Up And Light The Lights	Louis J. Reynolds	Marilyn Miller Reynolds
1992	Everything Old Is New Again	David A. Dussel	Cheri Blondeau Deykin
1993	Hallelujah Hollywood	John J. Meyer Jr.	Robyn Frances Shuh
1994	It's Our Party	John Joseph Hilbert Jr.	Jo Elda Young
1995	Oh! You Beautiful Doll	Melvin H. Dussel Jr.	Brooke Alyssa Deykin
1996	Dreams Really Do Come True	William Joseph Wallis	Linda Trahan Wallis
1997	Isis' 25th Anniversary	Larry L. Rolling Jr.	Roxanne Bejma
1998	Collectively Speaking	Errol A. D'Angelo	Sherrell Ann Gorman
1999	Dinner At Eight	Dr. Lance L. Webb	Debbie Lee Hadsell
2000	Just For The Fun Of It	Peter Ajan	Aimee Joyce Hyatt
2001	Fabulous Las Vegas	Paul V. Millet Sr.	Katherine Merritt Kolb
2002	Through The Years	Kenneth Oubre	Deborah Kelly
2003	Magic Of Music	Robert B. Hadsall	Judi East

KING ARTHUR

The legendary British King and his Knights of the Round Table have provided some of the most colorful and romantic tales in all of medieval lore. This former West Bank krewe, named after the noble monarch, was organized in 1977 by the youngest captain in the history of Carnival. The first three parades of the Knights were presented in the morning. In 1979, the group became the first West Bank men's organization to parade at night. The Knights of King Arthur moved its parade to New Orleans in 2001.

YEAR	THEME	KING ARTHUR	GUINEVERE
1978	It's A Graduate's Dream	Phillip Fricano Jr.	Ann Frances Bitoun
1979	King Arthur's Command Performance	Carl Scivicque Jr.	Kim Ann Scivicque
1980	Saturday Morning Matinee	Roy Jacobsen	Wendy Jacobsen
1981	Western World Adventures	Gary Allen Rogers	Rhonda L. Rogers
1982	Tour America On 4th Street Express	John H. Kentzel Jr.	Darlene Dale Blakey
1983	Halls Of Memories	Erroll Charles Jacobsen	Christi Jacobsen Rome
1984	Merlin's Festival Of Entertainment	Paul Barrois	Julie Ann Olsen
1985	Journey To A Foreign Land	Dale Bruce Sr.	Mary Rome Duet
1986	Journey Into King Arthur's Forest	Neil Paul Peterson	Vera Plaisance Vedros
1987	King Arthur's 10 Year Reunion	Michael J. Trupiano	Karen Packard DiMarco
1988	King Arthur's Royal Pastures	Calvin Floyd Linden	Loretta Persohn Brehm
1989	People In Louisiana	Ted Jaymes Badeaux	Cathy Danos Smith
1990	Arthur's Ave. Of Historical Adventures	Terry Lynn Braun	Carol Hebert Braun
1991	Earth Day 1991	Eugene Thacker	Jessica Pierce
1992	Turns 15, That's Music To Our Ears	Jerry Sellers	Miriam Johnson
1993	An Evening For Lovers	Thom Miller	Angie Fortino
1994	Ports Of Paradise Of Fact & Fiction	H. Lee Percival Jr.	Rosalind Cambre Oubre
1995	Somewhere Over The Rainbow	Johnny J. Rogers	Dawn Tassin Shaw
1996	Make Mine Manhattan	Brian Oubre	Patricia Lynn Richoux
1997	Dreaming — 20 Years Of King Arthur	Charles Turberville	Genevieve Ann Brown
1998	NO PARADE		
1999	. . . And You Thought We Were Dead	Marcel LeBlanc	Linda LeBlanc
2000	NO PARADE		
2001	Toto, We're Not On W'bank Anymore	Tony Clark	Melissa Mancuso Keller
2002	Our 25th Anniversary	Alan Dugas Jr.	Gayle Ponthieux
2003	What's The Big Deal? LA 1699-1803	Dwain J. Hertz	Lonnie Hobbel Pullins

MERCURY

This male and female Metairie krewe has as its mythological namesake, Mercury, the swiftest of the gods. This Roman deity, for whom the nearest planet to the sun is named, is the patron of travel and commerce. In Egyptian folklore, Thoth possessed the same basic characteristics, and Hermes is his Grecian counterpart. In earlier years, Mercury featured guest celebrities such as Shadoe Stevens, Alan Autry, Michael Morrison and Andy Kavovit. Mercury was founded in 1985.

YEAR	THEME	KING	QUEEN
1986	Mercury's Magnificent Movies	Bill Linck	Barbara Linck
1987	Merrymaking With Mercury	John M. McCoy	Cheryl Klibert Mart
1988	Mercury Salutes The History Makers	Santo Giliberto	Mary Maturano
1989	Birds Of A Feather	Terrance Apple	Mrs. Terrance Apple
1990	Music Mercury Please	Michael O'Brien	Mrs. Michael O'Brien
1991	Mercury In The Big Easy	Percy Penouilh	Tammy Dee O'Brien
1992	On The Wings Of Mercury	Antonio Mouriz	Mrs. Antonio Mouriz
1993	Give My Regards To Broadway	Thomas Davis	Catherine Cangelosi
1994	The Mercury Museum Of Fine Art	Felix Figueroa Sr.	Mrs. Felix Figueroa Sr.
1995	Memories Of Mercury	Felix Figueroa Jr.	July Mora
1996	Happiness Is . . .	James Otterpohl	Judy Keyser
1997	Mercury's Trippin' Out	Scott Arseneaux	Debra A. Guastella
1998	Mercury Salutes The United Nations	Gerald Parton	Diane Perez
1999	Mercury Loves The Movies	Bradley Richoux	Maitee Bretos
2000	Mercury Remembers The 20th Century	James C. LeNormand	Carolina Figueroa
2001	Naturally New Orleans	Timothy Pisciotta	Michelle Aukerman
2002	Mercury's People, Places & Events	Christopher Steinman	Jane Billings
2003	Mercury's Musical Heritage	Antoni Wilcox	Karin Toribio

Active Parading Krewes

MID-CITY

The Krewe of Mid-City, founded in 1933, is Carnival's fifth oldest parading organization, and is named for the neighborhood where its procession began through the 2001 season. In 1947 the club introduced animated floats to Mardi Gras, and its 1955 pageant, entitled *Candy*, featured the spraying of sweet fragrances from the floats. In 1963, the club introduced the "Greatest Bands in Dixie" contest. The youthful themes selected by this imaginative group make it a favorite among children. Mid-City's floats are colored with tin foil which gives them a unique appearance. Some throw items include the krewe's signature interlocking hearts and the French motto, *Pour La Joie De Vivre* — for the joy of life. Mid-City moved its parade to the uptown route for the 2002 season.

YEAR	THEME	KING	QUEEN
1934	Romance Of 1934	Charles Bourgeois Sr.	Mrs. Charles Bourgeois
1935	Familiar Themes Of Fairyland	Ernest Aiavolasiti	Mrs. Ernest Aiavolasiti
1936	Passion For Music	Paul Jamerson	Mrs. Paul Jamerson
1937	Dreams Of Youth	J. George Viosca	Mrs. J. George Viosca
1938	The Life Of King Tut Ankhámen	Connie F. Tullier	Mrs. Connie F. Tullier
1939	Familiar Airs	Dominick Marsiglia	Mrs. D. Marsiglia
1940	Playtime, Pastime Sports	Thomas J. Bourgeois	Mrs. Thomas Bourgeois
1941	Academy Awards	August W. Walsdorf	Mrs. August Walsdorf
1942-45	NO PARADES — WWII		
1946	Rio In The Times Of The Viceroys	John L. Lenfant	Mrs. John L. Lenfant
1947	Toyland	Joseph P. Barry	Mrs. Joseph P. Barry
1948	Uncle Remus Says . . .	Ben A. Latino	Mrs. Ben A. Latino
1949	Characters We Love	Robert A. Scivicque	Mrs. Robert A. Scivicque
1950	The Comics	Richard A. Campo	Mrs. Richard A. Campo
1951	Radio And Television Programs	Martin J. Paul Jr.	Mrs. Martin J. Paul Jr.
1952	The Circus	Arnold Wolfe	Mrs. Arnold Wolfe
1953	Once Upon A Time	Leslie B. Meyer	Mrs. Leslie B. Meyer
1954	Peter Pan	John A. Brady	Mrs. John A. Brady
1955	Candy	Peter V. Young	Mrs. Peter V. Young
1956	Magic	Nicola J. Tessitore	Mrs. Nicola J. Tessitore
1957	Songs Children Sing	Walter A. Vamprine Sr.	Mrs. Walter A. Vamprine
1958	Memories	S. Wallace Miller	Mrs. S. Wallace Miller
1959	A Day In The Park	Lloyd F. Gaubert	Mrs. Lloyd F. Gaubert
1960	Children's Hobbies	Peter Aiavolasiti	Mrs. Peter Aiavolasiti
1961	See the USA	E. Jack Hagan	Mrs. E. Jack Hagan
1962	Let's Go To The Beach	Joseph S. Zuppardo	Mrs. Joseph S. Zuppardo
1963	Everything From A To Z	Lewis E. Johnson	Mrs. Lewis E. Johnson
1964	Pages From A Coloring Book	Charles L. Mauer	Mrs. Charles L. Mauer
1965	Happiness Is Everything	Paul A. Menard Jr.	Mrs. Paul A. Menard Jr.
1966	Stories That Live Forever	Louis M. Rubio	Mrs. Louis M. Rubio
1967	Music For Everyone	M. Paul LeBlanc	Mrs. M. Paul LeBlanc
1968	A Tribute To Folklore	Tilghman Chachere Jr.	Mrs. Tilghman Chachere
1969	Did You Ever Say . . .	John L. Mascaro	Mrs. John L. Mascaro
1970	Chitty Chitty Bang Bang	D. Ed Pitiman	Mrs. D. Ed Pitiman
1971	Charlie My Boy	George B. Muller Jr.	Mrs. George B. Muller Jr.
1972	Games Children Play	William R. Martinez	Mrs.William R. Martinez
1973	One Man's World	John A. Mipro Jr.	Mrs. John A. Mipro Jr.
1974	Costumes Of Many Lands	Walter L. Wright III	Mrs. Walter L. Wright III
1975	LA . . . Cajuns, Creoles And Congé	George Johnston Sr.	Mrs. George Johnston Sr.
1976	The Colonies, Their Birds And Flowers	Odell Potter Jr.	Mrs. Odell Potter Jr.
1977	Fairy Tales From Around The World	Raymond Willhoft Sr.	Mrs. Raymond Willhoft
1978	Songs & Stories Of The Sea & Sailing	Larry A. Jehle	Mrs. Larry A. Jehle
1979	Bible Stories	Charles T. Sterken Jr.	Mrs. Charles Sterken Jr.
1980	Happiness Is . . .	Roy A. Hemelt	Mrs. Roy A. Hemelt
1981	Language Of The Flowers	Edgar J. Landry	Mrs. Edgar J. Landry
1982	Mid-City's Merry Menagerie	Melvin M. Holdsworth	Mrs. M. Holdsworth
1983	Our Golden 50's	Raymond Willhoft Jr.	Mrs. Raymond Willhoft
1984	Whole Lot Of Spinning Going On	Karl Senner	Mrs. Karl Senner
1985	Don't Rain On My Parade	Robert Nunez	Kim Marie Cronic
1986	Space Fantasies	Joseph Di Fatta Jr.	Mrs. Joseph Di Fatta Jr.
1987	Flight To Fairyland	John Lahare	Mrs. John Lahare
1988	Mid-City Sings Love Songs	Ralph Plaideau Jr.	Mrs. Ralph Plaideau Jr.
1989	Traveling Along, Singing A Song	Michael Haydel	Mrs. Michael Haydel
1990	All That's Gold	John Murray	Karen Snow
1991	Mid-City's Comic Rainbow	Norman Babin	Mrs. Norman Babin
1992	Mighty Mite Menu	Raymond Thibodaux	Mrs. R. Thibodaux
1993	Thanks, Betty Rae Kern	Harold Haydel	Mrs. Harold Haydel
1994	Les Bon Temps Roule	Mark Eaby Jr.	Gail Hartmann
1995	Check It Out . . . At the Library	Emmett Mercier Jr.	Mrs. Emmett Mercier Jr.
1996	Kaleidoscope Of Kings	Jay Smith	Diane Rosier
1997	Hold On To Your Hat	John Landry	Mrs. John Landry
1998	Forever Young At 65	Ralph Plaideau Sr.	Mrs. Robbie P. Holland
1999	Love Is In The Air	Joseph Baggett	Raimee Marmillion
2000	Magical Moments Of 20th Century	Eric Skrmetta	Julie LaNasa Lemoine
2001	A History Of Mystery	Gerard Braud	Michelle Swanner
2002	One Way Or The Other	John D. Miller	Jamie Lynn Blakeman
2003	Foiled Again	Clancy Dubos	Margo Dubos

MOMUS

The Knights are named for the god of mockery and entered the Carnival scene on New Year's Eve, 1872. Mardi Gras' third oldest krewe has an appropriate motto, *Dum Vivimus, Vivamus* — While We Live, Let Us Live. Historians agree that the most important parade of all time was the 1877 production, "Hades, a Dream of Momus." The parade featured a collection of demons, all recognizable as officeholders in the Carpetbagger Administration. In 1992, after presenting 86 parades in 120 years, Momus retired from the parade scene, but continues to stage an annual ball on the Thursday before Fat Tuesday.

YEAR	THEME	MOMUS	QUEEN
1872	The Talisman	Secret	None
1873	The Coming Races	Secret	None
1874 - 75	NO PARADES — CIVIL UNREST		
1876	Louisiana And Her Seasons	Secret	None
1877	Hades — A Dream Of Momus	Secret	None
1878	The Realms Of Fancy	Secret	None
1879	NO PARADE — YELLOW FEVER		
1880	A Dream Of Fair Women	Secret	None
1881	Scenes From Popular Subjects	Secret	Elise McStea
1882	The Ramayana	Secret	Jennie Kruttschnitt
1883	The Moors In Spain	Secret	Winnie Davis
1884	The Passions	Secret	Blanche Moulton
1885	The Legends Beautiful	Secret	Leila Bohn
1886	NO PARADE		
1887	Myths Of The New World	Secret	Cora Semmes
1888	NO PARADE		
1889	The Culprit Fay	Secret	Jennie Morris
1890	Paradise And The Peri	Secret	Gussie Glenny
1891	Palmer Cox's Brownies	Secret	Amelie Aldige
1892	Aladdin Or The Wonderful Lamp	Secret	Sallie Reeves Hewes
1893	The Legend Of The Four Leaf Clover	Secret	Ella Barkley
1894	The Fairies And The Fiddler	Secret	Louise Dunbar
1895	Mahabarata	Secret	Charlee Elliott
1896	Comic History Of Rome	Secret	Alice Buckner
1897	Domino	Secret	Lydia Finley
1898	Bal Masque	Secret	Katherine Eustis
1899	Cinderella, Of The Little Glass Slipper	Secret	Lena Logan
1900	Legends Of King Arthur's Court	Secret	May Waters
1901	Our Festivals	Secret	Myrthe Stauffer
1902	Byron's Poems	Secret	Fannie Buckner
1903	Myths Of The Red Men	Secret	May Schwartz
1904	Visions Of The World's Vanities	Secret	Carrie G. Charles
1905	Vathek, 9th Caliph Of The Abassides	Secret	Florence Kells
1906	Leaves From Oriental Literature	Secret	Daisy Charles
1907	The Quest For The Fountain Of Youth	Secret	Harriette Waters
1908	Aesop's Fables	Secret	Bessie Devlin
1909	Signs and Superstitions	Secret	Leo Callaway
1910	The Winged World	Secret	Alice Hardie
1911	The Language Of Flowers	Secret	Laura Hobson
1912	Chronicles of Momus	Secret	Susan Merrick
1913	Above The Clouds	Secret	Katherine Rainey
1914	Odds And Ends Of Nonsense	Secret	Dorothy Johnson
1915	Tales Of The How And Why	Secret	Elizabeth Carroll
1916	Pinocchio	Secret	Marcelle Grima
1917	Adventures Of Baron Munchausen	Secret	Lise Perrilliat
1918 - 19	NO PARADES — WWI		
1920	A Pierrot Ball	Secret	Mary Virginia Perkins
1921	Battle Of Don Carnival & Lady Lent	Secret	Martha Vairin
1922	The Dream Of Rosie	Secret	Ellene White
1923	Alice In Wonderland And Through The Looking Glass	Secret	Phro Broussard
1924	Jatakamala, Tales Of Buddah's Lives	Secret	Bessie Johnson
1925	Popular Quotations Of Long Ago	Secret	Lucille Hayward
1926	The Deities Of Greek Mythology	Secret	Jane Wall
1927	The Wonderful Adventures Of Nils	Secret	Peggy Fox
1928	Wonder Tales Of Old Japan	Secret	Eliska Tobin
1929	Sandman Stories	Secret	Josephine Solari
1930	Father Time's Holidays	Secret	Lucile Scott
1931	Broadcasting Old Favorites	Secret	Nina Pratt
1932	Snapshots From Movieland	Secret	Irene Rice
1933	Memories Of Long Ago	Secret	Olivia Bartlett
1934	Alexander The Great's Conquest Of Bactria, Sogdiana And Roxana	Secret	Catherine Eaves
1935	The Louisiana Purchase	Secret	Suzanne LaCour
1936	An Evening With Lafitte	Secret	Eleanor Harkey
1937	Operas Of Yesteryear	Secret	Katherine Hayward
1938	Legends	Secret	Marjorie Clarke
1939	Familiar Proverbs	Secret	May Miles
1940	Sayings We Learned In Childhood	Secret	Patricia Woodward
1941	Stories That Will Never Die	Secret	Carolyn Himel
1942 - 45	NO PARADES — WWII		
1946	Recollections Of The Past	Secret	Ellie Witherspoon
1947	Anniversaries	Secret	Isabel Joy Werlein
1948	The Songs Of Yesteryear	Secret	Joan Denis Ellis
1949	NO PARADE — RAINED OUT	Secret	Jean Gibbens
1950	Famous Loves and Lovers	Secret	Mary Foster
1951	NO PARADE — KOREAN WAR	Secret	Mary Barksdale Craig
1952	Momus Goes To The Opera	Secret	Joan Schwing
1953	King Arthur And His Knights	Secret	Martha Chaffe
1954	The Pleasures Of Momus	Secret	Mary Lee Burke
1955	Signs Of The Zodiac	Secret	Katherine Blair Moore
1956	Festivals Of The World	Secret	Helen Louis Scott
1957	A Tourist Discovers Louisiana	Secret	Charlotte S. Parker
1958	Stories Of The Ballet	Secret	Josephine Villere
1959	The Rubaiyat Of Omar Khayyam	Secret	Mitylene Floyd Parkam
1960	Birth Stones	Secret	Caroline Lyman
1961	A Momus Calendar	Secret	Clayton W. Nairne
1962	NO PARADE — RAINED OUT	Secret	Elizabeth M. Baker
1963	Momus Goes To The Movies	Secret	Cynthia Echols
1964	Ancient Religions Of The World	Secret	Lucie Minor Ewin
1965	Beowulf	Secret	Julie Munson Bartlett
1966	Adventures Of Baron Munchausen	Secret	Jane Vickery
1967	The Odyssey	Secret	Susan Andry
1968	NO PARADE — RAINED OUT	Secret	Nancy Barret Eaves

Active Parading Krewes

YEAR	THEME	KING	QUEEN
1969	Ten Flags Over Louisiana	Secret	Lise Allgeyer Matthews
1970	Eat, Drink And Be Merry	Secret	Margaret Todd Monrose
1971	The Weaker Sex	Secret	Morrell M. Trimble
1972	Merry Moments Of Momus	Secret	Susan Deslonde Baldwin
1973	Sing Along With Momus	Secret	Anne Martina Strachan
1974	In Vino Momus	Secret	Isabel Parham Waters
1975	The Grapes Of Mirth	Secret	Susan Price Stone
1976	Poor Richard's Almanac	Secret	Alice B. Parkerson
1977	Pandemonium Unveiled	Secret	Margaret B. Kostmayer
1978	Momus Deals	Secret	Shelly Lewis Devlin
1979	NO PARADE — POLICE STRIKE	Secret	Ruth Maginnis
1980	Aesop's Fables	Secret	Suzanne D. LeCorgne
1981	Now Playing Momus' Movies	Secret	Beverly Favrot Himel
1982	Comic Characters	Secret	Lillian M. LeGardeur
1983	Louisiana Wildlife	Secret	Dorothy Kemper Lyman
1984	Famous Cajuns	Secret	Katharine M. Gilly
1985	Where Y'at	Secret	Adair Freret Friedrichs
1986	Sing Along With Momus	Secret	Emily W. Alsobrook
1987	Games People Play	Secret	Catherine C. Webster
1988	Momus Goes To Church	Secret	Anne McIlwaine Chaffe
1989	They All Asked For You	Secret	Laura Favor Eastman
1990	Momus Visits The Aquarium	Secret	Eugenie M. Crusel
1991	Momus Brews A Toxic Roux	Secret	Catherine S. Monsted
Balls Only			
1992	Momus Goes A Trappin'	Secret	Julie Learned Phelps
1993	Momus Rolls The Dice	Secret	Lydia Adrienne Hardie
1994	Momus Dines Out	Secret	Mary Marshall Seaver
1995	Momus Monkey Shine	Secret	Virginia F. Preaus
1996	Momus Wings It	Secret	Megan Harold Menge
1997	125 Years Of Momus	Secret	Mary Elizabeth Moring
1998	Momus Goes To The Library	Secret	Allison C. Tessier
1999	Momus Reminisces	Secret	Shannon Stirling Burke
2000	Momus Predicts	Secret	Leigh Carroll Fenner
2001	Momus Spans the Century	Secret	Annie O'Laurie Fowler
2002	A Knight To Remember	Secret	Elizabeth W. Baldwin
2003	Momus Herald 1803 — The Louisiana Purchase	Secret	Emily Smith

MORPHEUS

The Krewe of Morpheus was founded in New Orleans in 2000 by a group of Mardi Gras veterans. This Carnival club is open to all sexes, races and ages. In Greek mythology, Morpheus was the god of dreams.

YEAR	THEME	KING	QUEEN
2002	A Reality Of Dreams (Or Not)	L. Thomas McClung	Bethany S. Lemoine
2003	Morpheus Treasures	Joey LeBlanc	Susan C. Pond

MUSES

In Greek mythology, the nine Muses were the daughters of Zeus. In New Orleans, several uptown streets bear their names. This club was founded in 2000 and is made up of a group of 600 women who describe themselves as "diverse in every way — ethnically, racially, and socioeconomically." The club conducts community outreach programs that involve school children and local artists in the design of Muses' throws and costumes.

YEAR	THEME	KING	QUEEN
2001	Muses' First Time	None	None
2002	Terrible Two's	None	None
2003	Museology	None	None

NAPOLEON

The life of Emperor Napoleon Bonaparte (1761-1821) provides a rich setting upon which this Metairie krewe has built its Mardi Gras celebration. The Corps de Napoleon was organized in 1980 in Jefferson Parish. The French motif employed by the male and female group allows for colorful adaptations of standard Carnival customs. The *Captaine des Corps* leads the parade, which features 4 period-style, horse-drawn carriages bearing the exquisitely costumed court. Napoleon has established a reputation for the high quality of its parade, which includes outstanding out-of-state bands.

YEAR	THEME	EMPEROR	JOSEPHINE
1981	Songs Of The South	George Koch	Cheryl Cossé
1982	Salutes Louisiana's Tricentennial	William Zeller	Brenda Zeller
1983	Napoleon's Menagerie	Delbert Frederick	Venessa Dalhouse
1984	Heroes And Heroines	George Koch	May Ball
1985	Napoleon Conquers The World	Chuck Adams	Valerie Adams
1986	Earthly Delights	William Zeller	Brenda Zeller
1987	Court Of Great Lovers	George Koch	Beverly LeBlanc
1988	A Salute To Broadway	Irvy Cossé III	Nicole Cossé
1989	March Of The Conquerors	Leslie Frederick	Tahmi Zeller
1990	Fright Night	Pete Perret	Hazel Perret
1991	Napoleon Rocks And Rolls	Robert Caire	Renee Caire
1992	Childhood Dreams	Delbert Frederick	Elizabeth Neider
1993	Napoleon Shoots For The Stars	Joe Gallo Jr.	Rachel Berg
1994	Napoleon Takes A Vacation	Howard Lindsay	Bette Lindsay
1995	Napoleon's Scrapbook	Darrell Bacon	Hazel Perret
1996	Napoleon's Theme Park	Irvy Cossé III	Trudy A. Ingersoll
1997	Star Date '97	Ronald Cheramie Sr.	Aimee Genin
1998	Oriental Odyssey	William Prepski	Virginia "Ginny" Prepski
1999	Adoring Duos	Randy Neider	Rosemarie Coble
2000	Ah-Some Opera	Mark Hildreth	Melissa B. Hildreth
2001	Exotic Realms	Francis Bremermann III	Denise Bremermann
2002	Aquatic Adventure	Stan Guidry	LaVerne Elaine Hooker
2003	Fantastic Festivals	Robert Caire	Renee' Caire

NOMTOC

New Orleans' Most Talked Of Club (NOMTOC) is the area's only all-black parading organization. Located on the West Bank of the Mississippi River, NOMTOC's Carnival activities are sponsored by the Jugs Social Club, which was organized in 1951. In addition to having provided a means of entertainment for its members and their guests, the Jugs have given generously to youth groups, schools, and numerous community civic programs. The size and quality of the NOMTOC procession have steadily grown since its inaugural 1971 parade, which rolled with six floats, one posse, and a half-dozen bands. NOMTOC's membership includes men and women.

YEAR	THEME	KING	QUEEN
1970	Mighty Monarchs Of History	Alden Lombard	Amentria M. Gaston
1971	Universal Soul Music	Edward P. Julien	Jan Yolanda Connor
1972	Saga Of The Dance	George Brown Sr.	Yvonne Delahoussaye
1973	Down Memory Lane	Warren L. Cook	Marie Ann Curry
1974	This Planet Earth	Rene Lombard	Melissa A. Goodreaux
1975	In Persuit Of Pleasure	Edward E. Cadres	Jan Mary Johnson
1976	Holidays USA	Ashton C. Mouton Sr.	Patrice V. McRhee
1977	The Good Things In Life	Arthur Clark Sr.	Flaire Remonda Clark
1978	Fantasy, Fiction And Fables	Emile A. Soupenné	Sheryl Ann Allen
1979	NO PARADE — POLICE STRIKE	John A. Brunet Sr.	Giselle Kandy Brunet
1980	Islands In The Sun	Ernest B. Brunet Jr.	Lynette Marie Hendrix
1981	NOMTOC's World-Wide Food Fest	Charles E. McDonald	Alexes Claire LaSalle
1982	Wish Upon A Star	Warren J. Green	Judy Ann Bizou
1983	Louisiana — A Dream State	Charles Southall	Karen Lynne Johnson
1984	Melodies We Remember	Louis F. Gilbert Jr.	Charlene Marie Levy
1985	NOMTOC Goes To The Movies	Alex C. LaSalle	Rene Caprice Lewis
1986	Twice Told Tales	Joseph Roy Allen	Wendy Angela Brunet
1987	Happiness Is . . .	William Jones Jr.	Fredrica Trinette Gordon
1988	Trip Around The World	William A. Bolds Sr.	Nikeitha Andrell Bolds
1989	Nature's Bounty	Curly Johnson Sr.	Kendra Lynn McGhee
1990	Sing Along With NOMTOC	Thomas J. Divens	Tracey R. Henderson
1991	Memories	Dave L. Addison Jr.	Tiffany Cassia Markey
1992	The NOMTOC Library	Eddie Mitchel	Naikia Michelle Lewis
1993	Moving Right Along	Eugene Michael Bart	Lattanya R. Gougis
1994	Saturday Matinee	James Henderson Jr.	Jennifer Denise Green
1995	Dance The Night Away	Gregory Laffair Sr.	Stephanie Lynn Green
1996	It's Party Time	Charles D. Ragas Sr.	Chloé Danielle Ragas
1997	Best Of Times	David Lee Lewis	Dekethia Letetia Lewis
1998	Beauties And Beasts	Orlandez L. Pierre	Adiata T. Devore
1999	Characters Of Our Childhood	Ed Debiew	Rehnen Allison Morgan
2000	NOMTOC's Musical Moods	Kenneth R. Ancar	Krystal Reneé Ancar
2001	NOMTOC's Events To Remember	Emmitt Cheri	Dannette Michelle Cheri
2002	This Island Earth	Alex Henderson-Dunn	Lillian HendersonDunn
2003	NOMTOC's Animal Planet	Roosevelt A. Swan	Courtney Lynn Swan

OKEANOS

The Krewe of Okeanos was organized in 1949 by civic-minded business leaders who were eager to bring a Carnival parade to St. Claude Avenue, their neighborhood's main street. The club is named for the Greek god of oceans and fertile valleys and is sponsored by the Sonaeko (Okeanos spelled backwards) Club. Okeanos presented its first ball and parade in 1950. The original parade route has changed, but the imaginative club continues to excel. In place of the traditional *bal masque*, the club presents an elegant Coronation Ball at which its queen is annually selected and crowned. The parade features two floats of female riders, mostly former members of the Krewe of Venus.

YEAR	THEME	KING	QUEEN
1950	Tales From Mother Goose	Tom Bridges	Elizabeth Joy Janssen
1951	The Land Of Enchantment	Anthony Bonomolo	Lucy Parola
1952	Famous Lovers In Operas	Walter Ranson	Shirley Jean Chive
1953	Arabian Nights	Thomas Taranto	Theodora Swan
1954	The Wonders Of Oz	Jack La Franca	Marie M. Rizzuto
1955	Famous Broadway Musicals	Carmello Russo	Gloria Angel Mangin
1956	Evil Men Of History	Marine Garica	Gwendolyn Armstrong
1957	Festivals Of Pan-American Countries	Salvadore P. Oddo	Nikki Oddo
1958	Great Literary Classics	Robert Muller	Olivia Russo
1959	Literary Fantasies	Victor Ogeron	Sandra Rita Long
1960	The Golden Era Of Gods	Joseph Bonomolo	Shirley Mae Bonomolo
1961	Thru The World's Kaleidoscope	Angelo Spinato	Joan Lynn Labadot
1962	Great Conquerors Of The Ages	Frank B. Spinato	Dianna Avriett
1963	Strike Up The Band	Harry Rosenthal	Marilyn Marsiglia
1964	History Of Man	Leon Walle	Suzanne Leah Doole
1965	Fairy Tales	Charles J. Jaeger Sr.	Ann Rae Davenport
1966	World's Great Festivals	J. Kenner Donnelly Jr.	Judith Catherine Traina
1967	Songs Of Famous Rivers	Bruce W. Leslie	Mary Ann Despaux
1968	World's Great Wonders	Alois J. Binder	Katherine Anne Traina
1969	Twice Told Tales	Baldo F. Mannino	Karen Patricia Paciera
1970	Show Business	Albert J. Saputo	Frances Ann Chisesi
1971	Famous Operas And Operettas	John Campo	Marian Johnson
1972	Great Conquerors Of History	Dr. Joseph P. Tedesco	Debbie Ann Craig
1973	New Orleans, This Is Your Life	John Kraus	Frances Bridget Pecoraro
1974	Tales Of Enchantment	Louis O. Reuther Jr.	Hollye Ann Sabrio
1975	World's Immortal Music	Henry A. Fabacher	Clara Frances Bourgeois
1976	Our American Heritage	Harold M. Perry Jr.	Bonnie Jo Schoenberger
1977	Man's Culture And Customs	Paul Paciera Sr.	Mary Ann Henricks
1978	Tell Me A Story	Lloyd J. Perret Sr.	Diane Marie Hebert
1979	Salute To Walt Disney	Andrew C. Hebert	Sue Ann Prejean
1980	Okeanos' World Of Music	Nicholas J. Lapara Sr.	Maria Kay Chetta
1981	The Realm Of Fact And Fiction	Dr. Donald J. Clausing	Denise Maria Aromy
1982	Exciting Events Of Childhood	Harold A. Martin Jr.	Barbara Ann Perrett
1983	People, Places, Things Remembered	Byrle L. Ladd	Yvette Prouet

1984	Happy Times — Happy Tales	Lloyd J. Perret Sr.	Sally Ann Lambert
1985	Let Okeanos Entertain You	Bernard W. Whittle	Judith Cristine Paciera
1986	Paging Through Pirate History	Earl A. Weiser Sr.	Theressa Marie Villa
1987	A Tribute To The Arts	J. Ronald Atchley	Shelly Merwin
1988	A Tribute To The Gods	Michael L. Martinolich	Sandra Gail Harber
1989	Remembering Places Of Interest	Daniel E. Jones	Wendy Hymel
1990	Magnificent Movies	Louis J. Huhner	Amy C. Tarantino
1991	Recollection Of Okeanos' Past	Dr. Harold T. Conrad	Melissa S. Lodrigues
1992	Naturally New Orleans	Nicholas J. Lapara Jr.	Schoen Robin Heier
1993	That's What I Like About The South	Thomas J. Heier Jr.	Tessa Maria Estopinal
1994	New Orleans' Music	Arthur R. Chalona Sr.	Summer Lauricella
1995	Louisiana Celebrates	Sam Imbragulia	Jennifer Kathleen Owens
1996	Bon Voyage	Lionel J. Smith Sr.	Cassie Jo Gonzalez
1997	Favorite Movies	Steve V. Campo	Kimberly A. Lassalle
1998	Adventures In Paradise	Augie Lapara	Katherine Leigh Fradella
1999	Go For The Gold	Frank Pace	Cheryl Ann Reine
2000	Ladies, Gents, Children Of All Ages	Lionel Smith Jr.	Kristin M. Reine
2001	Timeless Tales Of Childhood	William C. Larmeu Jr.	Angela Bruno
2002	Okeanos Goes To The Theatre	Vincent Savarese	Julie Ann Greiner
2003	Big Easy On The Move	Chef Andrea Apuzzo	Samantha Blackstock

ORPHEUS

The Krewe of Orpheus made history in 1994 when its first parade rolled with 700 members and was enthusiastically received by huge crowds. The organizers of Orpheus wanted to give the city of New Orleans and its guests a third consecutive parade in the tradition of Endymion and Bacchus. Because of the musical heritage of the founders of the club, including Harry Connick Jr., the group chose Orpheus as its namesake. Orpheus was the son of the Greek Muse, Calliope. The krewe's Leviathan float was the first to use fibre optic lighting. Among the celebrities to appear in Orpheus have been Anne Rice, Whoopi Goldberg, Glenn Close, Stevie Wonder, and Little Richard.

YEAR	THEME	KING	QUEEN
1994	Rhythm, Rhyme And Revelry	None	None
1995	The Lyrical Legend Of Orpheus	None	None
1996	The Music Of Mythology	None	None
1997	Tuneful Tales Of The Brothers Grimm	None	None
1998	Troubadour Tales	None	None
1999	World Premiers French Opera House	None	None
2000	Musical Metamorphosis	None	None
2001	Crescendos Of Creation	None	None
2002	Fiendish Fanfares Of Fantasy	None	None
2003	A Flourish Of Fetes And Feasts	None	None

OSHUN

Oshun, a figure comparable to the Roman's Venus, was the goddess of the fountain, love, wealth, and religion for the African people of Brazil, Haiti, and Cuba. Her symbol is the peacock and the fan. The club was founded in 1996 to provide members and their families a year-round outlet for wholesome entertainment and community service, and to present a beautiful street parade. Oshun calls its king "Shango."

YEAR	THEME	SHANGO	QUEEN
1997	Wide Wild World of Birds	None	Valeria Butler Williams
1998	African Folklore	Rickey Walker Sr.	Terrilaine Mackial Boyd
1999	All That Jazz	Broderick T. Adams	Deanne Clark Thomas
2000	Happy Holidays	Kevin Daughtry	Peggy Carter Severe
2001	Under The Big Top	Kermit Ruffins	Shelia White Jefferson
2002	New Orleans Is My City	Bryan Thomas Clark	Troy Bank Reimonenq
2003	Shades Of Blue	Jeffery Washington	Marilyn Monroe Clark

PEGASUS

Born of the blood of Medusa, the white winged horse of the mythological Grecian gods is the name of this New Orleans-based krewe founded in 1956 and chartered the next year. The club's slogan has deep meaning for its members — "Neither rain, nor cold, strike, nor hurricane's might." In 1965 Hurricane Betsy wiped out the krewe's costumes, its first parade in 1966 rolled in a deluge, and one of Pegasus' first balls was held in 15-degree weather. Nevertheless, the group overcame these obstacles and later became the first to skirt the 1979 New Orleans police strike by rescheduling its parade in suburbia. In 1999, the male and female club moved its parade from Tuesday to the second Saturday before Mardi Gras.

YEAR	THEME	KING	QUEEN
1966	Helz-A-Popin	John Kirchem Jr.	Crystal Smith Smith
1967	Man's Quest For Freedom	Leonard C. Ramon Jr.	Augusta Grab Yrle
1968	International Show Time	Norman J. Babin	Lorraine Smith Higgins
1969	The Year Of The Dragon	Robert H. Carnesi	Eileen C. Provensal
1970	Shakespeare, The Great Dramatist	Joseph A. Pavich	Deborah M. Dawson
1971	Vienna, City Of Song	David Nelson	Linda Spencer Williams
1972	With These Hands	George G. Bourgeois Jr.	Angel M. Donegan
1973	Happiness Is . . .	Ray A. Bentin	Debra LaNasa
1974	Richard Rogers, Man And His Music	Dr. Celeste G. Wichser	Frances Nelson Cradic
1975	Talk To The Animals	John S. Petty	Mary Frey Giolando
1976	Let Freedom Ring	Perry McMenamin Sr.	Mary Ann Licciardi
1977	Reflections	Leon E. Perret	Shirley McGovern Post
1978	Venetian Adventure	Charles L. Murray	Deborah Schlumbrecht
1979	Once Upon A Classic	Julien E. Pembo	Kerri Burrus Adams
1980	It's A Child's World	Maxime Landry	Mary Anne Majeste
1981	A Tale Of Enchantment	John A. Kiern	Maryann Liuzza
1982	I Hear America Singing	Kenneth E. Kopecky	Alexis Danielle Cooper
1983	Love Boat	Lt. Col. Karl Smith Jr.	Simone Yvonne Cooper
1984	Candies Of The World	Charles A. Mannina	Coleen Rose Albrecht
1985	Alien Lifeforms Visit Earth	John Puchot	Caliste Marie Boudreaux
1986	Our Bountiful Heritage	Robert A. Artigues	Terri Lynn Scroggins
1987	Something Old, Something New	Dr. Allan B. Cooper	Nichole Celeste Cooper
1988	Louisiana Fairs And Festivals	Ralph Morales	Karen Jayne Massey
1989	Pegasus Remembers . . .	Howard Massey	Melissa Ann Massey
1990	Pegasus Salutes Rock 'N Roll	Robin Couvillon	Holly Noel Scroggins
1991	Carnivals & Festivals Around World	John C. Todd	Suzanne Marie Todd
1992	Golden Books	General Karl Smith	Augusta Rose Yrle
1993	Hollywood Nights	Charles Scroggins	Stephanie Fair Ney
1994	Realms Of Fantasy	Anton Peter Yrle	Antonette Joublanc Yrle
1995	Comic Books And Strips	Arnold Giadrosich	Melissa Elline Todd
1996	Musicals On Parade	William C. Lewis Jr.	Angela Lynn Lewis
1997	Games Children Play	David Barkley	Julie Ann Johnson
1998	Circus, Circus	Karl N. Smith III	Jennifer Chantel Hall
1999	Songs The Whole World Sings	Joseph Michelli	Stephanie Michelli
2000	Prophecies	Kenneth L. Kopecky	Sarah Katherine Krekel
2001	Art In Legends And Myths	Clyde R. Coombs Jr.	Marylyn E. Womac
2002	Great Composers	Michael A. Britt	Mary Lee Coombs
2003	Out Of Africa	Sterling J. Hebert Jr.	Jeanne M. Livaudais

PONTCHARTRAIN

During the reign of Louis XIV, Pontchartrain was appointed as France's Minister of Marine. In his honor, Louisiana's largest lake bears his name. Chartered in 1975 as the decade's first new parade in Orleans Parish, the krewe derives its name from the lake along whose shore its parade was staged until 1991. The male and female club then moved its procession from New Orleans East to a downtown New Orleans route and has since changed the day of its parade from Sunday to Saturday. A highlight of the parade has been a marching band contest and appearances by local media celebrities.

YEAR	THEME	KING	QUEEN
1976	Children's Stories Of Great Americans	Joseph R. McMahon	Jenny Marie Wicks
1977	Super Friends And Super Foes	Carlo A. Montalbano	Lori Ann McGhee
1978	Classics Children Love	Judge Salvadore Mulé	Laurie Marie Boquet
1979	Dreams Of The Old Wild West	Roy F. Baas	Catherine Fay Clark
1980	Celebrates Happy Days & Holidays	C. L. Sarrat, Jr.	Alison Ann Fleury
1981	Pontchartrain Salutes The Winners	Captain J. Johnson	Karin Ann Tessier
1982	Come Fly With Pontchartrain	Robert J. Landry	Cheryl Ann Luscy
1983	Let's Play Games	J. Rudy Ruffino	Colleen Lee Fleury
1984	Pontchartrain's Circus	Roy R. LeBlanc	Katherine M. Berrigan
1985	Children's Fantasies	David J. Lamaire Sr.	Shelly E. Chiappetta
1986	Children's Bible Stories	Sal Cannizzaro	Marie Louise Hickham
1987	A Visit To The Magic Kingdom	Adrian G. Duplantier	Michelle K. Williams
1988	Pontchartrain Goes Wild	Guy A. Chiappetta	Suzette Marie Buchler
1989	Rhythms, Fables And Fairy Tales	Louis Cannizzaro	Jeanine Castrogiavanni
1990	Pontchartrain Jams To The Oldies	Dr. J. Castrogiavanni	Jennifer L. Bradford
1991	Movies, Music and Country	Dr. Richard Mautner	Kelly Elizabeth Buchler
1992	Things Mr. Mudbug Likes To Do	Raymond G. Perschall	Amy Kate Scandaliato
1993	Mr. Mudbug Entertains You	James John Buchler	Brandi Lynn Buchler
1994	Mythological Jambalaya	Stephen C. Martin	Stephanie Ann Martin
1995	Presents Song To Parade By	Peter Robert Buchler	Katherine Ann Buchler
1996	Pontchartrain Goes On A Honeymoon	Louis Casey Chadha	Rosamond Jane Jones
1997	Pontchartrain Plays Jeopardy	Gary J. Authement	Laura Catherine Spear
1998	Pontchartrain Presents "Love Is"	Jerry Lynn Tegan	Angela Marie Poulos
1999	"You Know The Old Saying"	Thaddeus Kilpatrick III	Elizabeth Ann Kilpatrick
2000	Celebrates 25 Years — Circus Style	George A. Gilligan	Stephanie M. Schlosser
2001	Nursery Rhymes — N. O. Style	Frank Charles Romano	Ashly Ivy Romano
2002	The Music Of Broadway	Frank Robert Arceri	Cynthia Ellen Lemmon
2003	Do Ya Know Where Ya At?	Richard C. Wheeler	Sacha A. G. Peiser

PROTEUS

Carnival's second oldest parading organization was founded in 1882. Known in Greek mythology as the shepherd of the ocean, Proteus was a god who acted as herdsman of Poseidon's seals. The old man of the sea possessed the gift of prophecy and the ability to change shape at will, a talent he used whenever rivals attempted to tap his wisdom. From its very first procession, Proteus has always presented elaborate parades and tableau balls. In 1893, the men introduced the custom of "call-outs," a method whereby ball maskers invite ladies in attendance to dance. Proteus did not parade from 1993-1999, but made a triumphant return in 2000 with a flambeaux-lit procession.

YEAR	THEME	PROTEUS	QUEEN
1882	Ancient Egyptian Theology	Secret	Ida Taylor
1883	The History Of France	Secret	Susie Richardson
1884	The Aeneid	Secret	Felice Burthe
1885	Myths And Worships Of The Chinese	Secret	May Bickham
1886	Visions Of Other Worlds	Secret	Mathilde Guesnard
1887	Andersen's Fairy Tales	Secret	Cecile Airey
1888	Legends Of The Middle Ages	Secret	Emma Theard
1889	The Hindoo Heavens	Secret	Edith Jennings
1890	Elfland	Secret	Emma Joubert
1891	Tales Of The Genii	Secret	Susan Miles
1892	A Dream Of The Vegetable Kingdom	Secret	Valentine Cassard
1893	Kalevala — Myths Of Finland	Secret	Virginia Nicholls
1894	Shah Nameh, The Epic Of The Kings	Secret	Alice Denis
1895	Asgard And The Gods	Secret	Louise Wiltz
1896	Dumb Society	Secret	Vera Boarman
1897	Orlando Furioso	Secret	Juanita Lallande
1898	A Trip To Wonderland	Secret	Laure Lanaux
1899	E Pluribus Unum	Secret	Pauline Menge
1900	Tales Of Childhood	Secret	Louise Ferrier
1901	Al Kyris The Magnificent	Secret	Alice G. Green
1902	Flora's Feast	Secret	Willey Denis

Active Parading Krewes

1903	Cleopatra	Secret	Olga Laroussini
1904	The Alphabet	Secret	Eliska Provosty
1905	The Rubaiyat	Secret	May Parkerson
1906	The Inspirations Of Proteus	Secret	Ella Levert
1907	The Queen Of The Serpents	Secret	Mrs. Alice Aldige
1908	The Light Of Asia	Secret	Olga Dunbar
1909	Romances Of Wales	Secret	Jean Gannon
1910	Astrology	Secret	Mary Ellis Leake
1911	The Last Days Of Pompeii	Secret	Dorothy Wilmot
1912	Zoroaster	Secret	Corinne McCloskey
1913	Adventures Of Telemachus	Secret	Josephine Janvier
1914	Gerusalemme Liberata	Secret	Gladys Cook
1915	Famous Lovers Of The World	Secret	Adele Ziegler
1916	Sherwood	Secret	Inez Lucille Ellis
1917	The Earthly Paradise	Secret	Mittie Clark
1918 - 21	*NO PARADES — WWI*		
1922	The Romance Of The Rose	Secret	Ethel Fox
1923	Myths & Legends Of N. A. Indians	Secret	Virginia Downman
1924	Netatua	Secret	Dorothy Gibbons
1925	Tales And Romances Of Old Japan	Secret	Adele Dunbar
1926	The Fair God	Secret	Ethel Homes
1927	Heroes & Heroines Of History, Legend	Secret	Helen McLellan
1928	Heroes Of History And Legend	Secret	Ruth Jahncke
1929	The Adventures Of Hajji Baba	Secret	Eleanor May Haggerty
1930	Scenes From Favorite Light Operas	Secret	Myldred Plauche
1931	Reminiscences Of History In Novels	Secret	Gladys Gelpi
1932	American Poet Lore	Secret	Marjorie Stair
1933	*NO PARADE — RAINED OUT*	Secret	Lorraine Nalty
1934	Retrospection Of Proteus	Secret	Elizabeth Eustis
1935	Irish Fairy Tales	Secret	Lydia C. Phillips
1936	Don Quixote De La Mancha	Secret	Lynn Hecht
1937	Spanish Fairy Tales	Secret	Mary Kernan Dart
1938	The Habitant And Other French-Canadian Poems	Secret	Marie Ella Gore
1939	Select Fables Of La Fontaine	Secret	Corinne Maunsell
1940	*NO PARADE — RAINED OUT*	Secret	Katherine A. Phillips
1941	The Immortal Songs Of Stephen Foster	Secret	Adelaide Rickert
1942 - 45	*NO PARADES — WWII*		
1946	Longfellow, The Poet	Secret	Louise Jahncke
1947	Strange Stories From Foreign Lands	Secret	Mary Margaret Todd
1948	Wonderful Adventures	Secret	Joan Rickert
1949	Famous Men And Women Of History	Secret	Eugenie LeDoux
1950	Holidays On Parade	Secret	Marjorie Ann Monroe
1951	*NO PARADE — KOREAN WAR*	Secret	Joy Nalty
1952	*NO PARADE — RAINED OUT*	Secret	Edwina Mae Saunders
1953	Famous Figures In Mythology	Secret	Margaret Lee Menge
1954	Proteus Through The Years	Secret	Blair Burnting
1955	*NO PARADE — RAINED OUT*	Secret	Vivian Gelpi
1956	The Realm Of Proteus	Secret	Sally Evans
1957	Great Stories Of The Sea	Secret	Constance W. Carriere
1958	The Hidden World	Secret	Katherine G. McCabe
1959	The Hobbies Of Man	Secret	Clara Boise Kemper
1960	New Orleans Through The Years	Secret	Anne Collier Pratt
1961	Love Is A Many Splendored Thing	Secret	Sheela Burke
1962	World Of Communication	Secret	Catherine T. Kerrigan
1963	The Streets Of New Orleans	Secret	Lorraine Jahncke
1964	The Life Of Hercules	Secret	Louise A. Gelpi
1965	Lost Cities In Fact And Fancy	Secret	Patricia Anne McCarroll
1966	Seers And Sorcerers	Secret	Ashley Claiborne
1967	Treasures Of The Earth And Sea	Secret	Kingsley Fitz-Hugh
1968	Mother Goose's Tea Party	Secret	Catherine C. Clark
1969	World Of Hans Christian Andersen	Secret	Marie Legendre Baldwin
1970	Tales Of The Tiny Folk	Secret	Elizabeth H. Mahorner
1971	Our Storybook Of The Sea	Secret	Pauline Simmons
1972	Stories In The Sky	Secret	Aileen C. Livaudais
1973	Tales Sea Shells Tell	Secret	Margaret L. Smallpage
1974	Living Jewels	Secret	Catherine Black Rainold
1975	Metamorphoses	Secret	Anne Kathleen Carriere
1976	American Ingenuity	Secret	Charlotte Waguespack
1977	A World In Your Garden	Secret	Michele Trimble Reynoir
1978	Creatures And Curious Cliches	Secret	Wendy Ann Kennedy
1979	*NO PARADE — POLICE STRIKE*	Secret	Elizabeth Leigh Carrere
1980	Harvest Of The Sea	Secret	Avery Buckner Bassich
1981	100th Anniversary	Secret	Virginia Stewart Kock
1982	Water Courses Of The Continents	Secret	Ruth Moore Winston
1983	Valentine Voyages	Secret	Constance Cox Barkley
1984	The Sun King	Secret	Ann B. Burlingame
1985	Frenchmen, Desire, Good Children	Secret	Mary V. Weinmann
1986	Noteable Notes From New Orleans	Secret	Lauren K. Jahncke
1987	Proteus Reviews Carnival	Secret	Kirsten Erwin Dahlberg
1988	Famous Firsts	Secret	Ann Elizabeth Geary
1989	Fantastic Voyages	Secret	Elizabeth Felder Stewart
1990	Bayou Lore	Secret	Sarah Goodrich Freeman
1991	Bayou Botanicals	Secret	Ashley Nell Counce
Balls Only			
1992	Wings Of Wonder	Secret	Jennifer E. Schmidt
1993	Dumb Society	Secret	Katherine B. Baldwin
1994	Cotton Centennial World's Exposition	Secret	Megan Claire Thompson
1995	Creatures And Curious Cliches Pt.2	Secret	Sarah Brandon Smart
1996	American Poet, Henry W. Longfellow	Secret	Ann Pratt Viguerie
1997	Strange Stories From Bayou Land	Secret	Elizabeth L. Christovich
1998	A Trip To Wonderland	Secret	Jane H. Heidingsfelder
1999	Snow Parade in 99	Secret	Dorothy V. Gambel
Parades			
2000	Flights Of Fantasy	Secret	Sallie McBee Dickson
2001	Tales For The Tiny Folk	Secret	Glenny Carrere Parker
2002	Bayou Flora And Fauna	Secret	Mary Avery McIlhenny
2003	Creatures And Cultures	Secret	Courtney A. Trufant

PYGMALION

Founded in 2000 by a group of Carnival veterans who professed the wish to strengthen the quality of parades scheduled for the first weekend of the Carnival parade season in New Orleans, this club chose the name Pygmalion. In ancient Greek mythology, Pygmalion was the king of Cyprus. He fell in love with a statue he created of a sea nymph, Galatea. The male and female group rolls on the uptown parade route.

YEAR	THEME	KING	QUEEN
2000	You Know You're In N.O. When . . .	Lloyd Brackney	Shannon Culotta
2001	Las Vegas On Parade	Joseph R. Berthelot III	Melody Cook Kirkwood
2002	Le Mer	Wade L. Verges	Jenny Ann Sciarrotta
2003	Pygmalion Sculpts The World	Nelson Paul Savoie	Brenda Newsom Verges

REX

Rex has been the international symbol of New Orleans' most famous holiday since his first appearance in 1872. The all male krewe is responsible for the concept of day parades, for the official Mardi Gras flag and colors — green for faith, gold for power, purple for justice — for the anthem of Carnival, "If Ever I Cease to Love," as well as for one of the most popular throws, the doubloon. Sponsored by the School of Design, the 600 men of Rex operate *Pro Bono Publico* — For The Public Good. Rex selects an outstanding civic leader to reign over Mardi Gras, and his queen is always a debutante.

YEAR	THEME	REX	QUEEN
1872	Triumphal Entry	Lewis J. Salomon	None
1873	Egyptian	E. B. Wheelock	Mrs. Walker Fearn
1874	Persian	W. S. Pike	Margaret Maginnis
1875	*NO PARADE — CIVIL UNREST*		
1876	Persian And Egyptian	Albert Baldwin	Cora A. Townsend
1877	Military Progress Of The World	Charles T. Howard	Caro Labatt
1878	The God Modernized	James I. Day	Jessie Hay
1879	The History Of The World	William Mehle	Courtney Leathers
1880	The Four Elements	Ambrose A. Maginnis	Alice Rathbone
1881	Arabian Nights Tales	H. C. Stringfellow	Cora Slocomb
1882	The Pursuit Of Pleasure	Hon. J. Shakspeare	Frances Isabel Morris
1883	Atlantis — The Antediluvian World	Hon. Jules Aldigé	Susie Richardson
1884	The Semitic Races	John Chaffe	Annie Howard
1885	Ivanhoe	James H. Maury	Celeste Stauffer
1886	The Triumph Of Aurelian	Burris D. Wood	Lena Jackson
1887	Music And Drama, Odds And Ends	Col. George Soulé	Louise Braughn
1888	The Realm Of Flowers	Harry Howard	Genevive Cottraux
1889	The Treasures Of The Earth	John G. Schriever	Cora Richardson
1890	Rulers Of Ancient Times	Sylvester P. Walmsley	Nita Shakspeare
1891	Visions	James S. Richardson	Bessie Behan
1892	Symbolism Of Colors	Robert S. Day	Carrie Spelman
1893	Fantasies	John Poitevent	Ella Sinnott
1894	Illustrations From Literature	Benjamin A. Oxnard	Mary Stewart
1895	Chronicles Of Fairyland — Fantastic Tales For Young And Old	Frank T. Howard	Lydia Fairchild
1896	Heavenly Bodies	Charles Janvier	Arthemise Baldwin
1897	On The Water — Real And Fanciful	Augustin B. Wheeler	Ethelyn Lallande
1898	Harvest Queens	Charles A. Farwell	Noel Forsyth
1899	Reveries Of Rex	Walter D. Denegre	Perrine Kilpatrick
1900	Terpsichore	Thomas J. Woodward	Rosalie Febiger
1901	Human Passions And Characteristics	Alfred Hennen Morris	Bessie Merrick
1902	Quotations From Literature	Matthew J. Sanders	May Van Benthuysen
1903	Feasts And Fetes	J. T. Witherspoon	Ingersoll Minge
1904	In The Realm Of Imagination	Frank B. Hayne	Josie Halliday
1905	Idealistic Queens	David Hennen Morris	Hazel Ellis
1906	In Utopia	Capt. Alex Halliday	Adrienne Lawrence
1907	Visions Of The Nations	Robert H. Downman	Pearl Wight
1908	The Classics Of Childhood	John J. Gannon	Elizabeth L. Maginnis
1909	The Treausres Of The King	Frank B. Williams	Edith Libby
1910	The Freaks Of Fable	Hunter C. Leake	Amelia Baldwin
1911	Arts And Sciences	William E. Stauffer	Rose B. West
1912	Phases Of Nature	George W. Clay	Lois Janvier
1913	Enchantments And Transformations	Hugh McCloskey	Dorothy Wilmot
1914	The Drama Of The Year	Crawford H. Ellis	Flores Howard
1915	Fragments From Song And Story	Ernest Lee Jahncke	Sadie Downman
1916	Visions From The Poets	John J. Mapp	Inez Lucille Ellis
1917	The Gifts Of The Gods To Louisiana	Charles H. Hamilton	Emily Percival Douglas
1918 - 19	*NO PARADES — WWI*		
1920	Life's Pilgrimage	John F. Clark	Elinor Bright
1921	Porcelain In Fact And Fancy	Sidney J. White	Dorothy Clay
1922	Romances Of River And Valley	Bishop C. Perkins	Marion Souchon
1923	A Fantasy Of The Sea	Frederick W. Evans	Emily Hayne
1924	Notable Women Down The Ages	Gustave B. Baldwin	Margaret Fayssoux
1925	Romances Of Fan Land	Leonidas M. Pool	Marguerite E. White
1926	The Music Of The Bells	Joseph P. Henican	Katherine Williams
1927	The Music Of The Ages	Eli T. Watson	Mildred Brown
1928	Transportation	Leon Irwin	Betty Watson
1929	Outline Of History	Williams H. McLellan	Beecye Casanas
1930	The Jewels Of Rex	Dr. Paul H. Sauders	Shirley Cordill
1931	The History Of The Drama	Edward E. Soulé	Gladys Gelpi
1932	1872 — Rex Scrap Book	A. B. Freeman	Yvonne White
1933	*NO PARADE — RAINED OUT*	Edgar R. DuMont	Mary Frances Buck
1934	The Conquest Of The Air	Charles W. Bouden	Laura Fenner
1935	Nature's Workshop	Garner H. Tullis	Barbara Bouden
1936	Romanian Fairy Tales	Reuben E. Tipton	Cora Stanton Jahncke
1937	Nature, The First Inventor	Albert B. Paterson	Jessie Wing Janvier
1938	Realms Of Earth, Sea And Air	Charles McLellan	Malcolm M. Tullis
1939	Belgian Fairy Tales	H. Grady Meador	Charlotte Hardie
1940	A Fantasy Of The Alphabet	George H. Terriberry	Katherine Phillips

1941	Gems From The Arabian Nights	Charles E. Fenner	Delphine Clark
1942 - 45	*NO PARADES — WWII*		
1946	Myths Of The Starry Hosts	Judge Wayne Borah	Emmy Lou Dicks
1947	What Is The Sea Shell Saying?	George G. Westfeldt	Henriette Vallon
1948	Dances Through The Ages	Dr. Alton Ochsner	Elizabeth Nicholson
1949	Louisiana — Utopia Of The South	Lester F. Alexander	Dolly Ann Souchon
1950	Adventures In Slumberland	Reuben H. Brown	Mary Brooks Soule
1951	*NO PARADE — KOREAN WAR*	George Janvier	Ann Simpson
1952	Panorama Of The Magic Sugar Egg	William Waller Young	Eugenie Penick Jones
1953	Origin Of Names Of States	Charles C. Crawford	Adelaide Wisdom
1954	Nature Creates, Man Invents	Leon Irwin Jr.	Phoebe Giles Williams
1955	Washington's Birthday And Life	Darwin S. Fenner	Harriet Smither
1956	Festivals Over The World	Edgar A. G. Bright	Patricia C. Henican
1957	Favorite Stories From Old Testament	Clifford F. Favrot	Charlotte S. Parker
1958	Hans Christian Andersen's Fairy Tales	Joseph Merrick Jones	Augusta A. Dinwiddie
1959	The Adventures Of Marco Polo	Richard West Freeman	Flora Sanders Fenner
1960	The Wonderful World Of Let's Pretend	Gerald L. Andrus	Stella Evans Farwell
1961	The Magic Of Music	Laurence M. Williams	Virginia Wayne Borah
1962	The Year Of The Circus	Eben Hardie	Linda Logan Monroe
1963	Wonderful World Of Brothers Grimm	Dr. Homer J. Dupuy	Helen Jospehine Grace
1964	The Wizard Of Oz	Clayton L. Nairne	Claudia T. Fitz-Hugh
1965	Once Upon A Rhyme	Harry B. Kelleher	Louise Person Smither
1966	Adventures Of Alice	Herbert G. Jahncke	Christine P. Westfeldt
1967	To The Ladies Bless Them All	Morgan L. Whitney	Susan Charest Dupuy
1968	New Orleans We Love You	Ernest C. Villere	Delia Lane Hardie
1969	Genesis Through Gemini	Hughes P. Walmsley	Henrietta Creevy Clay
1970	Classics Comics Cartoons	Ashton Phelps	Linda Jeanne Young
1971	Centennial Celebrations	Brooke H. Duncan II	Tina Louise Freeman
1972	A Tribute To Jules Verne	Leon Sarpy	Elizabeth Anne Nolan
1973	Kings & Queens Of Fantasy & Fact	Dr. Howard Mahorner	Lynn Agnes Favrot
1974	Twice Told Tales	Eads Poitevent	Anne Cameron Kock
1975	Creatures Of The Imagination	Harry McCall Jr.	Margaret Pratt Logan
1976	Jazz — A New Orleans Heritage	Frank G. Strachan	Alma Marie Atkinson
1977	Look To The Stars	Ulisse M. Nolan	Mary Jane Fenner
1978	Rex And The Masters	Edmund McIlhenny	Katherine S. Duncan
1979	*NO PARADE — POLICE STRIKE*	Laurance Eustis	Deborah H. Huger
1980	Flora Of The Realm	Morrell Feltus Trimble	Elizabeth W. Burke
1981	Ars Poeticas	John Williams Sims	Phyllis Cowser Saer
1982	Bicentennial Bourbon Louisiana	William B. Reily III	Katherine H. Waters
1983	The Sovereign's Symphony	John G. Phillips	Elinor Spicer Bright
1984	Royal Transit Authority	Edward B. Poitevent	Laura Louise Freeman
1985	Nature's Royalty	H. Devon Graham Jr.	Mary Stewart Smallpage
1986	The Royal Academy	George Denegre	Corinne Anais Young
1987	The Lure And Legend Of Gold	William W. Young Jr.	Adair Draughn Freeman
1988	Fabled Gods And Heroes	John D. Charbonnet	Deborah A. Tullis
1989	Lafcadio Hearn's Fantastics	Beauregard L. Bassich	Katherine Elise Ballard
1990	Audubon's Winged Splendour	Dr. John L. Ochsner	Anne Storey Charbonnet
1991	The Mystery And Magic Of Masks	Erik Johnsen	Elizabeth Shaw Nalty
1992	Voyages Of Discovery	B. Temple Brown Jr.	Elizabeth Kelleher
1993	Royal British Scribes	Roswell King Milling	Mathilde Bernard Villere
1994	Notable New Orleanians	James Marshall Cain	Anne Juden Sarpy
1995	Enchanted Beasts	Louis L. Frierson	Margaret L. Eastman
1996	King Arthur And His Knights	John G. Weinmann	Edwina B. Griswold
1997	If Ever I Cease To Love	Eli Watson Tullis	Anne Randsell Grace
1998	Royal Gems	Robert Henry Boh	Sidonie Swoop Villere
1999	The Golden Age Of Mardi Gras	Louis M. Freeman	Mary Louise Phelps
2000	Ancient Empires	Harry B. Kelleher Jr.	Dorothy Butler Dupuy
2001	Illustrious Illustrators	Denis H. McDonald	Niquette L. Kearney
2002	Royal Jazz	William F. Grace Jr.	Kathryn Lee Reily
2003	Bicentennial Of The La. Purchase	Richard W. Freeman	Shelby Scott Westfeldt

RHEA

The mythological Greek titaness, Rhea, known to all as the Mother of the Gods, was the daughter of Uranus and the mother of Zeus. The Krewe of Rhea began in 1969 as a female group and held its first three parades on Wednesday evenings in Metairie. Rhea was the first women's krewe to stage its pageant on Veterans Memorial Boulevard. For several years it was also one of a few suburban organizations that held its exclusive *bal masque* at the downtown Municipal Auditorium in New Orleans. Rhea parades on the first Sunday of the parade season.

YEAR	THEME	KING	QUEEN
1971	An Evening For Lovers	Harry P. Rosenthal	Vickie Soto
1972	That's What I Like About The South	Oscar Daniel Ernst Sr.	Amelia C. Carter
1973	When You Wish Upon A Star	John Joseph Livaccari	Patricia L. Livaccari
1974	Let Us Tell You A Story	Gary Kenneth Martin	Jane Lee Betpouey
1975	Yuletide At Mardi Gras	Harold Brett Jr.	Diane A. Brett
1976	N. O. The First-est City In America	John Joseph Livaccari	Cindy P. Burnette
1977	Rhea Reviews The Oscars	John Louis Simpson	Patricia C. Trupiano
1978	Around The World	Nick Giambelluca Sr.	Lynda G. Warshauer
1979	Rhea's Good Sports	August M. Spicuzza	Judy Spicuzza
1980	Rhea Remembers	Rych Henry Soto	Edley Ramagoz
1981	Music — The Voice Of The Soul	David Stephen Austin	Janice M. Strassel
1982	Rhea Takes A Holiday	John Wesley Cofhlin Jr.	Ann LaRocca Wright
1983	Rhea's Galactic Quest	Milton L. Strassel	Marlene K. Schwebel
1984	Rhea Books A World's Fair	Davey Lee Naquin Sr.	Betty Ann Bonura
1985	Through The Years	William Paul Grishaw	Johanna Coci Lapuyade
1986	Hot Time In The Old Town Tonight	Joseph M. Impastato	Mica Ann Impastato
1987	The Royal Gardens Of Rhea	Brent S. Lyons	Kelly Lynn Austin
1988	Rhea's Hit Parade	Anthony J. Cartozzo	Naomi Angelle
1989	Rhea Takes A Gamble	Donald A. Lochart	Frances Cartozzo
1990	Rhea's Roaring Twenties	Angelo Cartozzo Sr.	Shelly Ann Toujouse
1991	Circus Worlds Greatest Show On Earth	Joseph P. Fiore	Debra Kitchum
1992	Famous Ladies Of The Movies	David Stephen Austin	Tammy Austin Valenti
1993	Rhea Loves . . .	Francis Quigley	Lisa Lochart Cortez
1994	Rhea Dances	Harvey Julius Dupuy	Jill Gast Fischtziur
1995	Reflections In Silver	Edward L. Martina Sr.	Therese B. Patterson
1996	Through The Eyes Of A Child	Lawrence Caillouet	April Vandergriff
1997	Rhea Loves Louisiana	Philip F. Fricano Jr.	Valerie G. Dorignac
1998	Rhea's Broadway Ladies	Thomas Edward Miller	Dee Dee Casterlin
1999	Rhea's Juke Box	George Moore	Rhonda Lee Zanca
2000	Rhea's Blast From The Past	Chad Truer Kraemer	Alicia Andrea LaRocca
2001	Let's Party	Henry S. Patterson Jr.	Debra Ann Green
2002	Champagne Wishes . . .	Euwell M. Bankston	Sandra Dartez
2003	Celebrates Its "Three-Three" Year	Raleigh A. Castin	Sandra Kerner Castin

SATURN

Roman scholars thought this mythological figure so important that they named a planet and a day (Saturday) for him. Saturn was the god of agriculture, time and celebration. In his honor the ancients even called their festival of merrymaking the Saturnalia, an ancestor of Mardi Gras. The krewe was founded in 1983 and presented its first two processions in the City of Kenner, then moved its parade route to Metairie in 1986. The next year Saturn returned to Kenner, then moved to Orleans Parish in 1993. The male and female krewe presents a flambeau-lit, satirical parade.

YEAR	THEME	KING	QUEEN
1984	Saturn's World's Fare	Harrison J. Rinehard	Carol Shamp Cook
1985	Saturn's Stories Of Enchantment	Mave Paul Allemand	Debra Ann Gauthreaux
1986	Laissez Les Bon Temps Rouler	Raymond J. Enderline	Margaret Durand Herrle
1987	Broadway Melody	L. Neil Berry	Ann Berry
1988	Lets All Mask For Mardi Gras	Marcel M. Lashover	Hazel Perret
1989	Legends And Lore	Tony Redford	Susan Guttery
1990	The Sounds Of New Orleans	Jeffrey Ravanack	Nancy Lee Cornfield
1991	Exotic Birds And Flowers	Wade Andrew Berry	Crystal Elizabeth Berry
1992	The Beauty Of Nature	Joseph T. Picarella	Patricia G. Bennett
1993	Saturn's Shop Of Horrors	Marcel M. Lashover	Irene Tingler
1994	Infamous Last Words	Richard G. Breaux	Leslie Marie Medina
1995	Pandemonium On Parade	Jay Alvin Michell	Sally Ann Quinlan
1996	Triskaidekaphobia	Fred C. Buras	Cindy Larsen
1997	Jus Beans And Rice	L. Fair Hyams III	Caroline C. Williamson
1998	String Of Pearls	Thomas M. Stephens	Debra Dawn Amacker
1999	Saturn Goes Wilde	Fredrick M. Adams	Carrie Marie Green
2000	Greatest Stories Never Told	Ryan Blair Small	Nicole Joel Hebert
2001	Fallen Angles Lament	Harold Williamson Jr.	Irene Leon Grant
2002	America The Beautiful	Ronald J. Roberson Jr.	Elizabeth Kerr Milhous
2003	It Bugs Me	Brian Joseph Plauche'	Carolyn Precup Isbell

SHANGRI-LA

A central feature in James Hilton's famous 1933 novel, *Lost Horizon*, was a mythological kingdom where peace, love, tranquillity, and eternal youth prevailed. This female krewe chose that place as its namesake when it was formed in 1973. The club was first organized in St. Bernard with a membership of 280 women. Shangri-La's Carnival activities are annually sponsored by Kaly Nickta, Inc., whose Oriental motif is finely executed throughout the parade. Each year the Mystick Krewe of Shangri-La makes a scholarship donation to St. Michael's School for Special Children. In 2001, the parade moved to uptown New Orleans and included male members.

YEAR	THEME	KING	QUEEN
1974	A Journey To Shangri-La	Ferdinand G. Petrie	Audrey Chaplain
1975	Everything's Coming Up Roses	Charles E. Williams	Laura R. Bertaut
1976	I'm Damn Glad To Be An American	Roland E. Dobson	Renee B. Pusinelli
1977	Birds Of A Feather	Anthony J. Saladino	Lois Guste
1978	Return To Shangri-La	Bill Jastram	Lynn Schubert Cure
1979	Under The Big Top	Adam Peter Rauch	Shirley Saladino
1980	La Mer	Anthony L. Libasci Jr.	Delia Porche Perez
1981	When Knighthood Was In Flower	George P. McCarthy Jr.	Shirley B. Haley
1982	A Slice Of The Big Apple	William Finnan	Barbara Colomb Collura
1983	Encore	Richard Alvin Tonry	Catherine M. Favaloro
1984	I Am Woman	Samuel J. Carevich	Lois S. Eumont
1985	Fairy Tales Can Come True	Joseph P. Barreca	Monica Barreca Ohler
1986	Happiness Is . . .	Anthony J. Alfonso	Anna D. Tedesco
1987	Flora And Fond Memories	Carl L. Dieck Jr.	Rosemarie Hutzelmann
1988	I'll Take Manhattan	Anthony L. Palama	Paulette A. Zibilich
1989	Glittering Gems Of Shangri-La	Arnold Joseph Truxillo	Maria Correro
1990	Casinos Of The World	Raymond Willhoft Sr.	Agnes W. Hoffman
1991	The City That Care Forgot	Paul Patrick Mayer	Sherry T. Zimmermann
1992	Tomorrow The Stars	Charles Gallo	Jean H. Wild
1993	The Way We Were	Michael R. Duceung	Joycelyn S. Poumaroux
1994	A Salute To The Fine Arts	Richard I. Buchsbaum	Fae Esteves Renatza
1995	Dance To The Music	Mario G. Bogran Jr.	Diana Camille Caire
1996	It's My Party	Earl M. Pelitere Sr.	Bonnie R. Falgout
1997	It's Scentsational	Joseph S. Di Fatta Jr.	Rena S. Billiot
1998	Your Kisses Take Me . . .	Paul R. Verrette M.D.	Gerri Valene
1999	Once Upon A Time	Alan D. Daigrepont	Debbie M. Grumblatt
2000	Celebration 2000	Andre P. De La Barre	Margarita Bergen
2001	Shangri-La Comes To New Orleans	Mario G. Bogran Jr.	Patricia M. Bogran
2002	Florabundance	Paul M. Domitrovich	Ann B. Rando
2003	Oriented Expressed	G. Mark Owens	Debbie D. Grumblatt

SPARTA

Sparta was a city-state in southern Greece renowned for the strength and discipline of its people in ancient times. In 1981, after successfully staging tableau balls for nearly three decades, the Knights of Sparta exploded upon the parading scene with a traditional-style parade that also blended innovations employed by the newer krewes in

Carnival. The all-male parade is led by the captain aboard a white stallion, and he is followed by his shadow, a young boy who also rides a white steed. Until 2001, Sparta annually christened the St. Charles Avenue parade route. The club remains the first of the season to present flambeau carriers and a mule-drawn king's float.

YEAR	THEME	KING	QUEEN
1982	The Mighty Mississippi	Kevin Charpentier	Mrs. Rosario F. D'Amico
1983	L'Opera	Ray P. Brundrett	Debbie Ann Brundrett
1984	The Winged Kingdom	Dr. Onyx Garner	Penny Ann Whitlow
1985	That Broadway Rhythm	Dr. John P. Dunn	Mrs. F. A. Courtenay Jr.
1986	It's About Time	Dr. Herbert W. Marks	Mrs. Edward Conrad Jr.
1987	New Orleans Rediscovered	Dr. John P. Dunn	Kristine Simno Nielsen
1988	Stories Twice Told	Joseph Sanchez	Stacy Lynn Johnson
1989	Faubourgs De La Nouvelle Orleans	Yancy L. Pogue	Kathleen Prats Vogt
1990	Sparta's . . . Knights At The Oscars	Randy L. Brown	Ashley E. Andrews
1991	Heroes & Heroines Of Fact & Fiction	William Price Jr.	Tiffany R. Schneller
1992	Celebration Of Exploration	Michael H. Rodrigue	Lauren R. Courtenay
1993	Echoes From Golden Concert Stage	N. Carter Church	Mary A. Fitzmorris
1994	Down By The Riverside	Bobby S. Roberts	Stephanie N. Courtenay
1995	La Carnival International	D. Michael Vincent	Joy Lynn Charpentier
1996	Journey To Lost Civilizations	Greg Kahn	Alison L. Ramhofer
1997	Maestro's Magical Museum	Dr. Donald P. Bell	Veronica G. Bell
1998	Queen Of Hearts	Craig C. Andrews	Jeuné M.Rodrigue
1999	A Master's Touch	Captain J. Johnson	Erin Lee Cucullu
2000	Invitation To The Dance	Frank D'A. Foster	Stacy Renee Whitlow
2001	Celebrate The Glory That Was Sparta	Charles A. Andrews Jr.	Alanna C. Ramhofer
2002	Sparta's Poets Laureate	Mike Owen	Brandin E. Andrews
2003	A Knight At The Ballet	Wayne Cucullu	Holly Elizabeth Whitlow

THOR

Thor was the Norse god of thunder and rain for whom Thursday is named. The ancient Norsemen depicted him as a hammer-wielding hero riding a chariot that was drawn across the heavens by a team of goats. The Metairie-based parading krewe was founded in 1974. Its membership of both men and women made it unique. The krewe made history in 1986 by becoming the first parading club to stop issuing doubloons. In 1991, after a one-year merger with the Krewe of Mardi Gras, Thor returned to the parade scene on its traditional Monday evening, then moved to Wednesday in 1995.

YEAR	THEME	KING	QUEEN
1975	Legend Of Thor	NA From Krewe	NA From Krewe
1976	The Spirit Of America	Joseph Perry Stamm	Carole G. Morrison
1977	Thor Presents The Best Of Hollywood	NA From Krewe	NA From Krewe
1978	Symbols Of The World Of Thor	NA From Krewe	NA From Krewe
1979	Thor Enjoys The Good Life	NA From Krewe	NA From Krewe
1980	Thor Salutes The College Mascots	NA From Krewe	NA From Krewe
1981	America's Favorite Pastime — TV	NA From Krewe	NA From Krewe
1982	Thor's Festivals	Charles Ruppert	Mrs. Charles Ruppert
1983	Thor's Fantasy Island	Anthony P. Perpere	Mrs. Anthony P. Perpere
1984	Thor's TV Nostalgia	Richard Palmer	Elaine Palmer
1985	Thor's Children's Classics	John J. Hilbert Jr.	Pam Coste
1986	Thor Visits Las Vegas	E. J. Guillot	Karen Fischer
1987	Gone, But Not Forgotten	Henry Vicknair	Karen Nicoll
1988	Louisiana Festivals	William L. Soleto	Charleslyn Soleto
1989	Thor's Past Years	Arthur J. Coste	Helen G. Coste
1990	*NO PARADE - Merged With Mardi Gras*	NA From Krewe	NA From Krewe
1991	Thor's Gems Of The World	A. J. Perpere	Evelyn Perpere
1992	Thor's World Festivals	Todd Bergeron	Tracy Cantrell
1993	Music Of The Movies	Robin Pati	Tammy Soileau
1994	Thor Goes On Vacation	NA From Krewe	NA From Krewe
1995	Thor Dances The Night Away	Henry Vicknair	Jennifer Coste Collins
1996	If Ever I Cease To Love	Michael Rohli	Jacqueline McCloskey
1997	I Wish . . .	Jerry M. Virgadamo	Elizabeth C. Rizzuto
1998	On Tonight's Menu . . .	Vincent Catalanato	Carri Soileau
1999	Thor's Silver Anniversary	McKinley J. Cantrell III	Lindsey Labit
2000	As You Were Saying	Floyd J. Maronge	Rhonda Edmundson
2001	Festivals Of Louisiana	José Aponte Jr.	Jennifer Aponte
2002	Thor's Classic Cinema	Vincent Catalanato	Erin Godberry
2003	Dance To The Music	Joe Lonero	Erin Godberry

THOTH

Thoth is the Egyptian patron of wisdom and the inventor of science, art, and letters. He is traditionally represented by the body of a man and the head of an ibis. His mythological counterparts were the Greek Hermes and the Roman Mercury. The krewe was organized in 1947 in the uptown neighborhood and presented its first ball and five-float parade with 50 members the next year. Because it designs its parade route to pass in front of 14 institutions that care for persons with disabilities and illnesses, the men of Thoth have become known as the "krewe of the shut-ins." Its all-male membership topped 900 in 2003.

YEAR	THEME	KING	QUEEN
1948	Mythological Divinities & Demigods	Gilmore Dufresne	Gertrude Marie Hebert
1949	The Fantasy Of The Storybook	Edward A. Defresne	Merle Kugler
1950	Historic Europe	Allen F. Chappuis	Elizabeth Lambert
1951	Childhood Visions	Edward Marshall	Mrs. Edward Marshall
1952	Lovers Of Foreign Lands	Joseph Campisi	Mrs. Joseph Campisi
1953	Gamblers Paradise	Arthur A. Hinrichs	Mary M. Estopinal
1954	Tales From Fairy Land	Davis A. Horaister Sr.	Mrs. Davis Horaister Sr.
1955	The Age Of Chivalry	Frank J. Van Haelen	Mrs. Frank Van Haelen
1956	Folks From Storybook Land	Peter W. Murtes	Betty Jane Murtes
1957	Ancient China	Louis Joseph Barattini	Mrs. Louis Barattini
1958	Fairy Tales	John Van Vrancken	Mrs. John Van Vrancken
1959	Ancient Arabia	Frank Baggert	Mrs. Anna Baggert
1960	The Age Of Exploration	H. H. Baumgartner	Mrs. H. Baumgartner
1961	Evils And Superstitions	Ernest Nereaux	Patricia Jane Glinn
1962	Imagination And Fantasy	Milton Helmke	Regina Irma Helmke
1963	The Age Of Chivalry	Jacob Kerth Jr.	Jeanne Dale Buchert
1964	Gifts From The Mysterious East	Del Kern	Jeanne Dale Buchert
1965	Ole King Cole	Glyce L. Di Miceli	Marlene Mary Harris
1966	Tales Of Scheherazade	Robert V. Martin	Manice Amelia Theisges
1967	Leif The Lucky	Martin Mullen	Imelda Mary Kuebler
1968	A Legacy Of Names	Michael Fritcher	Elizabeth Jane Shenn
1969	Legends And Lore Of The Sea	Charles E. Wingerter	Karen Ann Nicholas
1970	Age of Myths, Their Gods & Heroes	Dom C. Schwab	Alicemarie Rey
1971	The Imperial Legacy Of Italy	Charles J. Bariani Jr.	Jo Ann Marie Caruso
1972	Famous Tales Of Fact And Fiction	Russell Amato	Jeanette Marie Lahair
1973	Man's Quest For Knowledge	Phillip Pecquet	Carmella Ann Albers
1974	The Magic Of Music	Christian O'Rourke Sr.	Barbara Ann Dupuy
1975	Movies Are Better Than Ever	Dominick Mumfrey Jr.	Stephanie Ann Hobart
1976	From the Pages Of Our History	Heyward E. Menasco	Anita Diana Miemeyer
1977	Stories Children Love	Anthony E. Stant	Tracie Jayne Bougon
1978	From The Master's Pen	Edward Niemeyer Jr.	Sandra Ann Niemeyer
1979	All Things Beautiful	Emery J. Lattimer Jr.	Margaret Ann Meyers
1980	Pages From Louisiana History	Charles Wingerter	Eydie M. D'Arcangelo
1981	Mexican Mosaic	Edgar D. Wragge Jr.	Dianne Marie Morreale
1982	Music — The Heart Of America	Ed Wragge Jr.	Denise Marie Rouzano
1983	A Song Of The South	Anthony M. Rizzuto	Lenette Marie Bordelon
1984	If Only I Could . . .	Dom C. Schwab	Sandra Faucheux Graci
1985	Classic Tales . . . Of Fact And Fiction	Peter G. Pauli	Sandra Pauli Gulley
1986	In the Days Of Camelot	Louis Reeg Jr.	Cathy Roch Schwab
1987	Thoth Remembers	Jack Wilson	Mary Elizabeth Tyler
1988	Feline Fantasies	Gerald Labit	Lisa Labit
1989	Dilemmas Of The Rich And Famous	Martin H. Siegel Jr.	Cynthia Argave
1990	Of Kings' Gold And Greed	Elroy C. Schwebel Jr.	Melissa L. Barrilleaux
1991	Which Witch Is Which	Leonard D. Simmons Jr.	Shelley M. Burke
1992	Backwater Buccaneers	Marvin J. Ackerman	Dana Rae Stumpf
1993	Thoth Tells Tales	Milton L. Donnell Jr.	Christine Renee Jones
1994	Thoth's Wild Weekend	Marion D. Landry	Lillian C. Couvillon
1995	Things That Go Bump In The Night	Alden G. Hagardorn	Kathy Sampere-Gorman
1996	That's The Way The Cookie Crumbles	Frank M. Provenza	Melissa Ann Pettingill
1997	Thoth's Golden Dynasty	Billy Dantagnan	Tiffiney Ann Trapani
1998	Strike Up The Band	Gary Genco	Monique A. Theriot
1999	In The Beginning	John Tessitore	Robin Eloise L'Hoste
2000	The Peasants Are Revolting!!	David M. Berggren	Kristen Virginia Gauchet
2001	Legends, Lore And Literature	W. Paul Theriot	Danielle E. Walker
2002	Broadway And The Silver Screen	C. J. Tessitore	Elizabeth C. Schoen
2003	Thoth's Wonderful World Of Color	Dr. Wynn Russo	Brenna M. Hoppmey

TUCKS

Known for its irreverence, the Krewe of Tucks began in 1969 as a rag-tag group of Loyola University students. The club takes its name from Friar Tucks, a defunct uptown pub where two college students decided to create their own Carnival krewe after unsuccessfully trying to become flambeau carriers. The parade has grown from a small nighttime parade of pick-up trucks into a procession of major proportions. In 1983 the parade became a daytime event and in 1986 the parade route finally stretched to downtown. Even though the club has grown in size and stature, Tucks has not lost its sense of humor. This group of 800 men and women toss more krewe-logo merchandise than any other club in Mardi Gras.

YEAR	THEME	KING	QUEEN
1969	PKT Presents	Charles Diethrich	Cheryl Porrier
1970	Rock Bottom Top Of Nothing, Bottom Of Everything	L. Eyraud and S. Signigilaro	Tony Coogan
1971	Acid Rock	Lloyd Frischhertz	Marcelle Livaudais
1972	Phi Kappa Theta Presents	NA From Krewe	Linda Cuccia
1973	My Ding-A-Ling	Kenneth Sidmore	Cathy Cronin
1974	American Graffiti	NA From Krewe	NA From Krewe
1975	Bayou Boogie	Captain Humble	Debbie Ruddy
1976	A Salute To The Zoo, A Zoo Review	John Moore	NA From Krewe
1977	Tucks In Outer Space	NA From Krewe	NA From Krewe
1978	Tucks Discovers Winter Wonderland	Ed Kurtz	NA From Krewe
1979	Tucks Goes To The Movies	NA From Krewe	NA From Krewe
1980	NA From Krewe	NA From Krewe	NA From Krewe
1981	NA From Krewe	NA From Krewe	NA From Krewe
1982	Tucks In Reverse	NA From Krewe	Rita Coolidge
1983	The Greatest Show On Earth	John Candy	NA From Krewe
1984	Cajun Creatures With All That Jazz	Eugene Levy	NA From Krewe
1985	Louisiana Lifestyles And Legends	Larry Bud Melman	Dixie Whatley
1986	Mardi Gras' Biggest Party	Dave Thomas	Faith Noullet
1987	Tucks On Vacation	Frank Arceri	Frances Radillo
1988	Tucks Time Machine Boats To Floats	Lucien Dauterieve	NA From Krewe
1989	Ghost Of A Chance	NA From Krewe	NA From Krewe
1990	No Pun Intended	Dr. Gerard DiLeo	Linda DiLeo
1991	Only In New Orleans	Dr. Frank Minyard	Chris Owens
1992	The World Is Our Playground	Pete Fountain	Susan Schiro Derais
1993	Tucks On A Silver Platter	Ronnie Kole	Patti Le Maire
1994	It's A Tucks World After All	Mickey Mouse	Karen Holzenthal
1995	Little City Hall Of Horrors	Dracus Morvant	Carol Mouledous
1996	Lose-iana Down The Tubes	Wayne Fontana	Rhonda Moecklin
1997	Tucks Rolls The House	Sidney Tiblier	Colleen Pillié
1998	30 "Note" Torious Off-Key Years	Tom Zitzmann	Kelle Reichert
1999	Tucks New Orleans Style	Rudy J. Cerone	Marie Cerone
2000	The Official Book Of Mardi Gras	Chip Seelig	Marcelle Frischhertz
2001	Toys For Tucks	Paul Peyronnin	Renee Bravo Spratt
2002	Tucks Does The Wild Thing	Ed Pluta	Liz Zitzman
2003	Tucks Smells Something Fishy In N.O.	Perry St. Raymond	Elizabeth Alford

Active Parading Krewes

ULYSSES

During the fabled Trojan War, Ulysses was a legendary leader of the Greek army. As King of Ithaca, he was known in Greek mythology for his cleverness and bravery. He was also a major character in Homer's *Iliad* and was the hero of *The Odyssey*. This West Bank krewe, named for the mythical warrior, was the brainchild of a group of Mardi Gras veterans who wanted to see the return of a Carnival parade in the Gretna neighborhood of Jefferson Parish on the weekend before Fat Tuesday. Ulysses was the first Carnival krewe to stage its ball at Blaine Kern's Mardi Gras World.

YEAR	THEME	ULYSSES	PENELOPE
1989	The Voyages Of Ulysses	Steve Ivicevich	Suzanna Johnson
1990	Ulysses Salutes New Orleans	Hugh Liles	Tracie Uzee
1991	Ulysses Takes A Vacation	Wayne J. LaJaunie	Darlene LeBoeuf
1992	Name That Tune	E. J. Babineaux	Gloria Weber
1993	Saturday Matinee	Duane D. Dunn	Stephanie Simoneaux
1994	Tell Me A Story	Malcom Dauenhauer	Millie Dauenhauer
1995	Cornucopia Of Entertainment	Ernest Bellunger	Mary Ann Wichers
1996	Laissez Les Bon Temps Rouler	Richard Maloney	Mary Busby
1997	25 Years Of Disneyworld On Parade	Raymond Brubaker	Lorri Brubaker
1998	Ulysses Celebrates Its 10th Anniv.	Al Wangerin	Donna Wangerin
1999	Salutes The Children's Classics	Neil Balsamo	Gayle Ponthier
2000	Yesterday Once More	Albert Deidrich III	Patricia Pinell
2001	Tastes Of Louisiana	Rob Erbes	Kit Murphey
2002	Ulysses Unites The World	Craig Hays	Sandy Guidry
2003	A Blast From The Past	Albert L. Deidrich	Patricia Pinell

ZEUS

Zeus was the highest deity on Mount Olympus and served as the ruler of all the gods of ancient Greece. In 1958, the men of the Krewe of Zeus presented the first nighttime parade ever held in a suburb of New Orleans. The club became the first such krewe to own its den and the first to provide reviewing stands for special children. The organization staged more than two dozen bals masques at the New Orleans Municipal Auditorium before changing formats in 1986. Zeus continues an ancient tradition by calling its doubloons "drachmas," and by employing the Greek motif throughout its parade and ball. Zeus is the oldest parading krewe in Metairie.

YEAR	THEME	KING	QUEEN
1958	The Realm Of Mother Nature	William Dwyer	Lynn Gay Knudsen
1959	The Land Of Make-Believe	Frederick Brown	Lillian Durabb Haber
1960	A Festival Of Favorite Songs	George J. Bode	Sandra Mathis Buras
1961	A Child's Dream Of Fantasy	Ernest Bertaut	Gay Melancon Sheppard
1962	Kaleidoscope	Clyde Hawk	Sandra S. Hakanson
1963	Musical Masterpieces	William Dwyer	Connie Favret Akers
1964	Over The Rainbow	Calvin Lee	Ann Riviere Morison
1965	An Evening With Sigmund Romberg	Edward Hienz	Janice Merle Strassel
1966	Shall We Dance	Patrick Copping	Elizabeth Bode Palmer
1967	Anniversary Gifts Of The Gods	John C. Boutall	Katherine B. Hoffman
1968	The World In A Festive Mood	Garland R. Rolling	Melanie C. Navazio
1969	A Master's Touch	John Foerster	Darlene Foerster Allen
1970	Midnight In Toyland	Al J. Hogan	Judith Ann Robichaux
1971	Showboat	William M. Justice	Fran Torney Braud
1972	That Fabulous Century 1800 - 1899	Roland A. Caire	Sharon Lee Andrews
1973	The Old South	Garland R. Rolling	Kathleen Martinez Leto
1974	Through Golden Opera Glasses	William H. Cobb	Vida Caire Crocker
1975	Encore, U.S.A.	Rivers J. Marchand	Winona Aguzin Gibbs
1976	Ten Flags In The Wind	Philip S. Lundgren	Geralyn O. Martinolich
1977	Literary Landmarks	Don J. Dupepe	Mary Alice Romero
1978	The Front Page	John Dingman	Barbara Linck Hodgson
1979	The Good, The Bad, The Ugly	Ray J. Black III	Shirley C. Malbrough
1980	Stories For The Young At Heart	Charles T. Nelson Sr.	Tina Quinlavan Heirsch
1981	Those Were The Days	Philip S. Lundgren	Erin Vezina Caruso
1982	That's Entertainment	Rene C. Bourgeois	Maura Vezina Owers
1983	Hooray For Hollywood	Harold M. Quinlivan	Judee Rodick Spansel
1984	Louisiana Welcomes The World	Whitney P. Theriot	Yvette Vezina Lacour
1985	Believe It Or Not	Alfred R. Woodruff	Teri Ann Carstens
1986	God's Creation, How Great Thou Art	Edward H. Doleac III	Kathleen Lawler Aubert
1987	Tradition Has It	William R. Scott	Kristen H. Porter
1988	Kartoons Kaleidoscope	Bobby R. Malbrough	Christine A. Betbeze
1989	And In The Center Ring	Samuel P. Oddo	Nanette E. Krumm
1990	Stay Tuned	Richard A. Kelly	Erin Clancy Hattier
1991	From These Waters	Henry W. Hof	Allison Lane Sutton
1992	Memories	Calvin R. Schultz	Stacey Lynn Schwebel
1993	Love Stories	Clarence A. Greco	Denise A. Caillouet
1994	Legends, Lore And Mythology	Joseph John Caruso	Heidi Elaine Dodd
1995	The Magic Of Music	Edmund H. McIntyre	Courtney Abercrombie
1996	Fairy Tales And Fantasies	George Orrin Avery	Jennifer Marie Colombo
1997	Ancient Cultures	Anthony W. Cannatella	Karynne Alise Hoffman
1998	Celebrations Around The World	Dennis Nalick	Phyllia Elizabeth Greco
1999	Zeus Presents Camelot	Salvadore H. Bartolotta	Erica Anne Crocker
2000	Zeus Summons Gods Of Olympus	Dr. Eugene Hoffman III	Erika K. Hoffman
2001	The Works Of William Shakespeare	Carl L. Giarraputo	Allison M. Malbrough
2002	The Best Of Broadway	Andrew Koslosky	Jeannine Malbrough
2003	Our World In Color	Anton "Pete" Yrle	Amanda Lynn McIntyre

ZULU

One of the season's most anticipated parades is presented by Zulu, named after the fiercest of the African tribes. Seven years before the black krewe's 1916 incorporation, the Zulu Social Aid & Pleasure Club's first King, William Story, spoofed Rex by wearing a lard can crown and by ruling with a banana stalk scepter. The most famous Krewe of Zulu king was Louis Armstrong, who ruled in 1949. Zulu's honor guard is called the Soulful Warriors, and they, along with Big Shot, Witch Doctor, Ambassador, Mayor, Provident Prince, Governor, and Mr. Big Stuff, all liven-up the Fat Tuesday crowd. Zulu was the first integrated Carnival club, and the Zulu coconut is among the most prized throws in Mardi Gras. (*Zulu officials report that parades prior to 1974 did not have themes.*)

YEAR	THEME	KING	QUEEN
1909		William Story	None
1910		William J. Crawford	None
1911		Alex Washington	None
1912		Peter Williams	None
1913		James Bolton	None
1914		Henry Harris	None
1915		John White	None
1916		John White	None
1917		James Robertson	None
1918 - 19	NO PARADES - WWI		
1920		Freddie Brown	None
1921		James Robertson	None
1922		Hebert Permillion	None
1923		Joseph Kahoe	None
1924		Adrian Hippolite	None
1925		Baley Robertson	None
1926		Joseph J. Smith	None
1927		Arnold L. Moss	None
1928		Henry Hicks	None
1929		Wurry Watson	None
1930		Paul Johnson	None
1931		Allen Leon	None
1932		Joseph Misshore	None
1933		Allen Leon	Mamie Williams
1934		Leopold LeBlanc	Virginia Coston
1935		Baptiste Giles	Josephine Smith
1936		Edward Hewlett	Regina Brooks
1937		Arthur Royal	Lillian Fiest
1938		Leopold LeBlanc	Katie Riley
1939		Allen James	Ora deLillie
1940		Emmanuel Bernard	Cola Carter
1941		Alonzo Butler	Rita Edwards
1942 - 45	NO PARADES — WWII		
1946		Clen Vandage	R. Vandage
1947		Joseph Warrington	Carrie Chapman
1948		James Smith	Edwina Robinson
1949		Louis Armstrong	Bernice Oxley
1950		William Poole	Alice Murphy
1951	NO PARADE — KOREAN WAR	Roland Brown	Louise Branch
1952		William Boykins	Bernice Butler
1953		Noel White	Marie Jones
1954		Manuel Wilson	Rosetta Robison Jackson
1955		Nathan King	Willa Mae Henderson
1956		Albert Hamilton	Gussie Baptiste
1957		William Boykins	B. Butler
1958		Alonzo Butler	W. Robertson
1959		Melvin Green	D. Madison
1960		William Poole	L. Walker
1961		Henry Johnson	L. Washington
1962		Melvin Green	L. Washington
1963		William Poole	R. Washington
1964		Edward Johnson	B. Johnson
1965		Milton Bienamee	J. Jones
1966		Alfred Barnes	A. Barnes
1967		Milton Bienamee	N. Warren
1968		William Boykins	B. Larrien
1969		Elizah J. Peters	A. Alexander
1970		Milton Bienamee	Lucille Caston
1971		Henry Berry	Cecile Landor
1972		Arthur Carter	Lillian Jackson
1973		Steve Johnson	Lucille Armstrong
1974	Zulu Soul	Morris F. X. Jeff Sr.	Pearl Morris
1975	The Soul Of Zulu Jazz	Harold Doley	Estelle Wilson
1976	NA From Krewe	Dr. Lawler Daniels Jr.	Maxine Holtry Daniels
1977	Zulu Sports Page	A. J. Mercadel	Janee Michelle
1978	NA From Krewe	Willie L. Papin	Lourde Russell
1979	NO PARADE — POLICE STRIKE	Joseph O. Misshore Jr.	Belva Misshore Pichon
1980	Zulu Visits The Screen	Elliott Boisdore	Adrianne Petit Mitchell
1981	Zulu In The Land Of Myths & Legends	John Elliot Adams	Rhonda M. Lombard
1982	Zulu Goes To The Big Apple	Charles L. Givens	Gloria Nicks
1983	Zulu's Book Of Nature	Jesse J. Balancier	Michelle Y. Baptiste
1984	Waterways Of The World	Alfred H. Gordon	Lawanda P. Gordon
1985	Stories Of Our Childhood	Eddie R. Carter	Sharon Jackson
1986	Zulu Celebrates	Louis Augustin	Juanita Lang
1987	Sing Along With Zulu	Fred Thomas	Marian H. Pierre
1988	Festivals And Holidays	Arthur Vigne	Desireé Glapion-Rogers
1989	Wonders Of Our World	Owens Haynes	Betty P. Wilson
1990	Happiness Is . . .	Keith E. Westherspoon	Virginia B. Johnson
1991	It's A Diamond Jubilee	Charles E. Hamilton Jr.	Linda M. Dixon
1992	Fabulous Festivals	James Russell	Ernestine L. Anderson
1993	Zulu Goes To The Classic Movies	Oscar Piper	Ellenese Brooks-Simms
1994	The Wonderful World Of Zulu	David Belfield	Angela K. Adams
1995	The Zulu Song Book	Straughter Prophet	Mattie Dorsey-Prophet
1996	Zulu Around The World In 80 Years	Louis R. Rainey Jr.	Rose A. Roché
1997	A Few Of Zulu's Favorite Things	Lawrence Robert	M.Antoine-Robért
1998	Zulu's Universal Music	Wallace Broussard	Oletha Signal-Broussard
1999	Characters Of Fact, Fantasy & Fiction	Dr. Myron Moorehead	Patricia C. Moorehead
2000	Zulu Enters The New Millennium	Roy E. Glapion Jr.	Desireé Glapion-Rogers
2001	Zulu 2001 "Happiness Is"	Melvin A. Armour	Rosemarie Armour
2002	Zulu's Book Of Nature	Louis Williams	Deidre M. Williams
2003	The Kingdom of Zulu	Gary A. Thornton	Beverly D. Thornton

Defunct Parading Krewes

The following section features major parading krewes, excluding children's clubs and preseason parades, that staged Mardi Gras processions 1924 - 2003.

ADONIS
The female Krewe of Adonis traditionally paraded in downtown New Orleans on the Saturday night before Fat Tuesday.

YEAR	THEME	KING	QUEEN
1949	New Orleans Salutes Latin America	Dudley J. LeBlanc	Sercet
1950	The Lone Star State	Sam E. Wilson Jr.	Mrs. Sam E. Wilson Jr.
1951	Pegasus, The Winged Messenger	Rene A. Curry	Sercet
1952	Louisiana, Our Heritage	Rosario A. Bologna	Sercet
1953	The Growth Of Cities And Nations	Jefferson J. Rebstock	Sercet
1954	The Coronation Ball Of Her Majesty	Calvin J. LeCompte	Sercet
1955	The International Ball Of Fashions	Dr. Benjamin R. Slater	Sercet
1956	This Is Vienna	Joseph Hingle	Sercet
1957	Memories Of A Decade	Robert Cohen	Sercet
1958	Festivals Around The World	Dominique C. Schwab	Sercet
1959	Oscars To Stars and Motion Pictures	Martin J. Paul Jr.	Sercet
1960	Enchanting Moments Of Music	Gerald G. Weems	Sercet
1961	Endowments Old World To America	Mett S. Carroll	Sercet
1962	Reminiscence Of Adonis	Roy R. Theriot	Sercet
1963	New Orleans, Its Streets & Traditions	Kenneth Philibert	Sercet
1964	Southern Reverie	Tom Gressaffe	Sercet

ALPHEUS
The male Krewe of Alpheus presented tableau balls from 1948-1978 in New Orleans, but staged their parades in St. Bernard on Monday night, eight days before Fat Tuesday.

YEAR	THEME	KING	QUEEN
1972	The Language Of Flowers	Secret	Jan Marie Villemeur
1973	Festivals Of The World	Secret	Dolores Lally LeBlanc
1974	Realities	Secret	Constance M. Comiskey

AMERICA
The male and female Krewe of America's purpose was to afford Fortune 500 executives the opportunity to ride in a New Orleans Mardi Gras parade on Fat Tuesday afternoon.

YEAR	THEME	KING	QUEEN
1998	From Sea To Shining Sea	None	None
1999	America On The Silver Screen	None	None
2000	Festival Time	None	None

AMOR
The Krewe of Amor was the first parading organization to include male and female members. This St. Bernard Parish group's membership topped 800 in the mid-1980s for its Friday before Mardi Gras night parade.

YEAR	THEME	KING	QUEEN
1970	A Toast To Love	E. Rodriguez	Janell Nunez
1971	Lovers Memories Of Our Childhood	Charles Villemeur Sr.	Bonnie Famularo
1972	Silver Screen's Greatest Lovers	William R. Tracy Jr.	Marion Boudreaux
1973	Everybody Loves A Circus	Curt Spicer	Marion Pohlman
1974	The Land We Love	Charles Rice	Marie Simmons
1975	Love Makes The World Go Round	Larry Gaff	Charmaine Roger
1976	Love That American Money	Earl E. Billiot	Louisa Suarez Poolych
1977	Those Lovable Monsters	John Long Sr.	Sandra Guepet
1978	Love Is ForThe Birds	Gary P. Hemelt	Leha Argus
1979	Everybody Loves A Circus	John Long Sr.	Sandra Guepet
1980	Love To St. Bernard On 200th Anniv.	John Ferrer Jr.	Mrs. John Long Jr.
1981	Love That Good Food	Jules Pat Massarini	Rita K. Gaff
1982	Love Songs	Joseph L. Romano	Louisa Suarez
1983	Loveliest Day Of The Year	Arthur Steams Jr.	Rose A. Broquet
1984	15 Years Of Lovely Memories	Charles A. Carollo	Betty L. Harvath
1985	The Night Was Made For Love	Sterling Constant	Pat Chassaniol
1986	Games We Love To Play	Forrest Singer	Tracy P. Mandola
1987	Amor Salutes Lovely Louisiana	Charles Castaing	Susan Leiva
1988	Love's A Universal Language	J. R. Guillot	Mary B. Petruccelli
1989	Amor's 20 Year Love Affair	Charles L. Villemeur	Trudy Constant
1990	Love The Kid In Us	Jack Choate	Amy Hughes
1991	For The Love Of . . .	Thom Crandall	Kimberly Cates
1992	When The Love Bug Bites	Charles Villemeur III	Tiffany Marie Leiva
1993	What A Lovely World	David M. Hemelt	Mary Hemelt

APHRODITE
The female Krewe of Aphrodite paraded for three years in New Orleans on Tuesday night, one week before Fat Tuesday.

YEAR	THEME	KING	QUEEN
1962	Gifts From God	Harry Rosenthal	Secret
1963	Mysteries & Wonders Of The World		Secret
1964	The World We Live In	Gary C. Turcotte Sr.	Secret

AQUARIUS
The St. Bernard Parish krewe, named after the eleventh sign of the Zodiac, featured male and female riders and paraded Monday night, eight days before Fat Tuesday.

YEAR	THEME	KING	QUEEN
1975	Aloha Hawaii	Claude Griffin	Elizabeth Sensebe
1976	America Celebrates The Holidays	Frank M. Cucinello Jr.	Bonnie Lensmeyer

ARABI
Founded in 1932 as a walking club, St. Bernard Parish's first Carnival organization was named for the community through which it paraded on Fat Tuesday.

YEAR	THEME	KING	QUEEN
1957	Beouf Gras	Lester Serpaz	Frances Bagneris
1958	Around The World In 80 Days	Roy Fortier	Frances Fortier
1959	Facts And Fictions	Melvin Seither	Adele Basford
1960	1/4 Century Of Memories	August Campagna	Mildred Campagna
1961	The Battle Of New Orleans	Jerome Eskew	Josie Eskew
1962	The Lost City Of Atlantis	Emile Bertucci	Shirley Bertucci
1963	Disneyland	John F. Rowley	Elizabeth Rowley
1964	Fairy Tales And Legends	Claude Meraux	Mae Meraux
1965	The Big Top	Fred Menge	Claire Menge
1966	Tales Of Yesteryear	Emile Prattini	Florence Prattini
1967	Great Battles Past And Future	Calvin Schench Jr.	Mrs. Calvin Schenck
1968	Tales Of Superstitions And Beliefs	Robert Torres	Myrtle Torres
1969	Native Dancers Of The World	Bruce Nunez	Joy Eskew Nowak
1970	Creatures Of The Earth	Victor Longo	Gail Sheridan
1971	Music And Songs To Remember	V. J. Campagna	Jane Campagna
1972	It's A Beautiful World	Leon Borja	Theresa Russell
1973	All The World Loves A Lover	Lionel Guillot	Sylvia Guillot
1974	Festivals Of America	Robert Angle	Joyce Angle
1975	In The Days Of King Arthur	Peter A. Perino	Marie Angle
1976	America — Fact And Folklore	Richard A. Tonry	Irene Tonry
1977	Arabi's Book Nook	Russell Amato	Margaret Jean Dow
1978	Come Sail The Sea With Arabi	Charles Pareti	Mary Lou Pareti
1979	Arabi's TV Odyssey	Wayne Mumphres	Victoria Mumphrey
1980	Arabi's Night At The Movies	Philip Creger	Doris Creger
1981	Scrapbook Of Themes Past	Allen Molero	Janet Molero
1982	Those Moments To Remember	Melvin Guerra	Judy Summerline
1983	Melodies Of Yesterday	S. Joe Griffith	Becky Fisher
1984	Golden Year, Happiness Is 50 Years	Richard W. Gallardo	Mrs. Jerry DeRoche
1985	Statue Of Liberty	Leon Borja	Glenna Lewis
1986	Treasures Of Arabi Pirates	Melvin Guerra	Merilyn G. Costanza

ASHANTI
The black, male and female Krewe of Ashanti rolled on the first Friday night of the parade calendar in New Orleans. The group merged with Vesta before disbanding.

YEAR	THEME	KING	QUEEN
1993	Salutes Great Kings, Queens Of Africa	Chester Pichon Jr.	Ann Cagnolatti
1994	Pays Homage To Animal Kingdom	Alvarez Brown Jr.	Ann Clark
1995	NO PARADE		
1996	Anansi The Spider	Pat Swilling	Iris Barnes

ASHANTI - VESTA
YEAR	THEME	KING	QUEEN
1997	We Love New Awlins	Patrict Sanders	Sheila Douglas

ATHENA
The male and female Krewe of Athena paraded on the weekend before Fat Tuesday in the afternoon in the Jefferson Parish City of Kenner.

YEAR	THEME	KING	QUEEN
1973	Athena And The Olympians	Charles L. Villemeur Jr.	Mrs. John Raffo
1974	The Enchanted World Of Music	Frankie Brent	Secret

ATREUS
The male and female krewe paraded on Fat Tuesday afternoon in St. Bernard Parish.

YEAR	THEME	KING	QUEEN
1983	The Silver Screen	Russel Amato	Claire McDonough
1984	Louisiana Lagniappe	Pat Massarini	Mrs. Pat Massarini
1985	Louisiana Parties	David Hemelt	Mrs. David Hemelt

CAMELOT
Named after the legendary city of King Arthurian lore, the male Knights of Camelot paraded in New Orleans on Sunday afternoon following the Krewe of Carrollton.

YEAR	THEME	KING	QUEEN
1997	Stories People Tell	Charles Detrez	Monique Detrez
1998	Camelot's Journey Through Music	Andrew J. Koslosky	Angela J. Waguespack

CARNIVAL
The Mystic Krewe of Carnival, a male and female krewe, paraded on Fat Tuesday afternoon in St. Bernard Parish following the St. Bernard truck parade.

YEAR	THEME	KING	QUEEN
1986	Fantastic World Of Fiction	Cary Degelos	Pipsie P. Armond
1987	Carnival Goes To The Movies	Kenneth Fox	Elizabeth Lehmann
1988	Traveling Through Dreamland	Mickey Prattini	Mrs. Mickey Prattini
1989	Come With Me By Land, Air & Sea	Brian Schaeffer	Stacie M. Wright
1990	Carnival's Captivating Stories	Timothy S. Satterlee Jr.	Jennifer A. Esposito

Defunct Parading Krewes

CARONIS
The goddess Caronis was the mythological wife of Cynthius. The female krewe staged its only parade on Saturday, February 19, 1949 in New Orleans.

YEAR	THEME	KING	QUEEN
1949	Famous Women Of History	John J. Grosch Sr.	Secret

CENTAUR
The Krewe of Centaur paraded with six floats on Friday, January 31, 1975 in the Jefferson Parish City of Kenner.

YEAR	THEME	KING	QUEEN
1975	Mardi Gras Comes To Kenner	Milton R. Walker Jr.	Darlene Miller

CHALIMAR
The male and female krewe named after the Chalmette neighborhood through which it paraded, rolled in St. Bernard Parish at night, six days before Fat Tuesday.

YEAR	THEME	KING	QUEEN
1976	Classic Characters	Jack Camhout	Dianne Warren
1977	Rivers And Their Songs	Jessie Varnado	Elanie McKenzie
1978	Chalimar's Childhood Classics	John Perret	Susan Wale
1979	It's A Small Small World	Albert Sanchez	Mrs. Lloyd D. Roshto
1980	Vactionland USA	John Degan	Joyce Degan

CRONUS
The youngest of the titans in Greek mythology was the name of this male krewe which paraded on Fat Tuesday on the West Bank in the New Orleans community of Algiers.

YEAR	THEME	KING	QUEEN
1953	Early American Explorers	Murphy J. Michel	Juanita De Mont Gould
1954	Gay Old New Orleans	Earl A. Molaison	Ina Claire Molaison
1955	Memoirs Of Alexander Dumas	Robert Paul Borne	Jacquelyn L. Gondrella
1956	Birth Of A Nation	Herbert E. Borne	Rowin Ann Harris
1957	NO PARADE		
1958	Arabian Nights	Secret	Katherine Caulking
1959 - 61	NO PARADES		
1962	Parade Had No Theme	Ray Meeks	Myrt Giordano
1963	Parade Had No Theme	Arthur Sevin	Joyce Meeks
1964	NO PARADE		
1965	Holiday In Space	Anthony Mazeika	Judy Turnage

CYNTHIUS
The male members of Cynthuis paraded in New Orleans the Tuesday night one week before Fat Tuesday. In 1951, they paraded the Saturday night before Mardi Gras.

YEAR	THEME	KING	QUEEN
1947	Books Of Oz	Secret	Ruth Mary Gaudet
1948	Tales From The Arabian Nights	Secret	Anna Nada Nedderman
1949	The Brownies	Secret	Adele Gertrude Broas
1950	King Arthur Knights Of Round Table	Secret	Louise Dorothy Castaing
1951	The American Way Of Life	Secret	Germaine C. Wells

DAUGHTERS OF EVE
The all female Krewe of the Daughters of Eve paraded on Tuesday night in St. Bernard Parish. The ladies named their king "Adam."

YEAR	THEME	KING	QUEEN
1973	In The Beginning	Danny R. Nicosia	Monica Ford
1974	Gotta Sing, Gotta Dance	George J. Dowd	Mrs. Stanley F. Weiss
1975	A Mariner's Dream	Eugene M. Reites Sr.	Linda Theresa Traina
1976	Festivities In Fireworks	Harold Gaspard	Mrs. J. W. Memphrey
1977	Eve's Night At The Opera	Anthony T. Losciuto	Mrs. Anthony Losciuto
1978	Come With Me To Sweetheart Tree	Stanley F. Weiss	Jane Bennett
1979	They All Asked For You	William O. Debruler Jr.	

DIANA
The Krewe of Diana, whose first ten parades were staged on Metairie Road, was the first woman's Carnival krewe to parade at night in Jefferson Parish.

YEAR	THEME	KING	QUEEN
1969	The Moon In All Its Splendor	Harry P. Rosenthal	Gemelle Martin Gavin
1970	Majestic Waters	Frank Genovese	Christine Mary Grilletta
1971	Monuments Of Progress	Frederick J. Grilletta	Carmen Sampere
1972	Nature Heralds Holidays	Robert T. Ramsey Sr.	Bell R. Laville
1973	Rare Collections	A. M. Bert Walker	Elsie Gautreau Colopy
1974	Tell Me A Story	Robert T. Ramsey Sr.	Deborah H. Swiber
1975	Today's Favorite Pastime	Anthony R. Lopez	Joan R. Sanders
1976	It's A Small World	Jack R. Grigsby Jr.	Audrey Di Constantino
1977	"Where? Louisiana, That's Where"	Harold A. Swiber Jr.	Loyce Daigle
1978	Odyssey To The Final Frontier	O. J. Zeringue	Christine G. Dureau
1979	Cajun Culture C'est Bon	Henry Bourgeois	Shirley Verbeek Switzer
1980	Fantasies And Dreams	Glennon S. Diket	Elsie Walker
1981	Dance, Dance, Dance	Erroll D'Angelo	Rosemary Watkins
1982	Ahoy! The Bountiful Sea	James A. Wysocki	Linda Tripp Hubert
1983	Let's Celebrate	Stephen J. Faucheaux	Mary Lee Penino
1984	Summertime	N. Carter Church	Christine G. Dureau
1985	High Spirits	Rubin Chandler	Miriam R. Chandler
1986	On A Shopping Dream	Joseph O. D. Dauzet	Mildred Dauzet
1987	Delectable Edibles	Xavier J. Grilletta Jr.	Madeline S. Walker
1988	Command Performance	Thomas O. Singelmann	Brenda Singelmann
1989	Could This Be Magic	Glennon S. Diket	Jamille Jude Robinson
1990	Bowl Bound	Vincent Di Constantino	Audrey Di Constantino
1991	Escape From Reality	Royce W. Mitchell	Ann Zedlitz Grilletta
1992	If I Was A Rich Man	Tracy W. Krone	Wanda Deimel Aizpurua
1993	Journey Through The 4th Dimension	Al Russell Jr.	Christine G. Dureau
1994	Our Universal Affair	Wayne G. LaBiche	Janie Jacob Billings
1995	Delightful Destinations	Carl C. Henderson	Brenda T. Singelmann
1996	Hail! It's Carnival Time	Rodney T. Loar	Lauren E. Schindler
1997	The British Invasion	Henry Luis Klein	Stephanie J. Dureau
1998	Exotic Experiences	Marcel M. Lashover	Mary Ann Hartle Robert
1999	Myths Or Mysteries	Gary Louis Herman	Midge Haase Herman

DRUIDS
Sponsored by the United Ancient Order of Druids, the Mystic Krewe of Druids followed, and sometimes preceded the Rex parade on Fat Tuesday.

YEAR	THEME	KING	QUEEN
1922	Everyman's Heaven	Richard H. Hamilton	Wilhelmine Young
1923	Once Upon A Time	William F. Durr	Sophie Flach
1924	Realm Of Flowers	H. E. Datz	Hilda Mehn
1925	Nature's Wonderland	Frank E. Sexton	Gertrude Ray
1926	The Story Of The Stars	B. J. Rosche	Vera Bayard
1927	Classic Transformations	Arthur J. Peters	Daisy Kramme
1928	Dieties Of Mankind	M. C. Calongne	Mary Hoffman
1929	In The Realm Of Fancy	Casimir Muller	Anita Debat
1930	Myths Of Greece And Other Lands	Dr. Philip Montelepre	Isabelle Hirth
1931	Lore And Legends Of The Northland	Charles Sintes	Mae Cullen
1932	Monsters Of Fable	M. J. Ostendorf	Esther Durr
1933	RAINED OUT		
1934	Makers Of History	George C. Austin	Gesina Smith

FRERET
The male krewe of Freret, named for the street where its procession started, was founded by a group of businessmen who wished to bring a Carnival parade to their uptown neighborhood.

YEAR	THEME	KING	QUEEN
1953	Arabian Nights	Henry McClelland	Elizabeth Peppo
1954	Sea Tales	Edward Jack Laporte	Barbara Marie Bourgeois
1955	Masqueraders	Jerry McKenna	Rosemary Donahue
1956	Dream Castle	Frank Barreca	Patricia Mary Kaiser
1957	Freret Fantasy	Joseph Barreca	Rosalie Ann Lucia
1958	Oriental Odyssey	Alvin P. Thibodeaux	Gayle Bachemin
1959	Imagination	Joseph A. Gallo	Patricia Dileo
1960	Hail Hawaii	Charles Villemeur Sr.	Jean Patricia Leman
1961	The American Indian	Melvin Leman	Carmen Corona
1962	Lafitte, The Pirate	Milton Winter	Diane Catherine Petit
1963	Mystery In Space	Raymond C. Russell	Dale Frances Mauffray
1964	The Growth Of American Industries	Frank Piper	Margaret Ann Wingfield
1965	Castle In The Sky	Ferdinand Petrie	Joan Marie Everett
1966	Painting By The Numbers	Joseph A. Barreca	Joyce Blondeau
1967	Six Flags Of Texas	Charles L. Villemeur Jr.	Kay Ann Villemeur
1968	New Orleans, Queen City Of South	Charles L. Villemeur Jr.	Jan Marie Villemeur
1969	The Golden Age Of Operetta	Lee Lafonte	Janel Mary Marx
1970	Fables From Land Of Magic Carpet	William E. Kramer Jr.	Mrs. Robert A. Stroud
1971	Music America Loves	Gene L. Young	Mrs. Robert E. Oliver
1972	Everything Is Beautiful	Henry S. Marx	Susan Marie Gallo
1973	The Eternal City Of Roma	Preston A. Marx Sr.	Geralyn C. Autin
1974	Oriental Splendors	James Wysocki	Jane Ann Hingle
1975	Mexican Treasures In Mosaic	Sal Osterhold	Diane Willmott
1976	America Discovers	William E. Kramer Jr.	JoAnn Barreca
1977	25 Years Of Parade	I. Nash Barreca	Lisa Barreca
1978	A Few Of Your Favorite Things	Stephen L. Barreca	Barbara Barreca
1979	It's Magic	James A. Wysocki	Mary Barreca
1980	Kiddie Matinee	George G. Guilbault Jr.	Paula Marx
1981	Parades Through Pages Of History	Joseph A. Barreca	Mary Barreca
1982	See America First	Preston A. Marx Sr.	Janel Marx
1983	Freret's Fiction & Folklore	Al Nelson	Yvonne Randazzo
1984	Fantasyland	James A. Wysocki	Kristen Barreca
1985	Salute To Great Monarchs	Benny A. Randazzo	Yvette Randazzo
1986	Holidays And Festivals	Emmett A. Barreca	Racquel Randazzo
1987	Sing Along With Freret	Robert Ritchie	Mary Catherine Casente
1988	Freret's Library	Joseph V. Gale Jr.	Paulette Gale
1989	Happiness Is	Peter A. Marx	Susan Ann Casente
1990	Through The Eyes Of A Child	Issac Palmer	Catherine Wolfe
1991	Freret Travels The Globe	Vincent J. Bertucci Jr.	Diana M. Sapia
1992	Freret's Fabulous 40th	Huw R. E. Summers	Rose Culotta
1993	A World Of Love	Dr. Joseph Michalik Jr.	Martha J. Brown

FRERET - PANDORA

YEAR	THEME	KING	QUEEN
1994	Children At Play	Ed Laporte	Deborah Cutcliffe

Defunct Parading Krewes

GEMINI
Although the male Krewe of Gemini presented only three parades on the West Bank on the Tuesday night before Mardi Gras, the krewe staged balls from 1958-1965.

YEAR	THEME	KING	QUEEN
1958	The Great Broadway Musicals	George G. Francke	Mrs. Preston Vinet
1959	NO PARADE		
1960	Strauss Waltz	Fred Barefoot	Mrs. Hazel P. Heffron
1961	The Mystery Of Fire	Mike Dema	Gloria Barefoot

HADERUS
The male and female Mystic Krewe of Haderus paraded only once in St. Bernard Parish, on Monday evening, February 11, 1980.

YEAR	THEME	KING	QUEEN
1980	Tales Of Fact And Fantasy	Clyde Taylor	Lorraine B. Taylor

HELIOS
The ladies Krewe of Helios, which paraded on Metairie Road, staged the first daytime parade ever held in Metairie, LA, on Saturday, February 8, 1958.

YEAR	THEME	KING	QUEEN
1958	Colorful Mexico	Gerson Z. Tolmas	Mary Coci
1959	Yester Years In Old New Orleans	Lloyd L. Baudier Sr.	Mrs. Bryan Lehmann Jr.
1960	Around the world In 80 Days	Charles P. Cole	Mrs. Giardino
1961	Superstitions	Jack Gurry	Cynthia Cella
1962	Toyland	Homer L. Manley	Mrs. Bell Laville
1963	Say It With Flowers	James F. Woodward	Patricia Baldridge
1964	Women Of Great Charm	John G. Fitzgerald	Aileen Howell Whitney
1965	NO PARADE		
1966	Gay Paree	Earl F. Moran Sr.	Windy Murphy
1967	Carnival Time	Patrick Burke Sr.	Nadine M. Capitano
1968	Precious Gems	Merlin G. Hudson Sr.	Mary Ann Capitano
1969	Nature's Moods	Edward J. D'Gerolamo	Nora Brent Everett
1970	An International Feast	Charles L.Villemeur Jr.	Mrs. Lloyd L. Baudier Sr.
1971	Mysterious Future	Leonard J. Vaccaro	Mrs. Jack J. Stewart
1972	Path Of The Tarot	Charles L.Villemeur Jr.	Audrey Childress
1973	Famous Festivals	Jack Joseph Stewart	Santa Quirk
1974	Broadway Ladies	Henry E. Williams	Regina Carol Almerico
1975	Hymn To The Sun	Robert Westerlund Jr.	Secret
1976	Heritage Of America	D. J. Olister	Patricia M. Friedrichs
1977	Down Memory Lane	Charles L.Villemeur Jr.	Mary Varner Drury

HERCULES
The male Krewe of Hercules paraded in the New Orleans neighborhood of Gentilly on the first Monday evening of the parade season.

YEAR	THEME	KING	QUEEN
1969	The Labors Of Hercules	John J. Landry Jr.	Mrs. John J. Landry Jr.
1970	Voyages Of Sinbad	Robert P. Jolet	Gayle Ann Jones
1971	Quest And Conquests Of Hercules	John E. Bacon	Mrs. John E. Bacon
1972	Greatest Rogues In History	Jules F. Bistes	Mrs. Jules F. Bistes
1973	In Quest Of Adventure	Pascal W. Japcke	Mrs. Pascal W. Japcke
1974	Myths, Magic & Mysticism	Angelo A. Paternostro	Mrs. Angelo Paternostro
1975	Hercules In Camelot	David J. Montgomery	Florence Montgomery
1976	The Evolution Of America	Bert Bannister	Mrs. Bert Bannister
1977	The Hercules Story Book	Terrence J. Gagliano	Mrs. Terrence J. Gagliano
1978	Hercules 10th Anniversary	Donald DeGeorge	Elizabeth Ann Pazos
1979	Hercules Goes Vacationing	Charles A. Imbornone	Carolyn B. Imbronone
1980	Mighty Warriors Of Yore	Brodus Krekel	Bonnie Ann Abadie
1981	Folkore Of Hercules	Joseph M. Bistes II	Candace D. Dubuisson
1982	Hercules Explores The Universe	Dennis J. Haydel	Mrs. David Montgomery
1983	Hercules' Island Adventure	Joseph S. Delaune	Therese Guenther
1984	Songs Of The River	David G. Trepagnier	Marianna deLaneuville
1985	Hercules Loves Music	James M. Smullen	Mary R. Sutton
1986	Hercules' Matinee	Michael K. Meyers	Diana H. Meyers
1987	Hercules Salutes America	John Munster	Trudy Benard Baudier
1988	Happy Twentieth Anniversary	Terrance Gomez	Pamela Schmidt
1989	Hercules' Favorite Things	John E. Munster	Pamela Aolman
1990	The Land Of Make Believe	Lind Latour	Tammy Bell
1991	Festivals Around The World	Joseph J. Taylor	Sylvia G. Taylor

HESPER
The teenage and adult Krewe of Hesper paraded in Kenner, LA, on Saturday afternoon on the first weekend of the Carnival parade calendar.

YEAR	THEME	KING	QUEEN
1972	The Wonderful World Of Gems	Sgt. Victor A. Nunez Sr.	Christine A. Bath Nunez
1973	Broadway Musicals Of The Past	Joseph R. Fertitta Sr.	Annetta C. Myers
1974	Come To The Mardi Gras	Robert J. Sekinger	Joyce Bounds

HESTIA
The Krewe of Hestia featured men, women, and children, and paraded in downtown New Orleans on the first Sunday night of the parade season. Telly Savalas and George Peppard rode as guest grand marshals.

YEAR	THEME	KING	QUEEN
1977	Family Fun In Television	None	Cynthia Kay Beaupre
1978	A Family Affair	None	Marilyn Beaupre

ICARIUS
Sponsored by men and women of the hotel industry, the Krewe of Icarius paraded on the first Sunday night of the parade season in New Orleans.

YEAR	THEME	KING	QUEEN
1982	Icarius Loves New Orleans	Charles Foti	Celeste B. McShane
1983	Icarius' Storybook	Jack Hines	Beverly Geiger
1984	A Journey Through Time	Ronnie Kole	Gardner Schneider
1985	Icarius Travels The Distant Lands	Sha-Na-Na	Sha-Na-Na

JASON
The male Knights of Jason paraded in Harahan, LA, on the Saturday night before Fat Tuesday for more than a decade. Its final two parades rolled on Metairie Road.

YEAR	THEME	KING	QUEEN
1964	Light Again, Life Again	Harold Toca	Darlene LaCava
1965	Center Ring	Earl J. Luminois	Mrs. Earl J. Luminois
1966	Babes In Toyland	Henry Collins	Jackie Collins
1967	Tales Of Winds And Waters	Charles L. Mauer	Mrs. Charles L. Mauer
1968	Many Faces Of New Orleans	A. J. Signorelli	Mrs. Albert J. Signorelli
1969	The Legend Of King Arthur	Robet O'Neil	Jo Ann Wigginton
1970	The Musical Theatre	Harold Brett Jr.	Mrs. Harold Brett Jr.
1971	Games People Play	Wayne F. Traverse	Leigh Traverse
1972	Jason Visits The Follies	Jesse M. Hartle Jr.	Mrs. Jesse M. Hartle Jr.
1973	Quest Of The Golden Fleece	Leonard J. Alleman	Mrs. Leonard Alleman
1974	Many Bayous Of Louisiana	Eric Tracy	Linda Tracy
1975	Children's Classics	Wesley Joseph James	Janet C. James
1976	Pride On Parade	Stanislas St.Pierre	Sandra LeBlanc St.Pierre

JEFLA
With its name signifying Jefferson (Parish) Louisiana, the male Krewe of Jefla paraded on the Sunday evening before Fat Tuesday in Gretna. Jefla merged with Midas in 1952.

YEAR	THEME	KING	QUEEN
1949	Fables Of Jefferson Parish	Louis Badelamento	Norma Calzada
1950	Say It With Love	John A. Flynn	Jeannette Martin
1951	King Jefla Visits Comicland	Joseph Chimento	Sidonia Terrebonne

JUNO
St. Bernard Parish's first female krewe rolled on the first Sunday evening of the parade season. Juno merged with Jupiter, became dormant for a decade, then returned as a solo krewe before disbanding in 1997.

YEAR	THEME	KING	QUEEN
1970	Written In The Stars	Frank S. Fiasconaro Jr.	Secret
1971	Our World And Welcome To It	Victor H. Longo Sr.	Secret
1972	I Love A Parade	George R. Bruno	Secret
1973	Phantoms And Phantacies	Robert V. Marten	Secret
1974	Sunday Night At The Movies	Kenneth A. Fox	Secret
1975	Destination New York	Leon F. Borja	Secret
1976	Let Freedom Ring	Rene A. Quentin Sr.	Secret
1977	NO PARADE		
1978	What's In A Name		Ethel McNabb
1979	I Am Woman		Mary Copeland
1980	Musicade	None	Barbera Bennett
1981	Flapdoodle	None	Marjorie Kelly
1982	We Love		Vera Newton
1983 - 84	*Merged With Jupiter*		
1985 - 94	NO PARADES		
1995	Somewhere In Time	Lawrence LeMeunier	Kathy Denley
1996	Fabulous Festivals	Philip A. Lapara	Bobbie Fontenot
1997	Wishes	Dennis Kazmierczak	Doreen Gamus

JUPITER
The male Krewe of Jupiter presented St. Bernard Parish's first night parade and was the first Carnival club from that area to stage a ball at the New Orleans Municipal Auditorium.

YEAR	THEME	KING	QUEEN
1969	The Divinities Of Mankind	Harry Rosenthal	Deborah Marie Reichert
1970	Triumphs And Disasters	Robert P. Perino	Cherry Louise Pepper
1971	The Performing Arts	Louis Munster	Cheryl Ann Collette
1972	So Proudly We Hail	Ivan Tetra	Susan Elizabeth Tedesco
1973	The Creation — Divine Faith	Leon Borja	Pamela Ann Boya
1974	Profiles In Courage	Ralph M. Roberts Jr.	Denise Ann Suarez
1975	Mardi Gras Many Splendored Thing	Ronald J. Vega	Bambi Lynn Gaffney
1976	America's Bicentennial	Mario Moranto	Kathy Elizabeth Regan
1977	I Write The Songs	Daniel McGovern III	Judy Ann Spicuzza
1978	Triumphs Of Arts & Sciences	Sidney D. Torres III	Garnet Marie Hill
1979	Fabulous Las Vegas	Vincent Ferrara	Lesley Ann Ferrara
1980	World Of Make Believe	Roger J. Haydel Jr.	Lisa Ann Guillot
1981	Precious Gems And Stones	Leon Borja	Tracy Ann Petruccelli
1982	Million Dollar Movies	Cola Long	Roxanne Louise Hill

Defunct Parading Krewes

JUPITER - JUNO

YEAR	THEME	KING	QUEEN
1983	Anything Goes	Harry P. Rosenthal	Deborah Yvonne Richard
1984	A Fair To Remember	Gerard Readeau	Mrs. Gerard Readeau

LOVE

The male and female Krewe of Love paraded only once in the City of Kenner, LA, on Tuesday, February 8, 1983, at night, one week before Fat Tuesday.

YEAR	THEME	KING	QUEEN
1982	Lovers And Sweethearts	Ed Muniz	Mrs. Ed Muniz

MARC ANTONY

Marc Antony paraded in Gretna, LA, on Thursday night. After a 7-year hiatus, they returned under the name Marc Antony and Merlin & Morganna, and rolled as a pre-season Sunday afternoon parade.

YEAR	THEME	KING	QUEEN
1984	Marc Antony's Conquest	Carl Scivicque	Kim Berrgren
1985	Music Maestro Please	Charles Moreau	Debbie Gautreaux
1986 - 91	NO PARADES		
1992	That's Entertainment	Robert Wilson, U.S.N.	Sue Prejean
1993	A Ticket To Broadway	Early Chaisson	Helen Bonura Leonard
1994	The Travels Of Marc Antony	Al LeConte	Ann Boggan

MARDI GRAS

Initially conceived as a composite parade of floats from other krewes, the male and female Krewe of Mardi Gras rolled at night for nearly two decades in Metairie, LA.

YEAR	THEME	KING	QUEEN
1975	Jefferson Parish Sesquicentennial	Larry Gibson	Virgie Overstreet
1976	200 Years Of History	Larry Villemeur	Jan Villemeur
1977	Friendship The Universal Language	Anthony Trumbaturi	Rose Trumbaturi
1978	The Gridiron's Greatest	Wayne Tyree	Kathy Cantrell
1979	I Wish	Ronald Burch	Mrs. Ronald Burch
1980	They're Playing Our Song	Terry Hodges	Tommye Brown-Hodges
1981	Alphabet Of Parade	George A. Hallal Sr.	Gloria R. Langlinais
1982	Like Grandma Used To Say	Rick Ashley	Mary Ashley
1983	Journey Thru Dreamland	Jacob Vallelungs	Kathleen K. Hertz
1984	Ten Cennial	McKinley J. Cantrell Jr.	Wanda Mary Cantrell
1985	The World Celebrates	Henry Vicknair	Roi-Lynn Manning
1986	Military Moments	Certice Corley	Mrs. Corley
1987	Color My World	William L. Soleto	Charleslyn Soleto
1988	Sinema Sensations	Anthony J. Perpere	Evelyn Perpere
1989	Naturally New Orleans	David Fontana	Susan Shelton
1990	Monopoly	Robert J. Ruiz	Lisa Ann Ruiz
1991	All That Glitters	David N. Noe	Victoria K. Noe
1992	Festivals Of The World	Robert Ruiz	Lisa Ann Ruiz
1993	And The Melody Lingers On	Arthur Coste Sr.	Helen Coste
1994	Just For The Fun Of It	William E. Causey	Virginia Marie Causey

MECCA

Originating in 1960, the Krewe of Mecca rolled on the first Saturday night of the parade season in New Orleans. The male krewe was named after the famous Islamic city. Mecca merged with Hestia and then Sparta before departing the parade scene.

YEAR	THEME	KING	QUEEN
1968	Disneyana — A World Of Fantasy	Harry Rosenthal	Mrs. Mitchell W.Herzog
1969	This Is America	Dr. Anthony Russo Jr.	Mrs. Frederick G. Podt
1970	Showcase Caribbean	Charles W. Wall Sr.	Mrs. Charles W. Wall Sr.
1971	The Best Of Broadway	Robert N. Samuels	Mrs. Robert N. Samuels
1972	All The World Loves A Clown	Jack Larue	Mrs. Andreas F. Reising
1973	Once Upon A Street	William P. Hindelang II	Gayle Doris Zoller
1974	Wish Me An Island	Joseph Costello III	Angeline M. Molinario
1975	Legends In Music	Clarence Champagne Jr.	Mrs. Terry J. Boffone
1976	Happy Birthday USA	Frederick C. Ebel	Betty Jean Yokers
1977	I Must Go Down In The Sea Again	Robert E. Thompson II	Shirley Thompson and Theresa Thompson
1978	The Valley Of The Kings	William P. Hindelang Jr.	

HESTIA - MECCA

YEAR	THEME	KING	QUEEN
1979	Myths & Fantasies	Al Copeland	Patti White Copeland
1980	Movie Mania	Sidney Bourdais	Jan Bodenger

SPARTA - MECCA

YEAR	THEME	KING	QUEEN
1981	Sparta's Golden Era Of Entertainment	Kevin L. Charpentier	
1982	The Mighty Mississippi	Francis A. Courtenay Jr.	

MIDAS

In 1952 the Gretna, LA, based Krewe of Jefla merged with the Krewe of Midas. The group paraded four times during the decade of the 1950s.

YEAR	THEME	KING	QUEEN
1952	Marvels Of Nature	Joseph Dentineo	Marilyn Cerniglia
1953	Louisiana Purchase	Henry Graf	Leverda Arcement
1954 - 55	NO PARADES		
1956	Folk Tales	Joseph Chimento	Louise Marcello
1957	NO PARADE		
1958	Broadway Musicals	Henry Urban	Louise Marcello

MINERVA

The female Krewe of Minerva paraded in New Orleans East on the Thursday evening before Fat Tuesday.

YEAR	THEME	KING	QUEEN
1977	Femmes Of Fame	Mark Durr	Myrlene Robinson
1978	Minerva's Journey Under The Sea	Irwin Bayard	Darnell Marr
1979	NO PARADE — POLICE STRIKE		
1980	Affair D'Amor	John Lofton Sr.	Christine Sauder
1981	Music, Maestro, Please	Joseph I. Jopes	Emelia Frazer
1982	Fun Is	Oren Welborn	Joyce Pedersen
1983	Seventh Heaven	Dr. W. J. Bradley	Judy Coker
1984	A Child's World Of Fantasy	Brodus Krekel	Tanya Roussett
1985	Love Makes The World Go Around	Matt Marr	Joann Cassisa
1986	Happy Birthday Minerva	Dr. W. J. Bradley	Dixie Duke
1987	NO PARADE		
1988	Minerva Returns	Orlando Aloe	Joan Wilkinson
1989	All That Glitters	Elmo Jack Wilkinson	April Mellen Wiebelt
1990	Crescent City Scenes	Alexander Gerhold III	Mary Jane Collins
1991	The Best Things In Life	J. Earle Collins	Jo Ann Bowles
1992	Let's Celebrate	Chuck Guzman	Erin Krumm

MOKANA

The New Orleans-based male Krewe of Mokana, founded in 1949, paraded on the first Saturday afternoon of the parade season.

YEAR	THEME	KING	QUEEN
1969	The Realm Of Man And Flower	Sercet	Elaine Marie Orr
1970	The Tarot Revealed	Sercet	Roxanne Lee Cox
1971	Creators And Connoisseurs	Sercet	Paula Carol Krebs
1972	Gateway To Art	Sercet	Susan Elizabeth Krebs
1973	Rendezvous Avec Temps	Sercet	Barbara Rebecca Givens
1974	The Mystique Of Witchcraft	Sercet	Sarah Agnes Rumage
1975	Les Deux Mondes	Sercet	Johnnie Ann Turcich

NEFERTARI

The female Krewe of Nefertari paraded on the West Bank on the Friday night before Fat Tuesday. Nefertari's king was called Pharaoh and the club's hexagon-shaped doubloons were unique.

YEAR	THEME	PHARAOH	QUEEN
1975	Women's World		Gladys Blanda
1976	American Fashion On Parade	Bill Senter	June Brockhoeft
1977	Ladies Of Distinction	William J. Boudreaux	Debra LeBlanc
1978	Mythical Goddesses	Barry Francis Boffone	Marylyn Brener
1979	Nefertari's Travels		
1980	Musical Moods Of Nefertari	Francis Buffone	Leone Geers
1981	John J. Audubon's Bird Sanctuary	Hilton Guidry	Emma Di Pascal
1982	Jewels Of Nefertari	Ronnie Lemoine	Judy Rivero
1983	Nefertari Visits The Islands	Irving Scheffler	Linda Miller
1984	Nefertari Reminisces	Eugene Orgeron	Hedy Keating
1985	Nefertari Relives History	Dudley Dufrene Sr.	Rita Berniker
1986	Nefertari Takes A Holiday	Earl Nash	Angelle Martin
1987	Movie Hits Of Yesterday	Santo Di Pascal	Bernice Jones
1988	You're Invited To A Party	Marty Martinez	Joyce Clemens
1989	Nefertari's Favorite Books	Ernest Arthur	Tricia Gautreaux
1990	Memories Of Childhood	Glynn Paulk	Catherine Sullivan
1991	You've Come A Long Way, Baby	Nick Stipelcovich	Joyce Gauthreaux
1992	This Planet Earth	Don Joseph Gautreaux	Lea Barras
1993	Monopoly Mania	Charles Moreau	Barbara LaJaunie
1994	Nefertari's 20 Years Of Memories	Floyd Martinez	Cecilia Langford
1995	That's Entertainment	Wayne Pipken	Sandra Dugas

NEPTUNE

The Metairie, LA, based male and female Krewe of Neptune paraded on the first Monday night of the parade season.

YEAR	THEME	KING	QUEEN
1996	Neptune Travels The World	Kenneth James Laizer	Elizabeth C. Rizzuto
1997	Neptune's Feelin' Festive	Melvin LeMane	Antionette Rizzuto

NIKE

The female Krewe of Nike paraded only once, on Wednesday, February 20, 1974, in the Gretna-Belle Chase neighborhoods on the West Bank.

YEAR	THEME	KING	QUEEN
1974	Fruits Of The Earth	Charles M. Miller	Doris Miller

OCTAVIA

The female Krewe of Octavia paraded on the first Saturday night of the parade season in Gretna, LA.

YEAR	THEME	KING	QUEEN
1980	Octavia's World Of Adventures		Laura Hannan

Defunct Parading Krewes

1981	Happy Days		
1982	It's A Small World		Kay Lascala
1983	Wish Upon A Star	Hilbert J. Morvant	Kathleen Matherne
1984	Hollywood On Parade		Sandra Chauvin
1985	Feminine Rulers		Pamela Fleege
1986	Is Everyone Having Fun	Robert Murray	Ethel Slayden
1987	Vacationing In Style	Troy Reed	Mrs. Malvin Orgeron

ORION
The female Krewe of Orion paraded in New Orleans.

YEAR	THEME	KING	QUEEN
1952	Heroines Of Opera	Col. William Bannon	Secret
1953	Her Majesty's Jewels	Edward J. McCoy	Secret
1954	Favorite Fairy Tales	A. J. Bartolotta	Secret
1955	The Alphabet Around The World	Anthony Commander	Secret
1956	Leaves From Literature	Edward A. Aragon	Secret
1957	Legend Of The Flowers	Salvador Centenni Sr.	Secret

PALMARES
The predominately black, male and female Krewe of Palmares featured a Brazilian motif and self-propelled floats. The club paraded in New Orleans following Pandora & Epimetheus on the first Saturday afternoon of the parade season.

YEAR	THEME	KING	QUEEN
1985	Palmares: The Brazilian Connection		Paula Pete
1986	Palmares Goes To Brazil	Jermaine Jackson	Josie Broughton

PANDORA
The female Krewe of Pandora paraded in the New Orleans neighborhood of Gentilly on the first Saturday afternoon of the parade season through most of its tenure, before moving downtown, accepting men (Epimetheus), and briefly merging with the male Krewe of Freret.

YEAR	THEME	KING	QUEEN
1968	The Magic Box	Dr. George J. Dimitri	Dianne G. Dimitri
1969	Pandora Explores The Abyssal Realm	Dr. Dominic C. Foti Sr.	Marie V. Foti
1970	Pandora In Psychedelphia	Pascal W. Japcke	Elise S. Japcke
1971	Oriental Mystique	Alfred E. Betzer	Dolores K. Betzer
1972	Latin Charisma	Lloyd A. English Sr.	Nimber A. English
1973	Gems Extrordinaire	Burnie B. Fowler	Kathleen C. Fowler
1974	Pandora, Femme Magnifique	Salvador A. Gambino	Jacqueline G. Barrere
1975	Pandora's Phantasia	Charles L. Murray	Gayle Ann Jones
1976	Pandora's La Nouvelle Orleans	John Landry Jr.	Lisa Betzer Landry
1977	Pandora In Retrospect	Ray Armstrong	Rose M. Armstrong
1978	Favorite Fables	Dr. James B. Stafford	Doris Cox Simon
1979	Poetic Arts	T. A. Pittman	Susan Pittman
1980	Rivers Of Romance	Justin M. Mutz	Elena Lyons
1981	Rhapsody In Color	Edward Niemeyer Jr.	Sandra Ann Niemeyer
1982	Elixir Of Life	Renard J. Falcon Jr.	Frances L. Falcon
1983	Captivating Capers	Albert F. Latour	Chetta Jones Latour
1984	Lullaby Of Broadway	George W. Haas Jr.	Carolyn Teresa Haas
1985	Magnificent Monarchs	Charles M. Micele	Lisa Kay Fowler
1986	Myths And Legends	James Seghers	Michelle Seghers
1987	Fantastic Flickers	Roy Pichon	Emilda Pichon
1988	Majestic Odyssey	George J. France Jr.	Patricia F. Danflous
1989	Pandora Welcomes Epimetheus	L. Roy Bandy	Barbara Ann Richardson
1990	Pandora & Epimetheus In Big Easy	Karl Kromer	Barbara Ann Richardson
1991	Pandora & Epimeth. Melody Lingers	Brodus Krekel	Letitia Krekel
1992	Pandora & Epimeth. Recall 25 Years	JackR. Wingerter	Dorothy G. Wingerter
1993	Prodicious Profiles	Wayne L. Vicknair	Margaret C. Parta

FRERET - PANDORA

1994	Children At Play	Ed Laporte	Deborah Cutcliffe

PHOENIX
The male Krewe of Phoenix paraded in the Jefferson Parish City of Kenner on the weekend before Mardi Gras.

YEAR	THEME	KING	QUEEN
1975	The World Of Phoenix Salutes . . .		Jeanne Zeller Misuraca
1976	New Orleans Scenes		Sercet

POSEIDON
Through most of its tenure, the Krewe of Poseidon paraded in the afternoon on the West Bank in the City of Gretna, LA, on the Sunday preceding Fat Tuesday.

YEAR	THEME	KING	QUEEN
1959	Gilbert And Sullivan	Whitney J. Zeringue	Mary Lee Griffin
1960	Festivals, Customs Of Countries	Sal Scanio Jr.	Gail Pitre
1961	Oriental Wonders	Jacob Gregory	NA From Krewe
1962	Products Of Louisiana	Joseph Licciardi	Loraine Zeringue
1963	Progress Thru Years To Outer Space	Robert E. Higgins	Elmire Begovich
1964	Show Business	Sam Territo	Ranell Carpenter
1965	Merrymakers Of England	Elliott Duffourc	Rosemary Bienvenue
1966	The Recordings Of Pete Fountain	William J. Mitchell	Melanie Ann Martin
1967	International Song Book	Charles M. Miller	Diane Marie Burnam
1968	Review Of The Past Ten Years	Russel Haas	Donna Durr
1969	Aladdin And His Magic Lamp	Gillis Molaison	Kathy Banquer
1970	The World And All Its Splendor	A. J. Cambre	Gail Cambre
1971	American Holiday	Linus W. Falgout	Debbie Martin
1972	Life And Its Environments	James Billings	Rhonda Billings
1973	Our Coloring Book	Phillip Martin	Patty Jane Danos
1974	Sing America Sing	L. J. Boudreaux Sr.	April Bergeron
1975	I Love A Parade	Edmond Orgeron Jr.	Stacy Marie Rodrigue
1976	New Orleans, Queen City Of South	Lloyd F. Giardino	Tammy Ann Lowery
1977	Games Children Play	Fallon P. Martin Sr.	Sarah Marie Martin
1978	Vacationland USA	Wilbert Schieffler	Sandra Cambre
1979	Everything Beautiful From A To Z	Ridy P. Brown Sr.	Nicole Leblanc
1980	Lights, Camera, Action	Charles R. Martin	Patti Buccola
1981	Music America Loves	Leonard J. Kinler	Vicki Buccola
1982	Holidays And Celebrations	Barnette Mahler Sr.	Paula Rhodes
1983	Historical Notes And Anecdotes	Nelson J. Cantrelle Jr.	Jodie Kass
1984	Dreams And Great Expectations	William DiMarco	Cristi Capdeville
1985	Dreams Of A Mariner	Vance J. Weinberger	Cynthia Ann Richard
1986	Poseidon's Wide World Of Sports	Warren J. Richard	Mellissa Ann Richard
1987	Poseidon's Fantasy World	Gary W. Pullins	Michelle-Marie Kinler
1988	Memories Of Yesterday	L. J. Richard	Stephanie Ann Richard
1989	Poseidon's Comics And Cartoons	Nelson J. Cantrelle III	Dawn Cantrelle
1990	A Musical Note	L. Bryan Blackburn	Colleen Elaine Arden
1991	Let the Good Times Roll	P. E. Gilligan	Peggy Jo Jones
1992	Poseidon's Literary Treasures	Gregory L. Dimak	Nicole Monique Kinler
1993	Travels Are Just For The Memories	August Creppel	Kimberly Kinler Breaux
1994	Poseidon Celebrates The World	Kirk J. Toups	Nicole Monique Kinler
1995	A Little Bit Of This, Little Bit Of That	Paul Bourg	Lonnie H. Pulliss
1996	NO PARADE		
1997	Poseidon Is Buzzin'	Jay Michael Ryals Sr.	Bonnie Ann Toups
1998	40 Years Of Poseidon Adventures	James S. Barrios Jr.	Juanita Acosta Kinler
1999	Love Makes The World Go Round	Eric Keith Combetta	Ceili Rose Acosta
2000	A Little Bit Of Luck	Mickey J. Plaisance Sr.	Amanda Lynn Pahnka
2001	Poseidon Is Naturally N'Awlins	David Gassenberger Sr.	Charmaine W. Mainieri
2002	Poseidon's Wild Kingdom	Edmund B. Ott Jr.	Lisa Marie Dufrene

ROMULUS & REMUS
The male and female Krewe of Romulus & Remus paraded only once, on Fat Tuesday, March 6, 1973, in Kenner.

YEAR	THEME	KING	QUEEN
1973	Behind Every Great Man	Danny Abramowiz	None

SAMSON & DELILAH
The male and female Krewe of Samson & Delilah paraded in St. Bernard Parish on Fat Tuesday afternoon following the Krewe of Arabi.

YEAR	THEME	KING	QUEEN
1983	Things And Stories I Love	Emile E. Prattini	Patricia A. Couture
1984	Man And His World	Kenneth A. Fox	Dorothy W. Edwards
1985	Facts, Fiction, Fables	Lucien Gioe	Mrs. Lucien Gioe

SELENA
The female Krewe of Selena paraded in New Orleans East on the Saturday afternoon before Fat Tuesday.

YEAR	THEME	KING	QUEEN
1977	It's A Small Small World	Leo Sider	Susan Sider Alcantara
1978	An Invitation To A Masquerade		Jacqueline M. Goldberg
1979	Tribute To King, Long Live His Music	John Scholl	Delores Accardo
1980	Selena Salutes The Bowls	Barry Nunez	Margie Short
1981	Oh You Beautiful Doll	Captain Alvin Short	Donna Marsh
1982	Las Vegas, Its Fabulous Strip	Anthony Serio	Carol Bernard
1983	If You Believe In Magic	Dennis Turgeau	Marlene Turgeau
1984	Happy Holidays	Donald Reinecke	Alice Reinecke
1985	Selena Tours The Caribbean	Robert Jones	Mrs. Buford Joni Jones
1986	Selena's Encore	Charles Rodriguez	Diane Rodriguez

SILENUS
The male Mystic Knights of Silenus paraded on Mardi Gras eve in the Jefferson Parish City of Kenner, LA.

YEAR	THEME	KING	QUEEN
1991	A Tale Of The Brothers Grimm	Aaron Broussard	Darlene Orgeron Cox
1992	Pirates Of The Caribbean	Edward Dosan	Bridget Cuevas

SINBAD
The Metaire, LA, based male and female Krewe of Sinbad paraded on Tuesday night, one week prior to Fat Tuesday. The club's king and queen were named Sultan and Scheherazade.

YEAR	THEME	KING	QUEEN
1990	The Voyages Of Sinbad	John Meyer	Monica Abney
1991	In The Land Beyond "Beyond"	Tim Lynch	Wendy Toca
1992	Shipwrecked In The Big Easy	Rick Michot	Janea Marie Ridgley
1993	Unsolved Mysteries	Stephen Offfner	Lynn Marie Waters
1994	Sinbad's Best Sellers	Gerald Roser Sr.	Michelle Lynch
1995	Tales Of The Lamp	William Seavers	Karen Louise Falcon
1996	The Last City Of Atlantis	Lloyd Robichaux	Meredith Leigh Gay
1997	The Treasures Of Ali Baba	Bruce E. Verrette	Kelli Elizabeth Rivere
1998	Search For The Sultan	Emile Gauchet II	Jennifer Lynn Dakin

Defunct Parading Krewes

THEBES
The black Krewe of Thebes paraded only once in New Orleans, on Monday, February 20, 1995.

YEAR	THEME	KING	QUEEN
1995	Precious Jewels	Warren Dent	Yvonne Jones

TITANS
The St. Bernard Parish, male and female Krewe of Titans paraded on the Wednesday night before Fat Tuesday.

YEAR	THEME	KING	QUEEN
1983	Wednesday Night At The Movies	Melvin Guerra	Marilyn G. Costanza
1984	America Remembers	Leonard Joseph Kinler	Kimberly Ann Kinler

VENUS
The first Mardi Gras parade presented by females was staged by the Krewe of Venus in 1941 in downtown New Orleans. For more than a half-century, the club paraded on the Sunday afternoon prior to Fat Tuesday.

YEAR	THEME	KING	QUEEN
1941	Goddesses	Irwein J. G. Jansen	Mrs. William O'Hara
1942 - 45	NO PARADES — WWII		
1946	Song of Yesterday	Dr. Charles J. Stewart	Mrs. Alexander Brown
1947	Jewels	William J. Gruber	Maxine DeLatour Moore
1948	Childhood Prose And Poetry	William L. Billups	Mary Cuccia
1949	Scenes From Nature	Julius B. Prager	Mrs. William L. Billups
1950	Famous Women Of Fact And Fiction	Niels Christopher	Aleda Saunders
1951	The Distaff Side Of History	Thurston B. Martin	Mrs. Thomas Roche
1952	Enchantments Of The Forest	Oswald P. McGregor	Mrs. Michael Mellaney
1953	Masques Of The Mardi Gras	Belmont J. Sanchez	Mrs. L. S. Planche
1954	Magic Moments Of Music	Troy R. Douthit	Mrs. Belmont J. Sanchez
1955	Les Masque Du Ballet	Elton A. Cigali	Mrs. Elton A. Cigali
1956	Favorite Operas	Norveil O. Alexander	Mrs. George Frisby
1957	John James Audubon, The Naturalist	Albert Chalona	Mrs. Thelma Cox
1958	Genesis Of Carnival	Earl T. Carr	Mrs. Preston Graham
1959	Heroines Des Classiques	Roland H. Meyer Sr.	Mrs. Metry I. Sherry
1960	Women Rulers Of The World	Octave M. Courrege	Mrs. Donald Franke
1961	Mythologies Of Mankind	Charles J. Turpin Sr.	Mrs. William O'Connor
1962	Fifteen Decisive Battles Of The World	Anthony P. Robino	Mrs. Ulysses G. Auger
1963	Command Performance	Mett S. Carroll Sr.	Jo Ann Carroll
1964	Cultures Of The World	Harry P. Rosenthal	Mrs. Anthony P. Robinol
1965	The Giants Of Literature	Dr. Anthony Russo Jr.	Mary H. Vandergrift
1966	Great Love Affairs	John J. Elms Jr.	Mrs. Frank Maubberet
1967	Great Tragedies Of Literature	John J. Walsh	Mrs. Cy Warner
1968	The Sounds Of Music	Harry P. Rosenthal	Secret
1969	The God Of Mirth Visits Many Lands	Frank S. Fiasconaro Jr.	Secret
1970	Carnival Pageantry Of 19th Century	Thomas J. O'Quin	Secret
1971	Les Opera Fameuse	Raphael J. Jones III	Secret
1972	The Flickers And The Stars	Harry P. Rosenthal	Secret
1973	The Powers Behind The Thrones	Octave M. Courrege Jr.	Secret
1974	Character Sketches Fact, Fiction, Drama	L. R. Ingram Sr.	Secret
1975	Legends True And False	Roy E. Walker	Secret
1976	Femmes Fatales In Espionage	David M, Goldberg	Secret
1977	China Revisted	William G. Keneker Jr.	Secret
1978	A Medley Of Operettas	Thomas C. Brandt	Secret
1979	Anniversaries And Their Symbols	Leon Gary Zoller	Secret
1980	Venus Toasts Tradition	Dr. Irving Sheen	Secret
1981	Tales Of Love, Fact And Fiction	Clifton E. Majoue	Secret
1982	Celebrations Of The World	Jacob R. Glaser	Secret
1983	Kingdoms & Fantasy Kingdoms	Edward Giroir	Secret
1984	Discover Italy	Sam Nicholas	Secret
1985	Myths And Legends	James F. Carson	Secret
1986	Celebrates 45 Sparkling Years	Henry Cunningham III	Secret
1987	Twentieth Century Women In Arts	Michael A. Pisciotta	Secret
1988	Love Transformed	Ralph F. White	Secret
1989	Women Who Changed The World	Roland H. Meyer	Secret
1990	Queens Of The Air	Michael Martinolich Jr.	Secret
1991	Legends In Gold	Philip S. Sunseri	Secret
1992	Famous Women Of New Orleans	Dr. Melvin J. Lescale	Secret

VIKINGS OF TYR
The male Vikings of Tyr paraded in St. Bernard Parish on the Wednesday night prior to Fat Tuesday. The club featured top-flight celebrities as its king, which it called "Odin".

YEAR	THEME	ODIN	QUEEN
1972	The Viking Age	Lief Erickson	Mrs. Alex Palama
1973	Great Conquerors	Peter Graves	None
1974	Famous Stories, Legends & Tales	Robert Reed	Doris D. Vincenti
1975	Great Battles Of History	McLean Stevenson	None

VULCAN
The male and female Krewe of Vulcan staged only one parade, on Tuesday, February 6, 1986 on the West Bank in Marrero.

YEAR	THEME	KING	QUEEN
1986	Vulcan's Debut To Mardi Gras	Jay E. Boyd	Kim Berggren

Queens of Oldest Active Ball Krewes

TWELFTH NIGHT REVELERS
Carnival's second oldest organization—the Twelfth Night Revelers—are so named because their annual ball is set for January 6, the religious feast day of the Epiphany, the 12th day of Christmas. TNR presented Carnival's first queen (1871), staged six parades during the 19th Century and uses a king cake to select its queen.

YEAR	QUEEN
1870	None
1871	Emma Butler
1872	Ada Bringier
1873	Mary Zacharie
1874	Louise Chiapella
1875	NO CELEBRATION
1876	Ada Bringier
1877	NO CELEBRATION
1879 - 83	NO CELEBRATION
1884	Alice Herndon
1885	Blanche Moulton
1886	NO CELEBRATION
1887	Leila Bohn
1888	NO CELEBRATION
1889, 90	King's Own Royal Guard replaced TNR and escorted Rex
1891	Nina Bisland
1892	Josephine Maginnis
1893	Louise Minor
1894	Fanny Eshleman
1895	Nora Glenny
1896	Mary Burton Hayward
1897	Lydia Winship
1898	Julia Palfrey
1899	Linda Miles
1900	Evelyn Penn
1901	Elise Richardson
1902	Louise McMillan
1903	Alice Stauffer
1904	Warrene Tutt
1905	Jessie Wisdom
1906	Edith Libby
1907	Gertrude Monroe
1908	Ruth Bush
1909	Laura Hobson
1910	Carrie Walmsley
1911	Sadie Downman
1912	Mary Elise Whitney
1913	Josephine Janvier
1914	Elizabeth Clarke
1915	Adele Ziegler
1916	Dorothy Sharp
1917	Mittie Clark
1918 - 19	NO CELEBRATION — WWI
1920	Lucille O'Kelley
1920	Marcelle Vallon
1920	Mary Virginia Perkins
1921	Dorothy Clay
1922	Emily Cook
1923	Maude Fox
1924	Minette Black
1925	Elizabeth O'Kelley
1926	Henryetta Bayle
1927	Frances Kittredge
1928	Eliska Tobin
1929	Gladys Hopkins
1930	Maude Butterworth
1931	Gwendelyn Baldwin
1932	Lorraine LaCour
1933	Mary Francis Buck
1934	Marigayle Hopkins
1935	Barbara Bouden
1936	Augusta Walmsley
1937	Jessie Wing Janvier
1938	Kathleen Eshleman
1939	Charlotte Hardie
1940	Sara Louise McLellan
1941	Mary Madison Ziegler
1942	Abby Orme Jackson — no ball
1943	Marie G. Souchon — no ball
1944	Suzanne Jones — no ball
1945	Nathalie Crumb — no ball
1946	Ruth Provosty
1947	Dorothy Henriette Vallon
1948	Lucile Bernard
1949	Brenda Moore
1950	Katherine Legendre
1951	Jean Huger
1952	Jane Bright
1953	Adelaide Wisdom
1954	Isabel Swoop Nott
1955	Arthe Walmsley
1956	Elise Marie Lapeyre
1957	Patricia Willoughby Burke
1958	Jackeen Kelleher
1959	Courtney-Anne Sarpy
1960	Judith Kemble Walshe
1961	Jeannette Limerick Bartlett
1962	Kate Adair Halsey
1963	Ann S. Wisdom
1964	Courtney Manard
1965	Ellenor Roger Clay
1966	Kathleen Maginnis
1967	Suzanne LaCour Wilkins
1968	Elizabeth Cromwell Maunsell
1969	Patricia Strachan
1970	Kay Jardine Hardie
1971	Arthemise B. Baldwin
1972	Ann Hastings Hobson
1973	Lynne Agnes Favrot
1974	Anne Cameron Kock
1975	Nancy E. Nolan
1976	Catherine Cook Flower
1977	Helen Eileen Eshleman
1978	Eugenie Elizabeth Huger
1979	Marie Louise Minor Barry
1980	Julia McCall Waters
1981	Charlotte Clayton Robinson
1982	Sidonie Scott Read
1983	Elaine F. Jones
1984	Courtney Bartlett Churchill
1985	Jacqueline L. Provosty
1986	Elizabeth Meredith Suthon
1987	Katherine McCall Whann
1988	Marie Louise Claiborne Perrilliat
1989	Eleanor Winship Bernard
1990	Elise Claiborne Lapeyre
1991	Sally Dart Hughes
1992	Jane Hayward Alpaugh
1993	Jane Blakemore Howard
1994	Anne Juden Sarpy
1995	Sara Evans Schmidt
1996	Susan Mary Hamilton
1997	Whitney Louise Eastman
1998	Celeste Claire Flower
1999	Elizabeth Lee Jahncke
2000	Elizabeth Flower Saer
2001	Charlotte Hardie Haygood
2002	Lindsey Ewing Powell
2003	Mary Rushton Dickson

ATLANTEANS
Named after the mythical sunken city, the god Poseidon has reigned over the elaborate tableau ball of the Atlanteans since its first presentation in 1891, entitled *The Lost Antilles*. Alice Roosevelt, daughter of future President Teddy Roosevelt, attended the 1901 Atlanteans ball.

YEAR	QUEEN
1891	Adele Blanc
1892	Lucia Miltenberger
1893	Annie C. Payne
1894	Evelyn Gasquet
1895	Nelie Dwyer

Queens of Oldest Active Ball Krewes

Year	Queen
1896	Penelope Chaffe
1897	Amelie Behn
1898	Erskine Kock
1899	Mary Matthews
1900	Nora Glenny
1901	Nora McLean
1902	Evelyn Krumbhaar
1903	Alice Monroe
1904	Cora Stanton
1905	Alice Miller
1906	Emma Grima
1907	Lucie Claiborne
1908	Gladys Fenner
1909	Maude Eustis
1910	Agnes T. George
1911	Katherine Legendre
1912	Marie Elise Whitney
1913	Marjorie Bobb
1914	Odile Lapeyre
1915	NO BALL
1916	Betty Bradford Wilkinson
1917	Mathilde Baldwin
1918 - 20	NO CELEBRATIONS — WWI
1921	Laura Kearny
1922	Marguerite Mason-Smith
1923	Nell Kearny
1924	Edwa Stewart
1925	Corinne Robin
1926	Emily Craig
1927	Helen McLellan
1928	Betty Watson
1929	Ethel Jane Westfeldt
1930	Myldred Plauche
1931	Adele Townsend Jahncke
1932	Alice Blanc Logan
1933	Mettha Westfeldt
1934	Virginia Logan
1935	Carolyn Gay
1936	Pamela Robinson
1937	Jane Cary George
1938	Malcolm M. Tullis
1939	Marjorie Leverich
1940	Gifford Glenny
1941	Anne Eshleman
1942	Elizabeth Mason-Smith — no ball
1943 - 45	NO CELEBRATIONS — WWII
1946	Anne R. Clark
1947	Alice P. Glenny
1948	Katherine Lucile Bernard
1949	Brenda Moore
1950	Virginia McConnell
1951	Mary Elizabeth Wisdom — no ball
1952	Emilie Lapeyre
1953	Penelope A. Fox
1954	Myldred Roberta Landry
1955	Eveline Gasquet Fenner
1956	Mathilde Bernard Villere
1957	Suzanne Penick
1958	Diana Bleecker Monroe
1959	Marcia Milling Monroe
1960	Stella Evans Farwell
1961	Catherine Reiss
1962	Regina Aglaé Soniat
1963	Ann Stuart Wisdom
1964	Courtney Claiborne Manard
1965	Susan Davidson
1966	Kathleen Maginnis
1967	Anne Brandon McIlhenny
1968	Penelope Eaves
1969	Helen Moore Sims
1970	Jean Louise McIlhenny
1971	Susalee Belser Norris
1972	Catherine Packard Williams
1973	Anne Ray Montgomery
1974	Katharine Adair Ewin
1975	Anne Beresford Fox
1976	Mary Neilson Watters
1977	Helen Eileen Eshleman
1978	Lydia Butler Williams
1979	Paula Hughes Murphy
1980	Yvette Eskrigge Young
1981	Penelope Adair Brown
1982	Susan Terrell Wolfe
1983	Lowell Davis Simmons
1984	Courtney Bartlett Churchill
1985	Barbara Crosby Bell
1986	Eleanor Terhune Ballard
1987	Sara Labouisse
1988	Eleanor Winship Bernard
1989	Anne Stuart Flower
1990	Rachel Beaird Tullis
1991	Miriam Crusel Wogan
1992	Darnell Kerr Preaus
1993	Cassandra Mitchell McIlhenny
1994	Margaret Timony Villeré
1995	Felicity Summerlin Strachan
1996	Virginia Logan Howcott
1997	Lady Catherine Reiss
1998	Elizabeth Grehan Poitevent
1999	Katharine McIlhenny Gardiner
2000	Ashley Lynn Phillips
2001	Stephanie McCampbell Claverie
2002	Adair Smith-Lupo Monroe Williams
2003	Virginia Zatarain Logan

ORIGINAL ILLINOIS

In 1895, former Chicago resident Wiley Knight formed Knight's School of Dancing in New Orleans and organized the Illinois Club, the first Carnival club for African Americans. Annual highlights of the ball are the introduction of debutantes and a father-daughter minuet-style dance called the "Chicago Glide."

YEAR	QUEEN
1895	Louise Fortier
1896 - 1929	NOT AVAILABLE FROM CLUB
1930	Alfretta Porter
1931	Dorothy M. Antonie
1932	Ruth Leona White
1933	Alvona Dorothy Keller
1934	NO CELEBRATION
1935	Lois Evelyn Green
1936	Doris Gaynell Taylor
1937	Dolores Andrea Baranco
1938	Bernice Marie Antoine
1939	Melba Theresa Baranco
1940	Julia Barbara Mitchell
1941	Dee Ione Geraldine Bowers
1942 - 45	NO CELEBRATIONS — WWII
1946	Mildred Badie
1947	Arthe C. Perrault
1948	Maxine Strange
1949	Genevieve Martin Bowles
1950	Beverly-Anna Baranco Avery
1951	NA From Krewe
1952	Jeannette Earline Stevens
1953	Shirley Antoine
1954	Evelyn L. Baranco
1955	Yvonne Amelie Denson
1956	Loma Linda Adams
1957	NA From Krewe
1958	Vera-Anna Imelda Baranco
1959	Selena Lilly Duncan
1960	Lennie Marie Davidson
1961	NA From Krewe
1962	Vivian Miranda Baranco
1963	Rogerwene E. Duncan
1964	NA From Krewe
1965	Joan Duplynn Rhodes
1966	Cynthia Marie Marshall
1967	Connie Ray Floyd
1968	Ann Marie Robinson
1969	Jewell Marie Tate
1970	Darlene Ann Barbarin
1971	Hermine Celeste Crump
1972	Maryellen Geri Harris
1973	Belva Marie Misshore
1974	Quivander Venice Magee
1975	Carla Vance Franklin
1976	Dorothy Denise Handy
1977	Gina Maria Eugere Rachal
1978	Cheryl Hyacinth Della Bowers
1979	Gabrielle Monique Turner
1980	Angela Celeste Baranco
1981	Anna Isabella Henry
1982	Kelli Danette Moorehead
1983	Richele Alvis Thomas
1984	Kayrya Adraiene Hutcherson
1985	Katherine Barbara Willard
1986	Yvette Marie Carter
1987	Evelyn Virginia Baranco
1988	Shelita Maria Cannon
1989	Lucille Alfonya Glin
1990	Erika René Turner
1991	Rogerwene C. Washington
1992	Roshawn Anitra Blunt
1993	Caneka Fawn Webb
1994	Amy Elizabeth Bryan
1995	Cassandra Katherine Gilyard
1996	Kinitra Brooks
1997	Janell Rose Batiste
1998	Shavon Theresa Charlot
1999	Brittany Evan Bailey
2000	Nicole Michelle Roberts
2001	Renata Marie Heim
2002	Cincia Liana Brooks
2003	Tiffany Karen Thomas

ELVES OF OBERON

The Elves entered the Carnival scene in 1895. With characters such as Oberon, Titania, and Puck, the mischievous Elves have always featured a dash of whimsy in their presentations. In 1930, the Elves of Oberon presented the first ball ever held at the New Orleans Municipal Auditorium.

YEAR	QUEEN
1895	Josphine Craig
1896	Virginia Logan
1897	Edith Buckner
1898	Louise Denis
1899	Connie Von Meysenbug
1900	Haydee Druilhet
1901	Louise Rainey
1902	Amelie Claiborne
1903	Elsie O'Connor
1904	Pauline Curran
1905	Stella Hayward
1906	Alba Beauregard
1907	Ruth Bush
1908	Eunice Williams
1909	Laura Merrick
1910	Polly Gordon
1911	Yvonne Stouse
1912	Adele Monroe
1913	Laura Hall
1914	Edith Clark
1915	Dorothy Spencer
1916	Inez Lucille Ellis
1917	Veva Penick
1918 - 21	NO CELEBRATIONS — WWI
1922	Bertha Manson
1923	Juanita Gelpi
1924	Margaret Fayssoux
1925	Elizabeth O'Kelley
1926	Katharine Williams
1927	Corinne Coyle
1928	Mildred Avegno
1929	Felicie Waguespack
1930	Anita M. Nolan
1931	Jane Bassett Hayward
1932	Betty Felder
1933	Stella Hebert
1934	Kitty Minor Logan
1935	Lydia Phillips
1936	Gladys Elizabeth Martin
1937	Jessie Wing Janvier
1938	Belen Wiltz Wagner
1939	Betsy Bourne Hackett
1940	Jane Audrey Read
1941	Cecile Airey Parker
1942	Corinne A. Eshleman
1943 - 45	NO CELEBRATIONS — WWII
1946	Betty Favrot Read
1947	Beverly Ann Favrot
1948	Yvonne Brown
1949	Marie Elise Amoss
1950	Carol Saunders
1951	Avery McLoughlin
1952	Deirdre Gibbons Burke
1953	Cynthia Wuerpel Rainold
1954	Lowell Landry
1955	Marietta Sinclair Moyer
1956	Carey Jean McLean
1957	Mettha Kathryn Eshleman
1958	Cynthia Ann Church
1959	Barbara Shields Breckinridge
1960	Jane Sanford
1961	Mary Ann McLellan
1962	Marguerite Anne Avegno
1963	Sally Lockett Chapman
1964	Ann Barrett Kennedy
1965	Martha Augusta Eshleman
1966	Kathleen Ford Boylan
1967	Meredith Turner Janvier
1968	M'Adele Scott Read
1969	Nicette Louise Gensler
1970	Kate Minor Eustis
1971	Julie St. Paul
1972	Julia Penn Mehurin
1973	Sally Chapman Westervelt
1974	Sidney St. John Eshleman
1975	Barbara Ann Geary
1976	Catherine Cunningham Barry
1977	Louise Grant Poitevent
1978	Mary Brooks Soulé Allen
1979	Eugenie Manget Lyman
1980	Mary Hamilton Chaffe
1981	Odette Henican McIntyre
1982	Adele Dugué Webster
1983	Marie Elizabeth Livaudais
1984	Mary Elizabeth V. Ives
1985	Susan Owen Hardtner
1986	Eleanor Eaton McClendon
1987	Katherine McCall Whann
1988	Elizabeth Marshall Breckinridge
1989	Katherine Glennon Hanemann
1990	Margaret Tomlinson Favrot
1991	Anne Campbell Rapier
1992	Patricia Brousseau Hardin
1993	Eleanor Shelby Burke
1994	Emily Inez Gautier Lapeyre
1995	Elizabeth Kendall Goodier
1996	Mary Margaret Burke
1997	Sarah Jackson Corder
1998	Isabel Teissier Strong
1999	Anne Teague Landis
2000	Marcelle Elise d'Aquin
2001	Lee Logan Charbonnet
2002	Mary Bache Kostmayer
2003	Elizabeth Kepper Brown

NEREUS

The sea god Nereus is the namesake of Carnival's ninth oldest krewe, founded in 1896. The club's one and only parade holds the distinction of being the only one whose float bodies were constructed on street cars. Logistical problems plagued the krewe but Nereus made Carnival history with its electric parade in 1900.

YEAR	QUEEN
1896	May Van Benthuysen
1897	Alys Laroussini
1898	Annie Soria
1899	Ethel Miller
1900	Maud Wilmot
1901	Alice Posey
1902	Martha Gasquet
1903	Corinne Marquez
1904	Mary Hosmer
1905	Vertilee Stanton
1906	Betty Werlein
1907	Nina Webster
1908	Anita Olivier
1909	Fannie Jackson
1910	Anina Legendre
1911	Louise Laplace
1912	Haydee Michel
1913	Anna Monot
1914	Margaret Thomas
1915	Edith Dart
1916	Emily Percival Douglas
1917	Cyril Collister
1918 - 22	NO CELEBRATIONS — WWI
1923	Nita LeGardeur
1924	Margaret Mae Moss
1925	Marjorie Ward
1926	Henryetta Bayle
1927	Lucy Mae Rainold
1928	Marcelle Coyle
1929	Louise Georgette Tusson
1930	Anita Nolan
1931	Kathleen Denechaud
1932	Rosa Freeman
1933	Mildred Porteous
1934	Jane Louise Grunewald
1935	Rosary Nix
1936	Irene Marrero
1937	Mary Kernan Dart
1938	Zelime Testart
1939	Eleanor Carrere
1940	Patricia Woodward
1941	Althea Huey
1942 - 45	NO CELEBRATIONS — WWII
1946	Katherine Laird
1947	Eva Stuart Voelker
1948	Janet Ann Northrop
1949	Eve Camille Butterworth
1950	Mary Brooks Soule
1951	Yvonne Anne Lacroix
1952	Helen Messick

Queens of Oldest Active Ball Krewes

Year	Queen
1953	Emily Percival Lang
1954	Janet Stella Sitges
1955	Elizabeth Carson Fox
1956	Nancy Weaks Trousdale
1957	Janet Elise Boisfontaine
1958	Lynn Kathryn Hammett
1959	Carolyn Marie Rowley
1960	Florence May Macdonald
1961	Ann Saunders Porteous
1962	Judith Ann Kelleher
1963	Mary Badger Marrero
1964	Nancy Elizabeth Story Kuhn
1965	Jean Dusenbury Culver
1966	Ann Marie Rowley
1967	Lucia Jacqueline Villere
1968	Elizabeth Dyer Eustis
1969	Ann Margaret Diaz
1970	Dale Marie Dane
1971	Martha Joanne Fromherz
1972	Eve Dibert Hammett
1973	Lisette Ann Charbonnet
1974	Kathleen Virginia Bohn
1975	Elizabeth Ann Pedrick
1976	Mary Satchie Snellings
1977	Anne Helena Delery
1978	Mary Broooks Soule Allen
1979	Catherine Margaret Cobb
1980	Mary Anderson Mackie
1981	Adrienne Gage Hammer
1982	Lizette Mary St. Paul
1983	Elizabeth Sumner Counce
1984	Charrette Marie Boogaerts
1985	Suzanne Elizabeth Schmitt
1986	Constance Sharp Cobb
1987	Jane Chambers Kelly
1988	Debra Jean Renandin
1989	Holly Marie Kuebel
1990	Helen Grant Jahncke
1991	Colleen Colton Eustis
1992	Margaret Maddix Kessels
1993	Genevieve Marie Hartel
1994	Gretchen Patricia Schonberg
1995	Mary Elise Lange
1996	Tricia Denise Schonberg
1997	Ashley Cowand Schonberg
1998	Ainslie Claire Blanke
1999	Heather Marie Redmann
2000	Emily Lacour Guiza
2001	Julie Roe Gambel
2002	Marion Dabney Landis
2003	Clare Colton

HIGH PRIESTS OF MITHRAS

The last Carnival krewe founded in the 19th Century is named for the exalted worshippers of Mithras, the mighty god of light in Persian mythology. The organization's first twenty-one tableaux balls were staged at the famed French Opera House on Bourbon Street which burned down in 1919.

YEAR	QUEEN
1897	Louise Joubert
1898	Marietta Wiltz
1899	Corinne Braughn
1900	Sophia Rogers
1901	Louise Cook
1902	Beatrice Gilmore
1903	Helen West
1904	May Norman
1905	Flora Sanders
1906	Mignon Goodrich
1907	Marguerite Maginnis
1908	Elise Hinderman
1909	Kate Nott
1910	Hilda Phelps
1911	Marion Monroe
1912	Lillian Urquhart
1913	Phillis Bush
1914	Margaret Montgomery
1915	Adela Pratt
1916	Alice Vairin
1917	Mildred Bobb
1918 -19	NO CELEBRATIONS — WWI
1920	Mabel Stouse
1921	Marguerite Larue
1922	Marion Souchon
1923	Corinne Hopkins
1924	Minette Black
1925	Alice Grima
1926	Noel Halsey
1927	Sedley Hayward
1928	Ethel Rea
1929	Gladys Hopkins
1930	Marjorie Brown
1931	Katherine Wolfe
1932	Katherine Turner
1933	Virginia Gore
1934	Nellie Sinclair
1935	Mildred Pratt
1936	Lenora McLellan
1937	Helen Simpson
1938	Marie Ella Gore
1939	Charlotte Hardie
1940	Helen Meyers
1941	Mary Sinclair
1942	Eleanor Pratt
1943 - 45	NO CELEBRATIONS — WWII
1946	Edith Helen Field
1947	Mary Margaret Todd
1948	Carol Black
1949	Joan Favrot
1950	Phoebe Helene de la Houssaye
1951	Ann Simpson
1952	Lelia Caron Lawson
1953	Virginia Meriwether
1954	Arthé Beardsley
1955	Vivian Gelpi
1956	Louise Marie Legendre
1957	Constance Wilbourn Carriere
1958	Marilyn Simpson
1959	Lolita Kahle Gelpi
1960	Paulette De La Vergne
1961	Lady Helen Hardy
1962	Linda Woods
1963	Mary Ellis Carrere
1964	Mary Madison Dickson
1965	Cecile LeBesque Grace
1966	Barbara Levert
1967	Mary Laura Ferry
1968	Elizabeth Cromwell Maunsell
1969	Edith Vail Smith
1970	Kay Jardine Hardie
1971	Sylvia Josephine Young
1972	Josephine Elizabeth Collins
1973	Margaret Lykes Carrere
1974	Corinne Lapeyre Barry
1975	Rand Riviere
1976	Shelley Rainold Hammond
1977	Sally Polk Huger
1978	Martha Bain Robinson
1979	Elaine Staed Finley
1980	Leslie Henican McIntyre
1981	Elise Charlotte Urquhart
1982	Susan Peters Bans
1983	Elaine Freidrichs Jones
1984	Joan Walet Hartson
1985	Catherine Pearce Butts
1986	Susan Penick Lane
1987	Tracey Noel Johnson
1988	Elise Leone Johnson
1989	Marilee Baker Keenan
1990	Elizabeth McGee Lane
1991	Helen Elizabeth Read
1992	Mary Hollis Wrighton
1993	Carolyn Bateman Hennesy
1994	Ashley Baldwin Leary
1995	Eleanor Maxwell Conway
1996	Catherine Barrett Downing
1997	Jane McCloskey Rapier
1998	Dorothy Wood Sarpy
1999	Mary Katherine Hardin
2000	Catherine Gordon Todd
2001	Margaret Blair Jacob
2002	Keenan Elizabeth Carrere
2003	Constance Airey Parker

OLYMPIANS

As an extension of the Youth Literary Society, founded in 1899, the Krewe of Olympians debuted in 1904. The club fell into abeyance from 1918-1934, but returned in 1935 and quickly became a member of Carnival's most prominent ball societies. Ball themes are usually topical and humorous.

YEAR	QUEEN
1904	Isabel Queen Homes
1905	Lolita Kahle
1906	Ellen P. Wilson
1907	Soline Delvaille
1908	Cora Spearing
1909	Marcelle Desporte
1910	Pocahontas Hendren
1911	Marie Theard
1912	Verna M. Pursell
1913	Marie Rouen
1914	Mary Jane Harrison
1915	Elizabeth Wisner
1916	Edvige Tiblier
1917	Beatrice Moulton
1918 - 34	ACTIVITIES SUSPENDED
1935	Etta Lou Elder
1936	Violet Grace Benedict
1937	Emma Marie Couret
1938	Zelime Marie Testart
1939	Eleanor Marie Carrere
1940	Jeanne Catherine Brown
1941	Helen Ann Charbonnet
1942	Mary Anna Rivet
1942 - 45	NO CELEBRATIONS — WWII
1946	Audrey M. Merritt
1947	Elaine Marie deVerges
1948	Elise Rita Charbonnet
1949	Lillian Marie Forstall
1950	Jean Marie Meric
1951	Effie Marie Stockton
1952	Marianna Belle Flowers
1953	Marie Minette Ferrier
1954	Janet Stella Sitges
1955	Mary Edna Clark
1956	Dorothy Plauché Rucker
1957	Marilyn Biddle Murphy
1958	Elizabeth Freret Hartson
1959	Dianne Mary Douglass
1960	Marion Clare McEnerny
1961	Leanne Marie Willoz
1962	Marion Merritt Blass
1963	Violet Benedict Collins
1964	Jeanne de Lery Capdevielle
1965	Rosemary Anne Charbonnet
1966	Margaret Couret Norman
1967	Mary Clare McEnerny
1968	Joan Biddle Murphy
1969	Michele Ann Tiblier
1970	Cheryl Ann Schafer
1971	Elizabeth Hughes Freret Luke
1972	Marguerite Louise Adams
1973	Lisette Ann Charbonnet
1974	Paulette Ann Charbonnet
1975	Leila Ann Thomas
1976	Ninette Marie Charbonnet
1977	Kim Marie De Sonier
1978	Michelle Putnam Nicaud
1979	Lizette Forstall St. Martin
1980	Alice Marie Charbonnet
1981	Cynthia Ann Schafer
1982	Holley Denechaud Hartson
1983	Nathalie Magdalene Forstall
1984	Elise Kempff Nicaud
1985	Enid Biddle Murphy
1986	Martha Close Borgman
1987	Holly Ann Nicaud
1988	Anne-Marie Rose Dardis
1989	Lisa Jane Sarrat D'Amour
1990	Katherine Elizabeth Harang
1991	Charlotte Adele Glas
1992	Stephanie Lee Sarrat
1993	Suzanne Bouchere Dardis
1994	Sally Ann Sewell
1995	Elizabeth Donovan Charbonnet
1996	Nicole Marie Charbonnet
1997	Julie Michel Sarrat
1998	Alison Jeanne Mouledoux
1999	Virginia Kelly Dunn
2000	Judith Margaret Barnes
2001	Lynne Elizabeth Dardis
2002	Jessica Renee Forstall
2003	Laura Durand Pennebaker

ATHENIANS

Athena was the goddess of wisdom and patroness of liberal arts. Carnival history was made by the Athenians at the 1933 ball. With the theme *King Solomon Receives Her Majesty, The Queen Of Sheba, And Kings, Queens, And Rulers Of All Nations In His Golden Palace In Jerusalem*, Athenians featured ten queens in its tableaux.

YEAR	QUEEN
1910 - 12	NO COURT
1913	Lucille Dugue Baker
1914	Katherine Kearny
1915	Marie Mason
1916	Anna Louise Cabrera
1917	Dorothy Mortimer
1918 - 21	NO CELEBRATIONS — WWI
1922	Mildred O'Connor
1923	Estelle Flaspoller
1924	Dorothy Gibbons
1925	Audrey Butler
1926	Lynn Robinson
1927	Elizabeth Westerfield
1928	Maud Werner
1929	Beecye Casanas
1930	Maud Butterworth
1931	Elizabeth Parker
1932	Margaret Henriques
1933	Cecile Airey
	Olga Nolan
	Gertrude Jahncke
	Lorraine Nalty
	Anne Green
	Juanita Perrin
	Brent Wickliffe
	Mildred Porteous
	Julia Hardin
	Alice Parker
1934	Mollie Hodges
1935	Murray Pearce
1936	Lynne Hecht
1937	Katherine Nolan
1938	Eugenie Lorrance Williams
1939	Elizabeth Claiborne Matthews
1940	Ellen Hewes Floweree
1941	Lucie Claiborne
1942 - 45	NO CELEBRATIONS — WWII
1946	Jeanne Watters
1947	Evelyn Ann Hodges
1948	Yvonne Claiborne
1949	Claire de la Vergne
1950	Susan Percy Hyams
1951	Laura Sussdorff — no ball
1952	Maureen Grundy
1953	Hanton de la Houssaye
1954	Gladys Gelpi McCarroll
1955	Arthe Marie Walmsley
1956	Joan Maude Glover
1957	Alice Elizabeth Duffy
1958	Donna Ann Odom
1959	Susan Ruth Kittredge
1960	Laura Jane Owens
1961	Eleanor May Tolbert
1962	Elizabeth Tyler Ball
1963	Sally Ann Kittredge
1964	Sheila Anne Richardson
1965	Patricia Ann McCarroll
1966	Ella Smith Montgomery
1967	Diane Elizabeth Alldredge
1968	Sandra Evelyn Salmen
1969	Deborah Gail Cromwell
1970	Stephanie Ellen Carter
1971	Lisette Katherine Verlander
1972	Rosalie Elizabeth Johness
1973	Janet Mathilde Andry
1974	Constance Claire Carrere
1975	Mary Hyland Brown
1976	Elizabeth Ann Lurry
1977	Diane Ellender Stall
1978	Catherine Christ Clerc
1979	Majorie Seibert Lurry
1980	Cecile Bertel Hyde
1981	Carol Anne Maddox
1982	Joyce Mary Delery
1983	Laura Elizabeth Hobson
1984	Adelaide Mackie Lautenschlaeger
1985	Margaret Lynn Bernhard
1986	Elizabeth Ann Caraway
1987	Mary Ashley Smith
1988	Elise Daniel Charbonnet
1989	Elizabeth Alma Slatten
1990	Elizabeth Cressend Schonberg
1991	Carol Eleanor Salassi
1992	Merriman Rebecca Powell
1993	Stacey Ann Colfry
1994	Courtenay Cate Graham
1995	Kristen Karlson Schonberg
1996	Georgia Gentry White
1997	Agatha Marie Fuller Roth
1998	Suzanne Elizabeth Alford
1999	Ashley Elizabeth Shreves
2000	Elise Springer Guidry
2001	Elizabeth Bolton Hassinger
2002	Bonnie Ann Cahoon
2003	Holly Elizabeth Wynne Verlander

African-American Ball Krewes of the Past and Present

African-American organizations that present Carnival balls have traditionally received little publicity in the mainstream media. This list, which is not comprehensive, was compiled primarily from the files of *The Louisiana Weekly*, 1925-2001, from *Sepia Mardi Gras* magazine, 1955, and *Tan Mardi Gras* magazine, 1972 and 1975 editions.

Aurelius Zuluranians
Aurora's Social & Pleasure Club
Autocrat Carnival Circle
Azaleas Club
B-Sharp Music Club
Bali Sports Social & Pleasure Club
Beau Brummell Club
Black Men of Labor Club
Black Pirates
Blooming Lillies Social & Pleasure Club
Blue Bird Sewing Circle
Blue Dahlia Social & Pleasure Club
Bon Temps
Boueno Damos Club
Breakfast Club
Bulls Aid Social & Pleasure Club
Bunch Club
C. C. Claver Club
Capetowners
Carnation Social & Pleasure Club
Carnival Tea-Flint Goodridge Hosptial
Charmettes Social Club
Children's Carnival Ball
Cotillion Social & Pleasure Club
Country Club Sports Social & Pleasure
Crescent City Claver Club
Crescent Jewels
Cuban Queens Carnival Club
Delta Sigma
Dilly Dally Social Club
Dukes of Winsor Social & Pleasure
Dunbars Social & Pleasure Club
Dunbar Aid & Pleasure Club
Echelons of '59 Social & Pleasure Club
El Diablos
Elite Sugar Babes
Elks
Eltros Social & Pleasure Club
Emeralds Social & Pleasure Club
Epicureans Club, Inc.
Esquires
Exclusive Ladies
Exclusive 20's Club
Exclusive Socialites Carnival Club
Exotic Ladies Social & Pleasure Club
Famous "G" Social & Pleasure Club
Fashionettes Gay Ball
Fine Arts Study Club
Fisher Mardi Gras Club

Friendly 12's Carnival Club
Four Roses
Gaiety Sewing Club
Gardenia Stitch & Chat Club
Gay Ladies
Gay Twenties
Gay 25's Social & Pleasure Club
Gaylords Ball
Girl Friends, Inc.
Golden Leaf Art & Rhythm Club
Golden Rods Social & Pleasure Club
Happy 20's Social & Pleasure Club
Hardettes
Hawkettes Carnival Club
Hi-Low Bidders Bicentennial Carnival
Imperial Bridge Club
J. L. L. Club
J. P .O.'s Social & Pleasure Club
Jet Set
Jewel Box Girls
Jolly Boys (also paraded in 1930s)
Joy Hawks
Juniorettes
Just Us Men Social & Pleasure Club
Kelly Stars Club
Kings & Queens Club
Klassy Kut Up Klub
Krewe of Aida
Krewe of Nefertiti
Krewe of Petronius
Krewe of Ramses Inc.
Ladies 38 Art & Charity Club
Ladies Bazaar
Ladies & Gents of Principle
Ladies Nites of Joy
Lady's Jolly Bunch Second Line Club
Lady Stars Social & Pleasure Club
Lady Southsiders Social & Pleasure
Las Companeras
Las Senoras Elegantes
Leisure Hour Embroidery Club
Les Ami Tou Jours
Les Beaux Modern Social & Pleasure
Les Dames Extraordinaires
Les Ecolier's Club
Les Equinois Club
Les Femmes Enchantress Club
Les Jeunes Femmes Club
Les Mesdames Mode

Les Toujour Ari
Local Union 169 Carnival Club
Lords & Ladies
Los Compenaris
Los Jovenes Senoras Autocrat Club
Luthurettes
Lyons Club
Madam Moiselle Sewing Circle
Majestic Club
Marchneil
Marigold Sewing Circle
Matadors Social & Pleasure Club
Merrymakers Autocrat Club
Mignonettes Social Club
Mikado Club
Millionaires Bridge Club
Modern Matrons Sewing Club
Modernettes
Modest Maidens
NAACP Youth Council Carnival Club
N. B. K.'s Club
New Orleans Creole Fiesta Club
Nile Queen
Nineteen Socialites Carnival Club
NOLA Whist & Pleasure Club
NOMTOC (The Jugs Social Club)
Orchettes
Orchid Girls
Original Dukes Club, Inc.
Original Exclusive 20's Social & Pleasure
Original Four Roses
Original Illinois Club
Original Ladies Bazaar Club
Original Les Equinois Club
Original Mikado Club, Inc.
Original Moderns
Original Smart Set Social & Pleasure
Original Stitch & Chat Club
Original Twenties
Original White Swans Social & Pleasure
Orleanians Club
Orleans Ladies
Paragon Club
Pink Carnation Club
P. L. C.'s
Phyllis Wheatly Club
Plantation Revelers Club
Popular Pals
Progressive Social & Pleasure Club

Psychedelics
Quartermen Club
Rainbow Social & Pleasure Club
Revolution Club
Rhinestones
Rosebud Art Club
Royal Aces
Royal 25 Club
Royalettes
2nd Movement Carnival & Social Club
S D C's
Sharks Social & Pleasure Club
Sigma Gamma Phi Carnival Tea
Silhouettes Social & Pleasure Club
Silver Swans
Smart Set Club
Social Hour Sewing Circle
Society of Social Celebrities
Society of Social Circle
Sophisticated 20s Social & Pleasure Club
Soulful Lites
Sportsmen Club
Stand Together Club
Stevenson's Academy of Hair Design
Straight Business School Carnival Club
Swans Club of Kenner
T T W Social Club
Tenawan
T G F's
The Bali Sports Social & Pleasure Club
Theta Rho
Toasts of the Vikings
Toujour Moi Social Club
Townsman
Twelve Regulars Social & Pleasure Club
Vagabonds
Vikings Krewe, Inc.
Vogue Sewing Club
Westside Revelers
Whiste
White Swan Ball
Winsomettes
Wonderful Boys Carnival Circle
Young Lady's 23 Club
Young Men Illinois
Young Men Orleanians
Young Men's 22 Social & Pleasure Club
Young Men's Twenty Club, Inc.
Zulu Social Aid & Pleasure Club

Mardi Gras Indians

Since at least 1884, African-Americans have masked as Indians and participated in Mardi Gras. The black Mardi Gras Indians are celebrated and cherished in New Orleans. The craftsmanship displayed by the men who design and create the magnificent Indian outfits (called suits) has earned worldwide praise. The chants the Indians sing have been the subject of study and the source of commercial success in the recording industry (*Big Chief*; *Jock-A-Mo*; *Iko, Iko*).

As with conventional Carnival clubs, the Indians have their own hierarchy. The groups are called tribes or gangs, and they are overseen by the leader who is called the Chief, or Big Chief. The Spy Boy's job is to scout for other Indian tribes and to report to the Flag Boy, who relays the message to the Chief.

Practice sessions are held, normally on Sunday evenings in taverns or nightclubs. On Fat Tuesday, Indians limit their activities to African-American neighborhoods. Customarily, they do not follow a prearranged route. The best reference book is *Mardi Gras Indians* by Michael P. Smith, Pelican Publishing, Gretna, LA in 1994.

In addition to their Mardi Gras appearances, the Indians march on the evening of St. Joseph's Day (March 19), and on Super Sunday, scheduled the third week in March.

This is a partial list of prominent tribes of the past and present.

Apache Hunters
Black Eagles
Black Feather
Blackfoot Hunters
Black Hawk Warriors
Carrollton Hunters
Cheyenne Hunters
Commanche Hunters
Creole Osceola
Creole Wild West
Diamond Stars
Eastern Cherokee
Eight Bad Men

Fi Ya Ya
Flaming Arrows
Geronimo Hunters
Golden Arrows
Golden Blades
Golden Eagles
Golden Sioux
Golden Star Hunters
Guardians of the Flame
Mandingo Warriors
Morning Star Hunters
Mohawk Hunters
Ninth Ward Hunters

Original Yellow Jackets
Red Frontier Hunters
Red, White and Blue
Second Ward Hunters
Seminole Hunters
Seminole Warriors
Seventh Ward Hunters
Seventh Ward Warriors
Shabke Hunters
The Hundred and One
Third Ward Terrors
Troubled Nation
White Cloud Hunters

White Comanche Hunters
White Eagles
Wild Apache
Wild Bogocheetus
Wild Magnolias
Wild Soua-tou-las
Wild Tchoupitoulas
Wild Treme
Young Brave Hunters
Young Cheyenne Hunters
Young Guardians of the Flames
Young Monogram Hunters
Yellow Jackets
Yellow Pocahontas

Walking Clubs

The Marching or Walking Clubs of New Orleans date from the mid-1880s. The Jefferson City Buzzards, founded in 1890, are the oldest surviving group. These small clubs usually march in front of, or in the middle of Mardi Gras parades. Brass bands sometimes accompany the walking clubs whose members hand out paper flowers in exchange for kisses.

Big Fifty Social Club of Gretna
Broad Street Carnival & Pleasure Clubs
Broadway Swells
Bwana Marching Club
Charlie's Saints Marching Club
Cleary Marching Club
Corner Club
Deep South Marching Club
Delachaise Carnival Club
Elenore Club
Frankie Brent's Chalice Club
Garden District Carnival Club
Jan Jans
Jefferson City Buzzards
Jefferson Royals
Kenner Trojans Marching Club
Lamplighter Club
Liberty & Chrysanthemum Social Clubs
Lyons Club
Marching Fools
Military Order of Cooties
Mistic Nites of JUMA
Mixed Breeds Carnival Club
Mondo Kayo
New Era Club
Original West Side Carnival Club
Peggy Landry's Silk Stocking Club
Pete Fountain's Half-Fast Walking Club
Sardonyn
Shady Ladies Marching Club
Silver Leaf Club
Sixth District Carnival Club
Sons of Rest
St. Flips
St. Roch Minstrel Club
Sultans of Swing
Tafluma Marching Club
Terrace Corner Marching Club
Tulane Pleasure Club
Turnbull Social & Carnival Club
Wampy Wamps
Westbank Marching Club
Winning Hand Social Club
Zele's
Zig Zag Marching Club

Active Krewes with Most Parades

More than 100 krewes have staged more than 2,300 Mardi Gras parades in New Orleans since Comus introduced the concept of themed processions with floats and maskers in 1857. The top 10 active clubs are:

	Krewe	Number of Parades
1.	Rex	122
2.	Proteus	97
3.	Zulu	82
4.	Carrollton	72
5.	Alla	64
6.	Mid-City	63
7.	Hermes	61
8.	Babylon	56
9.	Grela	56
10.	Thoth	56

Krewe Name Derivation

Since 1857, Carnival organizations in New Orleans have taken their titles from a variety of sources. This list includes krewes that paraded in 2003.

GREEK MYTHOLOGY
Aphrodite   Argus   Atlas
Bacchus   Chaos   Endymion
Hermes   Iris   Morpheus
Muses   Okeanos   Orpheus
Pegasus   Poseidon   Proteus
Pygmalion   Rhea   Ulysses
Zeus

ROMAN MYTHOLOGY
Adonis   Mercury   Saturn

EGYPTIAN MYTHOLOGY
Isis   Thoth

ARABIAN MYTHOLOGY
Aladdin

NORDIC MYTHOLOGY
Thor

AFRICAN MYTHOLOGY
Oshun

HISTORICAL FIGURES/GROUPS
Caesar   Centurions Cleopatra
Druids   Gladiators Napoleon
Pontchartrain   Zulu

NEIGHBORHOODS
Alla (Algiers, Louisiana)
Carrollton
Grela (Gretna, Louisiana)
Mid-City

ANCIENT CITIES
Babylon   Sparta

LITERARY CHARACTERS/ICONS
Bards   Excalibur
King Arthur   Tucks

FOREIGN WORDS
Aquila   d'Etat   Rex

MYTHICAL KINGDOM
Shangri-La

ACRONYM
NOMTOC
(New Orleans' Most Talked Of Club)

Truck Parades Past and Present

Organized truck parades have been a part of the New Orleans Carnival since 1935 when Chris Valley formed the Elks Orleanians. The group claimed the world's longest parade in 1973 with a 181-truck procession.

Krewe	Founding Date
Crescent City	1947
Elks Gretna	1983 - 2001
Elks Jeffersonians	1984
Elks Orleanians	1935
Krewe of Jefferson	1982
Krewe of St. Bernard	1975 - 1985

Parade Theme Categories

In 1997, the **Crescent City Doubloon Traders Club** published a list that detailed parade themes as they appeared on doubloons minted from 1960-1997. The top twenty-five theme categories, and the number of times they were used were:

175	Literature and Books
128	Music and Dance
108	Famous People
105	Anniversaries and Intros
83	Travel and Vacations
83	Dreams and Memories
78	New Orleans Area
70	Nature and Science
63	Movies
60	Mythology and Folklore
60	Mardi Gras, Masking & Parties
53	Holidays and Festivals
47	Rivers and Waters
42	American History
36	Broadway
35	Birds and Animals
33	Children and Toys
32	History and Landmarks
29	Magic and Mystical
27	World History
22	Louisiana History
20	Gambling and Games
20	Food and Drink
20	Flowers and Plants

Oldest Active Parading Krewes

First Parade	Krewe
1872	Rex
1882	Proteus
1915	Zulu
1924	Carrollton
1933	Alla
1934	Mid-City
1935	Elks Orleanians
1937	Hermes
1940	Babylon
1946	Choctaw
1947	Crescent City
1948	Grela
1948	Thoth
1950	Okeanos
1958	Zeus
1959	Iris
1959	Poseidon
1966	Pegasus
1967	Endymion
1969	Bacchus

Kiddie Parades Past and Present

In 1934 the Krewe of NOR (New Orleans Romance) provided the first opportunity for youngsters to participate in a Mardi Gras parade. Of the half-dozen children's clubs, only **Little Rascals**, founded in 1983, surived into the 21st Century.

Krewe	Founding/Ending Dates
NOR	1934-1949
Sprites	1968-1978
NOLAMISS	1972-1975
Pan	1972-1978
Oz	1981-1984

Little Rascals Themes & Royalty

The members of the **Krewe of Little Rascals** are boys and girls, ages 5 to 16. Named after Hollywood's most famous kids' group, the organization was founded in 1983 and is sponsored by the **Metairie Children's Carnival Club**. The Little Rascals pattern themselves after adult Carnival groups. Each year the krewe not only stages a parade, but also holds a ball at the Pontchartrain Center to which the public is invited.

YEAR	THEME
1983	Little Rascals Go To The Circus
1984	Salute Pets From Around The World
1985	Salute Space Adventures
1986	Little Rascals Love A Parade
1987	Things That Go Bump In The Night
1988	Laissez Les Bon Temps Rouler
1989	Little Rascals Read The Classics
1990	Little Rascals Do The French Quarter
1991	Little Rascals Salute Broadway
1992	A Dream Come True
1993	Celebrate Music, Music, Music
1994	Little Rascals Sports Odyssey
1995	Salutes Friends In Uniform
1996	Little Rascals Go To College
1997	Pride In Our Past, Faith In Our Future
1998	Little Rascals Around The World
1999	One Moment In Time
2000	Little Rascals Cajun Odyssey
2001	Proud To Be An American
2002	Salute The Louisiana Purchase
2003	Little Rascals Go Texan

YEAR	KING	QUEEN
1983	Trey Prats III	Jennifer Lowenherz
1984	Lewis Lemoine	Heather Munoz
1985	Joe Eurissa	Rebecca Bodenheimer
1986	Lance Cory	Tammy Juster
1987	Derek Schroeder	Beth Schroeder
1988	Jack G. Spittler Jr.	Sasha Cabrera
1989	Chad Pitfield	Mallory Messina
1990	Michael Guillot	Temi Mabe
1991	Casey Crouch	Amanda Avery
1992	Anthony Cox	Rachel Kay Spittler
1993	Brett Hancock	Mickal Gass
1994	Steven Michel	Allison Copeland
1995	Kavan Donegan	Christina Theriot
1996	Mark Berluchaux	Lesley Callahan
1997	Chris Cooke	Crystal Cabrera
1998	Matthew Cooke	Sarah Ricks
1999	Colin Berthelot	Christina Comeaux
2000	Peter Zuppardo II	Robyn Freeze
2001	Kieran Donegan	Rachael Trosclair
2002	Matt Zuppardo	Kaitlyn Pittfield
2003	Jared Hall	Vanessa Gale

LITTLE RASCALS' CAPTAINS

Jack G. Spittler Jr.
Rachel Kay Spittler
Rachel Kay Spittler, Anthony Cox
Crystal Cabrera
Rachel Kay Spittler, Crystal Cabrera
Matthew D. Cooke
Rachel Kay Spittler
Jared Hall, Vanessa Gale
Amanda Rose Tinkle,
    Jonathan Blake Tinkle

Past and Present Ball Krewes and their Founding Dates

Through the years, hundreds of Carnival organizations have come and gone, and records do not survive for many of them. This list includes many prominent krewes of the past and present.

Achaeans	1949	Iridis	1930
Achilles	1962	Janus	1949
Adonis	1948	Junior League of New Orleans	1935
Alexis	1973	Krewe of Agape Carnival Club	1991
Alhambra	1947	Krewe of Hades/Heralds	1967
Alpheus	1948	Lady Gardenias	1938
Amphictyons	1903	Late Night Revelers	1979
Ancient Scribes	1958	Les Marionnettes	1928
Anubis	1955	Les Mysterieuses	1896
Aparomest	1935	Les Papillions Sociaux	1981
Apollo	1929	Les Pierrettes	1946
Artemis	1970	Lord of Misrule	1922
Artemisians	1911	Lourdes	1948
Athenians	1910	Loyal Order of the Moose	1890
Atlanteans	1891	Maids of Troy	1948
Bal Masque	1950	Midas	1951
Bourbon Street Bounders	1919	Mithras	1897
Caliphs of Cairo	1937	Mittens	1901
Camen	1973	Moslem	1935
Caputanians	1951	Musica	1940
Carnival Revelers	1922	Mystery	1912
Caronis	1949	Mystic Club	1923
Carthage	1948	Naiads	1949
Children's Carnival Club	1926	Nemesis	1953
Cliquer's Club	1981	Neophermenos/Newcomers	1953
Consus	1897	Nereus	1896
Cynthius	1947	Niobeans	1946
David	1985	Nippon	1914
Disciples of Thespis	1874	Noblads	1937
Dorians	1938	Olympians	1903
Druids	1897	Olympus	1971
Electra	1889	Omardz	1936
Empyreans	1904	Orpheus	1938
Elenians	1936	Osiris	1916
Elves of Oberon	1895	Past Masters	1980
Epicureans	1947	Pericles	1948
Eros	1936	Phunny Phorty Phellows	1878
Eurydice	1941	Prince Charming	1981
Falstaffians	1900	Prometheus	1939
Fantasy	1945	Prophets of Persia	1927
Follies	1921	Ramses	1990
Friars	1948	Royal Dynamic's Social & Civic Club	1987
Grand Duke Alexis	1924	Royal Street Rounders	1949
Growlers	1882	Saint Bernard Jubilees	1970
Harlequins	1925	Sonians	1939
Harmony Club	1896	Squires	1963
Hebe	1949	Theron	1948
Helena	1955	Titanians	1914
Hera	1949	Twelfth Night Revelers	1870
Hypatians	1935	Uhuru Social Club	1984
Imperial Reception of Alexis	1970	Virgilians	1939
Independent Order of the Moon	1881	Yami	1911
Indra	1917	Young Men's Hebrew Association	1900

Oldest Active Non-Parading Krewes

In the history of Carnival, more than 150 organizations have presented balls. Of those that lasted into the 21st Century, here are the oldest krewes and their founding dates.

1857	Mistick Krewe of Comus
1870	Twelfth Night Revelers
1872	Knights of Momus
1891	Atlanteans
1895	Illinois Club
1895	Elves of Oberon
1896	Nereus
1897	Mithras
1903	Olympians
1910	Athenians
1912	Mystery
1916	Osiris
1923	Mystic Club
1925	Harlequins
1926	Young Men Illinois
1927	Prophets of Persia
1928	Les Marionnettes
1935	Moslem
1936	Eros
1937	Caliphs of Cairo

Gay Carnival Clubs

The first gay Carnival Club, the Krewe of Yuga, was founded in 1959, but did not present its first official ball until 1962. The St. Bernard Cultural Center was the home of most gay balls in the 1970s and 1980s. Later, most krewes moved to the Municipal Auditorium and opened admission to the general public.

Amon-Ra	1967
Armeinius	1969
Celestial Knights	1976
Dasimé	
Dirty Dottie	c1980
Ganymede	1968
Ishtar	1981
Krewe of David	1984
Lords of Leather	1984
Memphis	1976
MKA (Apollo)	1970
Olympus	c1970
Perseus (New Orleans)	
Petronius	1962
Phoenix	c1973
Polyphemus	1982
Satin & Sequins	c1975
Satyricon	2003
Yuga	1959
Vista	1982

Mardi Gras Collectibles

Mardi Gras has generated its own unique ephemera. Paper collectibles from the festivities generally fall into three categories: (1) those produced by the organizations that stage the public parades and private balls; (2) those produced by New Orleans businesses involved in Mardi Gras; and (3) commercially produced items associated with the annual celebration.

Since 1857 when the first official parade was held, more than 2,500 Mardi Gras processions have rolled during the Carnival season in New Orleans. An incredible 7,500 balls have also been presented. Original watercolor renderings of each float, costume and tableau ball setting were created before the finished product was executed by local artisans.

During the period 1874-1941, entire parades were commemorated by a series of giant broadsides called "Carnival Bulletins." These chromolithographs measure 48" x 28" and depict all of the floats in each parade. Engraved invitations, admit cards, dance cards, and programs accompanied each Carnival ball. In the early years, many of these die-cut pieces were produced in Paris. Those that have survived the damp New Orleans climate stand as a testament to the high art of color lithography from the late-19th Century.

The most collectible paper items are krewe specific and include:

Carnival Bulletins	ball invitations
ball programs	ball dance cards
ball admit cards	costume plates
commemorative publications	float plates

Mardi Gras Archives

For a complete list of archival sources, see http://nutrias.org/gnoa/mgguide/contents.htm. The city's most extensive collections of Mardi Gras memorabilia are housed in the following institutions:

Louisiana State Museum
751 Chartres St., NOLA 70116
504-568-6968

Special Collections Howard Tilton Memorial Library
Tulane University
6823 St. Charles Avenue. NOLA 70118
504-865-5643

Historic New Orleans Collection
533 Royal Street, NOLA 70130
504 523-4662

New Orleans Public Library
219 Loyola Avenue, NOLA 70112
504-596-2610

On Display

Mardi Gras memorabilia is on permanent display at:

Louisiana State Museum
751 Chartres, NOLA 70116
504-568-6968

Treasure Chest Mardi Gras Museum
4213 Williams Blvd., Kenner, LA 70062
504-468-7231

Blaine Kern's Mardi Gras World
233 Newton St., NOLA 70114
504-361-7821

Carnival Celebrity Guests

ARGUS
- 1975 Barbara Eden
- 1976 Kay Starr
- 1977 Phyllis Diller
- 1978 Shirley Jones
- 1979 Cathy Lee Crosby
- 1980 Connie Stevens
- 1981 Loretta Swit
- 1982 Dianne Ladd
- 1983 Shari Lewis
- 1984 Lee Meredith

ASHANTI
- 1994 Harold Sylvester

BACCHUS
- 1969 Danny Kaye
- 1970 Raymond Burr
- 1971 Jim Nabors
- 1972 Phil Harris
- 1973 Bob Hope
- 1974 Glenn Campbell
- 1975 Jackie Gleason
- 1976 Perry Como
- 1977 Henry Winkler
- 1978 Ed McMahon
- 1979 Ron Howard
- 1980 Pete Fountain
- 1981 Marine Sgt. J. McKeel Jr. (Hostage in Iran)
- 1982 Dom Delouise
- 1983 Charlton Heston
- 1984 Kirk Douglas
- 1985 Lorne Green
- 1986 John Ritter
- 1987 William Shatner
- 1988 Alan Thicke
- 1989 Billy Crystal
- 1990 Dennis Quaid
- 1991 Steve Guttenberg
- 1992 Gerald McRaney
- 1993 Harry Connick Jr.
- 1994 Claude Van Damme
- 1995 John Larroquette
- 1996 Dick Clark
- 1997 Tom Arnold
- 1998 Drew Carey
- 1999 Jim Belushi
- 2000 Luke Perry
- 2001 Larry King
- 2002 Nicolas Cage
- 2003 Jon Lovitz

BARDS OF BOHEMIA
- 1984 Rudy Vallee
- 1985 David Wolper, Tommy Walker
- 1988 Marguerite Piazza
- 1989 Ross Hunter, Lionel Hampton, JoAnne Worley, Lee Meriwether, Nancy Sinatra
- 1991 Brad Edelman
- 1992 Harry Blackstone Jr., Marguerite Piazza, Mrs. Rudy Vallee, Johnny Mann
- 1993 Dr. Joyce Brothers
- 1994 Rhonda Shear, Carol Connors
- 1995 Charlene Tilton
- 1996 Frankie Laine, Ben Vereen
- 1997 Harry Blackstone Jr.
- 1999 Brad Little
- 2000 Emeril Lagasse

CAESAR
- 1987 Billy Martin
- 1988 Patricia Brant (Miss LA)
- 1989 Mickey & Minnie Mouse, Roger Rabbit
- 1990 Teenage Mutant Ninja Turtles
- 1991 Garfield & Odie
- 1992 Snoopy & Peanuts
- 1993 Bugs Bunny
- 1994 Will Clark
- 1995 Weird Al Jankovic, Flintstones
- 1996 Power Rangers, NFL Quarterbacks
- 1997 Cast of "Star Trek Deep Space Nine"
- 1998 Batman, Robin & Riddler
- 1999 Rug Rats
- 2000 WCW Wrestlers, Nitro Girls
- 2001 Blues Clues
- 2002 Animaniacs
- 2003 Wild Thornberries

ELKS ORLEANIANS
- 1951 Hopalong Cassidy

ENDYMION
- 1974 Doc Severinsen
- 1975 Dyan Cannon, Bobby Vinton
- 1976 Alice Cooper, Wolfman Jack, Jerry Vale
- 1977 Gino Vanelli, Penny Marshall, Cindy Williams, Vikki Carr
- 1978 Cheryl Ladd, Wayne Newton, Fats Domino
- 1979 Charo, K.C. & Sunshine
- 1980 Engelbert Humperdink
- 1981 Neil Sedaka, Suzanne Somers
- 1982 Captain & Tennille, Kool & Gang
- 1983 Lou Rawls, Crystal Gayle, Kool & Gang, Doc Severinsen
- 1984 Tom Jones, Kool & Gang, Fats Domino, Doc Severinsen
- 1985 Wayne Newton, Fats Domino, Melissa Manchester
- 1986 Paul Anka
- 1987 Kirk Cameron, Jeremy Miller, Tracey Gold,
- 1988 Dolly Parton, Heather Locklear, Roy Orbison Smokey Robinson, Spuds McKenzie, Miami Sound
- 1989 Fred Savage, Hall & Oates
- 1990 John Goodman, Chicago, Four Tops
- 1991 Ken Olin, Patricia Wettig
- 1992 Ken Rogers, Patrick Duffy
- 1993 Steven Seagal, Beach Boys
- 1994 Stephen Stills, Jeannie Cooper, Corbin Bernsen Frankie Valli
- 1995 Chuck Norris, Huey Lewis, K.C. & Sunshine, Richard Karn
- 1996 Kool & Gang, Johnathan Silverman, Donna Summer
- 1997 David Schwimmer
- 1998 Jerry Springer, Jack Wagner, Ian Ziering, K.C. & Sunshine Band
- 1999 Emeril Lagasse
- 2000 Britney Spears
- 2001 Frankie Muniz
- 2002 Jason Alexander
- 2003 Aaron Carter

GLADIATORS
- 1974 George Blanda
- 1975 Kenny Stabler
- 1976 Johnny Bench
- 1977 Bert Jones
- 1978 Joe Ferguson
- 1979 Ray Guy
- 1980 Norris Weese
- 1981 Billy Kilmer
- 1982 Sonny Jurgenson
- 1983 Danny Abramowiz
- 1984 Archie Manning
- 1985 Richard Todd
- 1986 Brian Hansen
- 1987 Morten Anderson
- 1989 Will Clark
- 1990 Stan Brock
- 1991 Gil Fenerty
- 1992 John Tice
- 1993 Tommy Barnhardt
- 1994 Rich Mauti
- 1995 Jerry Pellegrini
- 1996 Tom Dempsey
- 1997 Bobby April
- 1998 Brett Bech
- 1999 John Fourcade
- 2000 Ron Swoboda

GRELA
- 1998 Milton Berle
- 1999 Rick Springfield
- 2000 Sammy Kershaw

HESTIA
- 1977 Telly Savalas, Billy Carter
- 1978 George Peppard

HESTIA/MECCA
- 1979 Frankie Avalon
- 1980 James Darren

JUNO
- 1980 Ferlin Husky

LITTLE RASCALS
- 1993 Spanky McFarland

MECCA
- 1977 Evel Kneivel
- 1978 Ernest Borgnine

MERCURY
- 1988 Gary Pucket
- 1989 Shadoe Stevens
- 1990 Alan Autry, David Hart
- 1991 Michael Morrison, Jon Hensley, Andy Kavovit
- 1992 Macy & Thorne

NAPOLEON
- 1981 Andy Gibb
- 1982 Dr. John

OCTAVIA
- 1988 Jermaine Jackson

ORPHEUS
- 1994 Little Richard, Vanessa Williams, Dan Aykroyd
- 1995 David Copperfield, Delta Burke, James Brown
- 1996 Jay Thomas
- 1997 Quincy Jones, Better Than Ezra
- 1998 Stevie Wonder
- 1999 Sandra Bullock
- 2000 Whoopi Goldberg
- 2001 Whoopi, Glenn Close
- 2002 New York Fire & Police
- 2003 Travis Tritt

PALMARES
- 1986 Jermaine Jackson

PONTCHARTRAIN
- 1976 Red Buttons
- 1988 Will Clark
- 1991 Allen Toussaint
- 1992 Bart Simpson

SINBAD
- 1990 Archie Manning

THOR
- 1979 Louis Nye
- 1980 Marty Allen
- 1981 San Diego Chicken
- 1982 Boog Powell
- 1983 Eddie Mekka

TUCKS
- 1982 Rita Coolidge
- 1983 John Candy
- 1986 Larry Bud Melman

VIKINGS
- 1972 Leif Erikson
- 1973 Peter Graves
- 1974 Robert Reed
- 1975 McLean Stevenson

ZEUS
- 1977 Bob Cummings
- 1978 Johnny Rusk
- 1979 Pat O'Brien
- 1980 Dick Clark
- 1981 Buddy Hackett
- 1982 Sandi Duncan

ZULU
- 1949 Louis Armstrong
- 1980 Woody Herman
- 2003 Spike Lee

Same Name, Different Krewes

With just so many mythological figures from which to choose, it is not surprising that different Carnival organizations have sometimes chosen the same deity as their namesakes. In most cases, a new group has adopted the name of a defunct club. The one exception is the Krewe of Orpheus which is used by both a Mandeville club (started in 1987) and by a New Orleans krewe, chartered in 1994. Others to share names were:

Adonis	Aphrodite
Apollo	Argonauts
Bacchus	Diana
Druids	Jupiter
Pandora	Ulysees
Vulcan	

Foreign Language Mottoes

Several krewes have mottoes which they imprint on their doubloons and other official merchandise. Eight such clubs that feature foreign language sayings are:

Caesar — *Vini, Vidi, Vinci* — I came, I saw, I conquered

Comus — *Sic Volo, Sic Jubeo* — As I will it, there will be joy

d'Etat — *Vivite Ut Veitatis, Vehatis Ut Vivatis* — Live to Ride, Ride to Live

Mid-City — *Pour La Joie De Vivre* — For the joy of living

Momus — *Dum Vivimus, Vivamus* — While we live, let us live!

Rex — *Pro Bono Publico* — For the public good

Rhea — *Magna Mater* — Great Mother

Saturn — *In Horam Vivere* — Live for the Moment

Royal Oddities

This list features solo rulers and those with special nomenclature for their krewe royalty:

Aladdin	King Aladdin, Queen Jasmine
Alla	Maharajah & Maharanee
Babylon	King called Sargon
Bacchus	Bacchus is a god, no queen
Caesar	Emperor & Empress
Chaos	No queen
Choctaw	Chief, Princess
Cleopatra	No king
d'Etat	King called Dictator, no queen
Druids	King called Arch Druid, no queen
Gladiators	Caesar and Empress
King Arthur	King Arthur & Guinevere
Muses	No king or queen
Napoleon	Emperor & Josephine
Orpheus	No king or queen
Oshun	King called Shango
Proteus	Proteus is a god
Rex	Rex means king
Ulysses	Ulysses & Penelope

Doubloon Kings

According to statistics compiled by Jamie Montgomery for the *Crescent City Doubloon Traders Swapper's Guide*, some 128 New Orleans area parading krewes struck a total of 17,411 doubloons in various colors, thicknesses and materials, from 1960 through 2003. The top ten clubs in terms of doubloon production are:

Krewe	Types Minted
Thoth	580
Bacchus	549
Zulu	520
Iris	457
Alla	454
Endymion	413
Carrollton	397
Rex	375
Shangri-La	357
Mid-City	352

Parade Components

In 2002, the *Mardi Gras Guide* published a quantitative analysis of Mardi Gras parades held in a three-parish area the preceding year.

Parades	53
Floats	1,061
Trucks	326
Marching Bands	588
Jazz/Brass Bands	66
Dance/Marching Groups	226
Drill Teams/ROTC/Color Guards	111
Shriner Units	93
Equestrian Units	151
Captains/Riding Lieutenants	187
Convertibles/Antique Cars	193
Flambeaux/Flares	191
Radio Station Vehicles	75
Police/Fire/Medical	137
Service Vehicles	220
Miscellaneous Units	95
TOTAL UNITS	3,773

Float Builders/Designers

Since the 1950s, Blaine Kern has been the preeminent float builder in New Orleans. Other companies include Cantrell & Son, the Barth Brothers, Louis Masset, Royal Artists, and Henri Schindler. During the first part of the 20th Century, Soulie & Crassons, and later, the Deutschmann Brothers also produced floats.

Many artists have designed parades through the years. Among the most prominent pre-WWII designers were Jennie Wilde, Ceneilla Alexander, Carlotta Bonnecaze, Charles Briton, Bror Wikstrom, Leda Plauche, and Louis Fischer.

Economic Impact

Since 1977, economist Dr. James McLain has published an annual study of the effects Carnival has on the economy of New Orleans.

Year	Millions	Year	Millions
1986	$239.2	1994	$660.0
1987	$275.3	1995	$929.1
1988	$309.6	1996	$810.6
1989	$330.6	1997	$800.8
1990	$487.9	1998	$840.7
1991	$499.1	1999	$956.9
1992	$579.9	2000	$1,056.0
1993	$567.7		

Sponsoring Organizations

Parading krewes are chartered as non-profit organizations. The corporate names are often different from the public krewe names. Some of the more interesting titles are:

Alla
Great Golden Gryphon Society

Aquila
Eagles' Nest, Inc.

Bards of Bohemia
Paidia Club, Inc.

Caesar
Roma Club

Centurions
Harahan - RiverRidge Carnival Club Association

Ancient Druids
Golden Acorn Society

Hermes
Semreh Club

Napoleon
Cohorts Civic League, Inc.

NOMTOC
Jugs Society

Okeanos
Sonaeko Club

Pegasus
Victory Club

Proteus
Crescent Club

Rex
School of Design

Rhea
Greek Goddess Social Club

Shangri-La
Kaly Nickta

Sparta
Spartan Society

Zeus
Metairie Carnival Club

St. Tammany Parades

On the northshore of New Orleans, parades are annually staged in the cities of Covington, Mandeville, and Slidell.

Krewe	Founding date
Slidellians	1960
Olympia	1966
Perseus	1970
Troy	1984-2000
Dionysus	1985
Eve	1986
Orpheus	1987
Selene	1997
Flora	1988-2000
Millennium	2002

Mardi Gras Dates By Year

Year	Day	Year	Day	Year	Day
1857	Feb. 24	1929	Feb. 12	2001	Feb. 27
1858	Feb. 16	1930	Mar. 4	2002	Feb. 12
1859	Mar. 8	1931	Feb. 17	2003	Mar. 4
1860	Feb. 21	1932	Feb. 9	2004	Feb. 24
1861	Feb. 12	1933	Feb. 28	2005	Feb. 8
1862	Mar. 4	1934	Feb. 13	2006	Feb. 28
1863	Feb. 17	1935	Mar. 5	2007	Feb. 20
1864	Feb. 9	1936	Feb. 25	2008	Feb. 5
1865	Feb. 28	1937	Feb. 9	2009	Feb. 24
1866	Feb. 18	1938	Mar. 1	2010	Feb. 16
1867	Mar. 5	1939	Feb. 21	2011	Mar. 8
1868	Feb. 25	1940	Feb. 6	2012	Feb. 21
1869	Feb. 9	1941	Feb. 25	2013	Feb. 12
1870	Mar. 1	1942	Feb. 17	2014	Mar. 4
1871	Feb. 21	1943	Mar. 9	2015	Feb. 17
1872	Feb. 13	1944	Feb. 22	2016	Feb. 9
1873	Feb. 25	1945	Feb. 13	2017	Feb. 28
1874	Feb. 17	1946	Mar. 5	2018	Feb. 13
1875	Feb. 9	1947	Feb. 18	2019	Mar. 5
1876	Feb. 29	1948	Feb. 10	2020	Feb. 25
1877	Feb. 13	1949	Mar. 1	2021	Feb. 16
1878	Mar. 5	1950	Feb. 21	2022	Mar. 1
1879	Feb. 25	1951	Feb. 6	2023	Feb. 21
1880	Feb. 10	1952	Feb. 26	2024	Feb. 13
1881	Mar. 1	1953	Feb. 17	2025	Mar. 4
1882	Feb. 21	1954	Mar. 2	2026	Feb. 17
1883	Feb. 6	1955	Feb. 22	2027	Feb. 9
1884	Feb. 26	1956	Feb. 14	2028	Feb. 29
1885	Feb. 17	1957	Mar. 5	2029	Feb. 13
1886	Mar. 9	1958	Feb. 18	2030	Mar. 5
1887	Feb. 22	1959	Feb. 10	2031	Feb. 25
1888	Feb. 14	1960	Mar. 1	2032	Feb. 10
1889	Mar. 5	1961	Feb. 14	2033	Mar. 1
1890	Feb. 18	1962	Mar. 6	2034	Feb. 21
1891	Feb. 10	1963	Feb. 26	2035	Feb. 6
1892	Mar. 1	1964	Feb. 11	2036	Feb. 26
1893	Feb. 14	1965	Mar. 2	2037	Feb. 17
1894	Feb. 6	1966	Feb. 22	2038	Mar. 9
1895	Feb. 26	1967	Feb. 7	2039	Feb. 22
1896	Feb. 18	1968	Feb. 27	2040	Feb. 14
1897	Mar. 2	1969	Feb. 18	2041	Mar. 5
1898	Feb. 22	1970	Feb. 10	2042	Feb. 18
1899	Feb. 14	1971	Feb. 23	2043	Feb. 10
1900	Feb. 27	1972	Feb. 15	2044	Mar. 1
1901	Feb. 19	1973	Mar. 6	2045	Feb. 21
1902	Feb. 11	1974	Feb. 26	2046	Feb. 6
1903	Feb. 24	1975	Feb. 11	2047	Feb. 26
1904	Feb. 16	1976	Mar. 2	2048	Feb. 18
1905	Mar. 7	1977	Feb. 22	2049	Mar. 2
1906	Feb. 27	1978	Feb. 6	2050	Feb. 22
1907	Feb. 12	1979	Feb. 27	2051	Feb. 14
1908	Mar. 3	1980	Feb. 19	2052	Mar. 5
1909	Feb. 23	1981	Mar. 3	2053	Feb. 18
1910	Feb. 8	1982	Feb. 23	2054	Feb. 10
1911	Feb. 28	1983	Feb. 15	2055	Mar. 2
1912	Feb. 20	1984	Mar. 6	2056	Feb. 15
1913	Feb. 4	1985	Feb. 19	2057	Mar. 6
1914	Feb. 24	1986	Feb. 11	2058	Feb. 26
1915	Feb. 16	1987	Mar. 3	2059	Feb. 11
1916	Mar. 7	1988	Feb. 16	2060	Mar. 2
1917	Feb. 20	1989	Feb. 7	2061	Feb. 22
1918	Feb. 12	1990	Feb. 27	2062	Feb. 7
1919	Mar. 4	1991	Feb. 12	2063	Feb. 27
1920	Feb. 17	1992	Mar. 3	2064	Feb. 19
1921	Feb. 8	1993	Feb. 23	2065	Feb. 10
1922	Feb. 28	1994	Feb. 15	2066	Feb. 23
1923	Feb. 13	1995	Feb. 28	2067	Feb. 15
1924	Mar. 4	1996	Feb. 20	2068	Mar. 6
1925	Feb. 24	1997	Feb. 11	2069	Feb. 27
1926	Feb. 16	1998	Feb. 24	2070	Feb. 11
1927	Mar. 1	1999	Feb. 16	2071	Mar. 3
1928	Feb. 21	2000	Mar. 7	2072	Feb. 23

Mardi Gras Dates By Day

1857 - 2003

Times	Date	Year
0	Feb. 3	
1	Feb. 4	1913
0	Feb. 5	
4	Feb. 6	1883, 1894, 1940, 1951
3	Feb. 7	1967, 1978, 1989
2	Feb. 8	1910, 1921
5	Feb. 9	1864, 1869, 1875, 1932, 1937
5	Feb. 10	1880, 1891, 1948, 1959, 1970
5	Feb. 11	1902, 1964, 1975, 1986, 1997
6	Feb. 12	1861, 1907, 1918, 1929, 1991, 2002
6	Feb. 13	1866, 1872, 1877, 1923, 1934, 1945
5	Feb. 14	1888, 1893, 1899, 1956, 1961
3	Feb. 15	1972, 1983, 1994
6	Feb. 16	1858, 1904, 1915, 1926, 1988, 1999
7	Feb. 17	1863, 1874, 1885, 1920, 1931, 1942, 1953
5	Feb. 18	1890, 1896, 1947, 1958, 1969
3	Feb. 19	1901, 1980, 1985
3	Feb. 20	1912, 1917, 1996
6	Feb. 21	1860, 1871, 1882, 1928, 1939, 1950
6	Feb. 22	1887, 1898, 1944, 1955, 1966, 1977
4	Feb. 23	1909, 1971, 1982, 1993
5	Feb. 24	1857, 1903, 1914, 1925, 1998
5	Feb. 25	1868, 1873, 1879, 1936, 1941
5	Feb. 26	1884, 1895, 1952, 1963, 1974
6	Feb. 27	1900, 1906, 1968, 1979, 1990, 2001
5	Feb. 28	1865, 1911, 1922, 1933, 1995
1	Feb. 29	1876
7	March 1	1870, 1881, 1892, 1927, 1938, 1949, 1960
4	March 2	1897, 1954, 1965, 1976
4	March 3	1908, 1981, 1987, 1992
5	March 4	1862, 1919, 1924, 1930, 2003
6	March 5	1867, 1878, 1889, 1935, 1946, 1957
3	March 6	1962, 1973, 1984
3	March 7	1905, 1916, 2000
1	March 8	1859
2	March 9	1886, 1943

Mardi Gras Cancelations

In the time since the first Comus parade gave birth to the present celebration of Mardi Gras, there have been thirteen years when the festivities were completely canceled or severely limited.

1862-1865	Civil War
1875	Political unrest
1918-1919	World War I
1942-1945	World War II
1951	Korean War (limited activities)
1979	Strike by New Orleans Police canceled 13 Orleans parades

Parade Growth

The celebration of Mardi Gras in New Orleans has grown from a single-day event that included only one parade in 1857, to a twelve-day festival that features more than 50 processions. Stats are for adult, float parades only.

Year	Parades	Year	Parades
1860	1	1940	7
1870	2	1950	9
1880	3	1960	20
1890	4	1970	33
1900	5	1980	51
1910	5	1990	53
1920	6	2000	46
1930	5		

Fat Tuesday Weather

Year	Date	Rainfall	Temp. (hi/lo)	Year	Date	Rainfall	Temp. (hi/lo)	Year	Date	Rainfall	Temp. (hi/lo)
1872	Feb. 13	0	Unavailable	1915	Feb. 16	0	61° 48°	1962	March 6	0	55° 37°
1873	Feb. 25	0	Unavailable	1916	March 7	Trace	79° 64°	1963	Feb. 26	.17"	55° 48°
1874	Feb. 17	Trace	75° 64°	1917	Feb. 20	.10"	83° 68°	1964	Feb. 11	0	55° 43°
1875	Feb. 9	.44"	57° 42°	1918-19	WWI canceled Mardi Gras			1965	March 2	.71"	57° 52°
1876	Feb. 28	0	73° 62°	1920	Feb. 17	.51"	52° 42°	1966	Feb. 22	0	63° 37°
1877	Feb. 13	.37"	62° 53°	1921	Feb. 8	.03"	77° 69°	1967	Feb. 7	0	44° 32°
1878	March 5	0	68° 46°	1922	Feb. 28	Trace	70° 60°	1968	Feb. 27	0	71° 44°
1879	Feb. 25	0	74° 51°	1923	Feb. 13	Trace	82° 68°	1969	Feb. 18	0	55° 35°
1880	Feb. 10	0	70° 51°	1924	March 4	Trace	75° 55°	1970	Feb. 10	0	60° 31°
1881	March 1	0	66° 50°	1925	Feb. 24	0	69° 55°	1971	Feb. 23	0	63° 38°
1882	Feb. 21	.02"	73° 55°	1926	Feb. 16	0	62° 47°	1972	Feb. 15	.90"	71° 49°
1883	Feb. 6	0	73° 54°	1927	March 1	2.12"	66° 41°	1973	March 6	Trace	74° 61°
1884	Feb. 26	0	70° 53°	1928	Feb. 21	Trace	61° 46°	1974	Feb. 26	0	54° 31°
1885	Feb. 17	0	66° 43°	1929	Feb. 12	0	51° 32°	1975	Feb. 11	.07"	78° 52°
1886	March 9	.07"	69° 49°	1930	March 4	0	56° 40°	1976	March 2	Trace	80° 64°
1887	Feb. 22	.09"	81° 63°	1931	Feb. 17	0	78° 54°	1977	Feb. 22	.04"	76° 42°
1888	Feb. 14	0	79° 47°	1932	Feb. 9	0	83° 67°	1978	Feb. 7	Trace	39° 31°
1889	March 5	0	62° 50°	1933	Feb. 28	.26"	59° 50°	1979	Feb. 27	0	65° 35°
1890	Feb. 18	0	79° 54°	1934	Feb. 13	0	63° 46°	1980	Feb. 19	0	74° 50°
1891	Feb. 10	.02"	52° 44°	1935	March 5	.08"	76° 66°	1981	March 3	0	70° 52°
1892	March 1	0	56° 43°	1936	Feb. 25	Trace	78° 62°	1982	Feb. 23	0	81° 49°
1893	Feb. 14	.14"	76° 50°	1937	Feb. 9	.43"	60° 53°	1983	Feb. 15	.39"	67° 40°
1894	Feb. 6	0	64° 43°	1938	March 1	0	64° 45°	1984	March 6	.07"	50° 42°
1895	Feb. 26	0	69° 49°	1939	Feb. 21	1.69"	62° 47°	1985	Feb. 19	0	62° 49°
1896	Feb. 18	0	62° 37°	1940	Feb. 6	1.29"	59° 54°	1986	Feb. 11	0	40° 32°
1897	March 2	Trace	76° 57°	1941	Feb. 25	0	67° 60°	1987	March 3	0	70° 46°
1898	Feb. 22	0	59° 39°	1942-45	WWII canceled Mardi Gras			1988	Feb. 16	0	59° 33°
1899	Feb. 14	Trace	38° 22°	1946	March 5	0	76° 62°	1989	Feb. 7	Trace	44° 36°
1900	Feb. 27	Trace	70° 54°	1947	Feb. 18	0	74° 49°	1990	Feb. 27	0	72° 52°
1901	Feb. 19	0	68° 50°	1948	Feb. 10	0	45° 35°	1991	Feb. 12	0	68° 46°
1902	Feb. 11	0	54° 34°	1949	March 1	Trace	55° 43°	1992	March 3	0	72° 53°
1903	Feb. 24	0	66° 46°	1950	Feb. 21	0	74° 44°	1993	Feb. 23	0	66° 44°
1904	Feb. 16	0	62° 49°	1951	Feb. 6	.51"	68° 50°	1994	Feb. 15	Trace	63° 33°
1905	March 7	Trace	75° 60°	1952	Feb. 26	.45"	56° 44°	1995	Feb. 28	1.71"	69° 55°
1906	Feb. 27	0	60° 44°	1953	Feb. 17	.20"	63° 46°	1996	Feb. 20	0	76° 55°
1907	Feb. 12	0	73° 48°	1954	March 2	0	68° 49°	1997	Feb. 11	0	52° 36°
1908	March 3	.01"	79° 59°	1955	Feb. 22	1.04"	58° 42°	1998	Feb. 24	0	69° 45°
1909	Feb. 23	.45"	79° 55°	1956	Feb. 14	.03"	72° 60°	1999	Feb. 16	0	76° 50°
1910	Feb. 8	.13"	66° 50°	1957	March 5	.30"	70° 53°	2000	March 7	0	77° 54°
1911	Feb. 28	0	76° 56°	1958	Feb. 18	0	48° 29°	2001	Feb. 27	0	80° 62°
1912	Feb. 20	.20"	75° 62°	1959	Feb. 10	.36"	79° 69°	2002	Feb. 12	0	58° 41°
1913	Feb. 4	0	57° 43°	1960	March 1	Trace	50° 45°	2003	March 4	Trace	67° 58°
1914	Feb. 24	.29"	45° 32°	1961	Feb. 14	0	77° 54°				

Mardi Gras Reading List

Mardi Gras has been the subject of scores of books. This selected bibliography contains primary reference works, some of which are available through New Orleans libraries, new and used book stores, and on the web at www.bookfinder.com.

General Mardi Gras History

The Mistick Krewe: Chronicles of Comus and His Kin
Perry Young
Standard Printing Co., NOLA
1931, 1979

Carnival and Mardi Gras in New Orleans
Perry Young
Harmanson's, NOLA
1938

Mardi Gras
Robert Tallant
Doubleday & Company, New York, NY
1948

New Orleans Carnival and its Climax, Mardi Gras
Thomas DiPalma
Homes Printing Co., NOLA
1953

New Orleans Masquerade Chronicles of Carnival
Arthur LaCour, Stuart Landry
Pelican Publishing, Gretna, LA
1952, 1957

Mardi Gras — A Pictorial History of Carnival in New Orleans
Leonard Huber
Pelican Publishing, Gretna, LA
1977

Mardi Gras! A Celebration
Mitchel Osborne, Errol Laborde
Picayune Press, NOLA
1981

Mardi Gras Indians
Michael P. Smith
Pelican Publishing, Gretna, LA
1994

Mardi Gras New Orleans
Henri Schindler
Flammarion, Paris
1997

Mardi Gras Treasures, Invitations of the Golden Age
Henri Schindler
Pelican Publishing, Gretna, LA
2000

Mardi Gras Treasures, Float Designs of the Golden Age
Henri Schindler
Pelican Publishing, Gretna, LA
2001

Mardi Gras Treasures, Costume Designs of the Golden Age
Henri Schindler
Pelican Publishing, Gretna, LA
2002

Krewe Specific Books

If Ever I Cease to Love
Charles Dufour, Leonard Huber
School of Design, NOLA
1970

A Chronicle of the First Century of the Knights of Momus
Charles Dufour
Knights of Momus, NOLA
1971

Bacchus
Myron Tassin
Pelican Publishing, Gretna, LA
1975

50th Anniversary Krewe of Alla
Richard Dixon
Golden Gryphon Society, NOLA
1981

Krewe of Proteus: The First 100 Years
Charles Dufour
Upton Printing, NOLA
1981

Mardi Gras and Bacchus
Myron Tassin, Buddy Stall
Pelican Publishing, Gretna, LA
1984

Silver Memories, Endymion 25th Anniversary 1967-1991
Arthur Hardy Ent. Inc., NOLA
1990

Bacchus XXV Anniversary 1968-1993
Bonnie Warren
Bacchus, Inc. NOLA
1994

Marched The Day God, A History of the Rex Organization
Errol Laborde
The School of Design, NOLA
1999

Periodicals

Official Mardi Gras Program
L. R. Philbrook
NOLA
Annually 1946-1949

Mardi Gras New Orleans
Thomas Lupo
NOLA
Annually 1963-1969

Arthur Hardy's Mardi Gras Guide
Arthur Hardy Enterprises, Inc.
NOLA
Annually 1977-2003

Index

A
African-American Carnival: 66, 108
anti-discrimination legislation: 76
Armstrong, Louis: 53, 58, 63, 69
Ash Wednesday: 5, 42, 51
Athenaeum: 31

B
Baccha-Whoppa: 74
Bacchanalia: 4
Bacchusaurus: 74
bal masque: 7-9, 25, 28, 31, 54, 64, 84
ball krewes: 105, 110
Baranco, Angela Celeste: 75
Bathurst: 16
Bayoue du Mardi Gras: 5
Bedouin Arabs: 8
bingo games: 79
Boardman, Vira: 36
boeuf gras: 4, 17, 52, 64, 66, 84
Bonnecaze, Carlotta: 36
Boston Club: 46, 76
Bourbon Street Awards: 69
Briton, Charles: 24
Buffalo Bill's Wild West Show: 45
Butler, Emma: 14

C
call-out section: 36, 37
captain: 84
Capt. Eddie's S.S. Endymion: 78
carnelevamen: 5
Carnival celebrities: 111
Carnival (defined): 5, 6, 84
Carnival Bulletins: 33, 83
Carnival Krewes:
    Achaens: 59
    Adonis (New Orleans): 100
    Adonis (West Bank): 86
    Aladdin: 86
    Alhambra: 59
    Alla: 59, 60, 62, 77, 86
    Alpheus: 59, 100
    Amon-Ra: 69
    America: 79, 100
    Amor: 67, 76, 100
    Amphictyons: 52
    Ancient Druids: 77, 86
    Ancient Scribes: 64
    Aphrodite (New Orleans): 100
    Aphrodite (St. Bernard): 67, 74, 86
    Apollo: 56
    Apollonians: 52
    Aquarius: 100
    Aquila: 74, 86
    Arabi: 64, 100
    Argonauts: 52
    Argus: 71, 74, 79, 87
    Armeinius: 69
    Artemesians: 52
    Ashanti: 100
    Athena: 100
    Athenians: 31, 54, 59, 107
    Atlanteans: 31, 46, 47, 52, 59, 105
    Atreus: 100
    Atlas: 74, 87
    Babylon: 59, 61, 64, 87
    Bacchus: 11, 30, 62, 67-69, 71-76, 88
    Bards of Bohemia: 59, 74, 88
    Barkus: 78
    Caesar: 74, 75, 77, 88
    Caliphs of Cairo: 59
    Camelot: 100
    Capetowners: 59
    Carnival: 100
    Caronis: 101
    Carrollton: 59, 61, 68, 71, 88
    Centaur: 101
    Centurions: 74, 89
    Chalimar: 101
    Chaos: 77, 82, 89
    Choctaw: 45, 60, 76, 89
    Cleopatra: 74, 89
    Comus: 9-14, 22-27, 35-40, 42, 46, 49, 51, 59, 64, 76, 80, 83, 89
    Consus: 46, 51
    Crescent City: 60
    Crewe of Clones: 80
    Cronus: 64, 101
    Cynthius: 101
    d'Etat: 79, 90
    Daughters of Eve: 101
    Diana: 67, 76, 101
    Dorians: 59
    Druids: 56, 101
    Electra: 42
    Elenians: 59
    Elks Orleanians: 60
    Elves of Oberon: 31, 46, 48, 59, 106
    Empyreans: 52
    Endymion: 62, 67-68, 70-71, 76, 77, 80, 90
    Eros: 59
    Excalibur **77,** 91
    Falstaffians: 52
    Freret: 64, 76, 101
    Freret / Pandora: 101
    Gemini: 64, 102
    Gladiators: 74, 91
    Grela: 62, 91
    Haderus: 102
    Harlequins: 31, 56, 59
    Helios: 64, 65 102
    Hercules: 67, 76, 102
    Hermes: 59, 60, 77, 78, 83, 91
    Hesper: 102
    Hestia: 102
    Hestia / Mecca: 103
    High Priests of Mithras: 31, 46, 51, 59, 107
    Icarius: 102
    Indra: 52
    Iris: 56, 59, 64, 77, 92
    Isis: 74, 92
    Jason: 67, 102
    Jefla: 102
    Juno: 102
    Jupiter: 67, 102
    Jupiter / Juno: 103
    King Arthur: 74, 76, 92
    Krewe du Vieux: 80
    Les Marionettes: 56, 59
    Les Mysterieuses: 46, 49
    Love: 103
    Marc Antony: 103
    Mardi Gras: 75, 103
    Mecca: 67, 103
    Mercury: 74, 92
    Mid-City: 59, 60, 68, 82, 93
    Midas: 64, 103
    Minerva: 103
    Mistick Merry Bellions: 41
    Mittens: 52
    Mokana: 67, 103
    Momus: 22-27, 31, 32, 36, 38-46, 56, 59, 76, 82, 93
    Morpheus 77, 94
    Moslem: 59
    Muses: 77, 82, 94
    Mystery: 31, 57, 59
    Mystic Club: 31, 56, 57, 59
    Mystic Maids: 52
    Naiads: 59
    Napoleon: 74, 94
    Nefertari: 76, 103
    Neptune: 103
    Nereus: 31, 46, 48, 51, 52, 59, 106
    Nike: 103
    Niobeans: 59
    Nippon: 52
    Noblads: 59
    NOMTOC: 74, 94
    NOR: 58
    Octavia: 103
    Okeanos: 64, 94
    Olympians: 31, 54, 59, 107
    Omardz: 59
    Original Illinois: 46, 49, 56, 75, 106
    Orion: 64, 104
    Orpheus: 62, 76, 77, 80, 82, 95
    Oshun: 95
    Osiris: 31, 59
    Palmares: 104
    Pandora: 67, 76, 104
    Pegasus: 67, 95
    Petronius: 69
    Phoenix: 104
    Phunny Phorty Phellows: 31, 41, 42, 50, 74
    Pontchartrain: 74, 76, 95
    Poseidon: 64, 77, 104
    Prometheus: 59
    Prophets of Persia: 31, 56, 59
    Proteus: 31, 36-40, 46, 48, 51, 52, 58, 59, 76, 83, 95
    Pygmalion: 96
    Rex: 16-21, 24, 26, 28, 29, 31-35, 38, 40-48, 50- 57, 59, 60, 62, 64-67, 74-77, 83, 96
    Rhea: 74, 97
    Romulus and Remus: 104
    Samson and Delilah: 104
    Saturn: 74, 76, 79, 97
    Selena: 104
    Shangri-La: 74, 76, 97
    Silenus: 59
    Sinbad: 104
    Sparta: 74, 97
    Sparta / Mecca: 103
    Sprites: 67
    Thebes: 105
    Thor: 74, 98
    Thoth: 62, 77, 98
    Titans: 105
    Titanians: 52
    Tucks: 67, 77, 98
    Twelfth Night Revelers: 14, 15, 22, 24, 26, 31-33, 35, 42, 59, 105
    Ulysses: 74, 99
    Underwear: 80
    Venus: 59, 61, 71, 76, 105
    Vikings of Tyr: 105
    Virgilians: 59
    Vulcan: 105
    Well Known Gentlemen: 31, 49
    Yami: 52
    Young Men Illinois Club: 56
    Young Men's Society: 31
    Yuga: 67, 69
    Zeus: 64, 70, 99
    Zulu: 52, 53, 58, 62, 63, 66, 67, 74, 76, 99
Carnival Palace: 32
Carnival season (defined): 5
Carpetbag: 25, 26
Catholic Church: 5, 6, 13, 15
Chicago Glide: 49
Children's Carnival Club: 56, 59
childrens' krewes: 109
Churchill, Charles: 9
Civil War: 12, 16, 26, 32
commercializing Carnival: 79
Connick, Harry Jr.: 77
Costume De Rigueur: 28
Cotton Centennial Exposition: 40, 44
court: 84
Cowbellian deRakin Society: 9
Creole: 7-9, 15, 29, 36, 54
Creole Wild West Indian: 45
Crescent Club: 36
Crisp's Variety Theater: 11
Czechoslovakia: 67, 75

D
Darwin, Charles: 24
Daughters of the Confederacy: 27
Davis, Varina: 27
debutante: 29
den: 84
defunct parading krewes: 100
doubloon: 67, 68, 70, 75, 84, 112

Index

Downman, Robert H.: 21
Dryburg Abbey: 38
Duke and Duchess of Windsor: 64

E
EBay: 81
Easter: 6
economic impact: 112
Ellison, Joseph: 9
Epiphany: 6, 14, 15
Ernest N. Morial Convention Ctr: 76
Exposition Hall: 31

F
Fairchild, L. W.: 50
Fat Tuesday (defined): 5
Fat Tuesday weather: 114
favor: 84
Fete du Soleil: 4
Fisher, Louis Andrews: 56
flambeau: 39, 80
float builders: 112
Fountain, Pete: 67
French Opera House: 14, 22, 27, 31, 33, 36, 42, 46, 51, 52, 55
French Quarter parades: 70
Frozen Charlotte: 15

G
Gallier, James: 31
Gay Carnival clubs: 69, 82, 110
Gem: 10
Gen. Benjamin "Spoons" Butler: 25
Gen. D. H. Hill: 24, 27
Gen. John J. Pershing: 52
Gen. Robert E. Lee: 20, 24, 27
Gen. T. "Stonewall" Jackson: 24, 27
Governor Don Antonio Ulloa: 6
Governor Henry Clay Warmoth: 19
Governor Marquis de Vaudreuil: 6
Governor William Claiborne: 7
Grand Duke Alexis Romanoff: 16-19
Grand Opera House: 47, 48
Greatest Bands in Dixie: 68
Gretna: 62, 77, 78

H
Hades, a Dream of Momus: 22, 26
Harmony Club: 50
Harrah's Casino: 76
Hill, Nannie: 27
Hope, Bob: 71
Howard, Frank T.: 50

I
Iberville: 5, 6, 83
If Ever I Cease to Love: 19, 40, 66
invitation: 84
Internet: 81

J
Jackson, Julia: 27
Jefferson City Buzzards: 46, 47, 75
Jefferson Parish: 62, 64, 65, 70, 75, 77, 78, 79, 81

K
Kaye, Danny: 69
Kelly, John: 53
Kern, Blaine: 58, 62, 76, 78, 112
king cake: 15, 73, 84
King Kong: 74
King of Carnival: 16
Korean conflict: 64
Kraft, Michael: 9
krewe (defined): 9, 84
krewe name derivation: 109

L
La Salle Conde: 6
Leavitt, Mel: 62
LeBlanc, Leopold: 53
Lee, Mary: 27
Lee, Mildred: 27
Leviathan: 77
Libby, Edith: 52
Little Rascals: 109
Louis XIV: 4, 5, 20
Louisiana Club: 23
Louisiana State Museum: 81
Louisiana Superdome: 70, 72, 76
Lundgren, Philip S.: 70
Lundi Gras: 74, 84
Lupercalia: 4

M
Maginnis, Josephine: 27
Mardi Gras Q & A: 84
Mardi Gras cancelations: 113
Mardi Gras collectibles: 110
Mardi Gras colors: 15, 17, 48, 85
Mardi Gras dates: 85, 113
Mardi Gras (defined): 5, 84
Mardi Gras dictionary: 84
Mardi Gras Indians: 45, 80, 108
Mardi Gras themes: 86, 109
Mardi Gras Mask-a-thon: 73
Mardi Gras memorabilia: 81
Mardi Gras Museum: 81
Mardi Gras reading list: 114
Mardi Gras Royalty, how chosen: 85
Mardi Gras Royalty, lists: 86
Mardi Gras World: 76
Maury, James H.: 41
Mayor Charles Waterman: 11
Mayor Marc Morial: 83
McLain, Dr. James: 83
meeting of the courts: 40, 80
Metoyer, John L. Jr.: 53
Miller, Nettie: 27
Milton, John: 11
Mobile: 9, 11, 16
Monday King: 20
Moss, Arnold L.: 53
mules: 64
Municipal Auditorium: 36, 58, 59, 61, 64, 70, 72, 76
Muniz, Ed: 80
Mythology: 109

N
Neiman, Leroy: 83
New Orleans Cotton Exchange: 36
New Orleans Police Dept.: 72, 74
Nicholls, Francis T.: 26

O
Odd Fellows Hall: 31, 49
Orpheuscapade: 77

P
parade components: 112
parade format: 85
parade ladders: 73
Paradise Lost: 11
Pemberton, John: 21, 39
Pickwick Club: 12, 46
Pointe du Mardi Gras: 5, 83
Poitevent, Emily: 49
Pontchartrain Center: 76
Pope, Dr. John H.: 11
President Jefferson Davis: 24, 27
President Teddy Roosevelt: 52
President Ulysses S. Grant: 22, 25, 26
President William Howard Taft: 52
Pro Bono Publico: 57
Purple, Gold and Green: 15, 17, 48

Q
Quadroon: 6
Queens of ball krewes: 105

R
Reconstruction: 16, 24, 40
Richardson, Susie: 41
Rivergate Convention Center: 69
Rodrigue, George: 83
Roosevelt, Alice: 52
Rosenthal, Harry P.: 68
Russell, James: 53

S
Sala, George Augustus: 39
Salle d'Orleans: 7
Salomon, Lewis: 16
Saturnalia: 4
Schindler, Henri: 81, 112
School of Design: 17, 64
Scott, Sir Walter: 22
September 11, 2001: 78
Seventh Dist. Carnival Assoc.: 56, 61
Sharpe, H. Alvin: 67
Signal, Solomon: 75
signature floats: 74, 77
Sinnott, Emma: 27
Smith, Thad: 9
Soulé, George: 57
Sousa, John Philip: 45
St. Augustine Marching Band: 72
St. Charles Hotel: 30
St. Charles Theatre: 31
St. Tammany Parades: 112
Steward, Ovide: 53
Story, William: 53
Strikers: 9
Super Bowl: 78
super krewes: 68, 69, 77, 78, 85
Symbolism of Colors: 17, 48

T
tableau ball: 10, 30
Taylor, Dorothy Mae: 76
Tea Drinkers: 9
Teunisson, J. N.: 39
The Academy of Music: 31
The Missing Links to Darwin's Origin of the Species: 25
The Mistick Krewe: 58
Theatre d'Orleans: 8
Theatre St. Phillipe: 7
Thompson, Lydia: 18, 19
throws: 56, 67, 75, 84
trash: 85
Truck Krewes: 109
Triumphs of Epicure: 13
Twelfth Night: 6, 9, 15

V
Varieties Theatre: 12, 16, 25, 32

W
WDSU: 62
WSMB: 58
Walking Clubs: 47, 109
Wikstrom, Bror Andrews: 50
World Wars: 52, 61
Wu, Ting Fang: 52

Y
Young, William Waller: 65

Z
Zulu coconut: 53